Siegel's

EVIDENCE

Essay and Multiple-Choice Questions and Answers

Fifth Edition

BRIAN N. SIEGEL
J.D., Columbia Law School

Revised by

Arthur Best
Professor of Law
University of Denver
Sturm College of Law

Published by Wolters Kluwer Law & Business in New York.

Wolters Kluwer Law & Business serves customers worldwide with CCH, Aspen Publishers, and Kluwer Law International products. (www.wolterskluwerlb.com)

To contact Customer Service, e-mail customer.service@wolterskluwer.com, call 1-800-234-1660, fax 1-800-901-9075, or mail correspondence to:

> Wolters Kluwer Law & Business
> Attn: Order Department
> PO Box 990
> Frederick, MD 21705

The authors gratefully acknowledge the assistance of the California Committee of Bar Examiners, which provided access to questions on which some of the essay questions in this book are based.

Printed in the United States of America.

1 2 3 4 5 6 7 8 9 0

ISBN 978-1-4548-0928-9

SFI Certified Chain of Custody
Product Line Contains At Least
20% Certified Forest Content
www.sfiprogram.org
SFI-00756

About Wolters Kluwer Law & Business

Wolters Kluwer Law & Business is a leading global provider of intelligent information and digital solutions for legal and business professionals in key specialty areas and respected educational resources for professors and law students. Wolters Kluwer Law & Business connects legal and business professionals as well as those in the education market with timely, specialized, authoritative content and information-enabled solutions to support success through productivity, accuracy and mobility.

Serving customers worldwide, Wolters Kluwer Law & Business products include those under the Aspen Publishers, CCH, Kluwer Law International, Loislaw, Best Case, ftwilliam.com, and MediRegs family of products.

CCH products have been a trusted resource since 1913 and are highly regarded resources for legal, securities, antitrust and trade regulation, government contracting, banking, pension, payroll, employment and labor, and healthcare reimbursement and compliance professionals.

Aspen Publishers products provide essential information to attorneys, business professionals, and law students. Written by preeminent authorities, the product line offers analytical and practical information in a range of specialty practice areas from securities law and intellectual property to mergers and acquisitions and pension/benefits. Aspen's trusted legal education resources provide professors and students with high-quality, up-to-date and effective resources for successful instruction and study in all areas of the law.

Kluwer Law International products provide the global business community with reliable international legal information in English. Legal practitioners, corporate counsel, and business executives around the world rely on Kluwer Law journals, looseleafs, books, and electronic products for comprehensive information in many areas of international legal practice.

Loislaw is a comprehensive online legal research product providing legal content to law firm practitioners of various specializations. Loislaw provides attorneys with the ability to quickly and efficiently find the necessary legal information they need, when and where they need it, by facilitating access to primary law as well as state-specific law, records, forms and treatises.

Best Case Solutions is the leading bankruptcy software product to the bankruptcy industry. It provides software and workflow tools to flawlessly streamline petition preparation and the electronic filing process, while timely incorporating ever-changing court requirements.

ftwilliam.com offers employee benefits professionals the highest quality plan documents (retirement, welfare, and non-qualified) and government forms (5500/ PBGC, 1099, and IRS) software at highly competitive prices.

MediRegs products provide integrated health care compliance content and software solutions for professionals in healthcare, higher education and life sciences, including professionals in accounting, law and consulting.

Wolters Kluwer Law & Business, a division of Wolters Kluwer, is headquartered in New York. Wolters Kluwer is a market-leading global information services company focused on professionals.

Introduction

Although law school grades are a significant factor in obtaining a summer internship or entry position at a law firm, no formalized preparation for finals is offered at most law schools. For the most part, students are expected to fend for themselves in learning how to take a law school exam. Ironically, law school exams may bear little correspondence to the teaching methods used by professors during the school year. At least in the first year, professors require you to spend most of your time briefing cases. This is probably not great preparation for issue-spotting on exams. In briefing cases, you are made to focus on one or two principles of law at a time; thus, you don't get practice in relating one issue to another or in developing a picture of an entire problem or the entire course. When exams finally come, you're forced to make an abrupt 180-degree turn. Suddenly, you are asked to recognize, define, and discuss a variety of issues buried within a single multi-issue fact pattern. Alternately, you may be asked to select among a number of possible answers, all of which look inviting but only one of which is right.

The comprehensive course outline you've created so diligently, and with such pain, means little if you're unable to apply its contents on your final exams. There is a vast difference between reading opinions in which the legal principles are clearly stated and applying those same principles to hypothetical essay exams and multiple-choice questions.

The purpose of this book is to help you bridge the gap between memorizing a rule of law and *understanding how to use it* in an exam. After an initial overview describing the exam-writing process, you see a large number of hypotheticals that test your ability to write analytical essays and to pick the right answers to multiple-choice questions. *Read them—all of them!* Then review the suggested answers that follow. You'll find that the key to superior grades lies in applying your knowledge through questions and answers, not through rote memory.

GOOD LUCK!

Table of Contents

Essay Answers

Multiple-Choice Questions

Multiple-Choice Answers

Table and Index

Preparing Effectively for Essay Examinations

To achieve superior scores on essay exams, a law student must (1) learn and understand "blackletter" principles and rules of law for each subject, (2) analyze how those principles of law arise within a test fact pattern, and (3) clearly and succinctly discuss each principle and how it relates to the facts. One of the most common misconceptions about law school is that you must memorize each word on every page of your casebooks or outlines to do well on exams. The reality is that you can commit an entire casebook to memory and still do poorly on an exam. Our review of hundreds of student answers has shown us that most students can recite the rules. The students who do **best** on exams are able to analyze how the rules they have memorized relate to the facts in the questions, and they are able to communicate their analysis to the grader. The following pages cover what you need to know to achieve superior scores on your law school essay exams.

The "ERC" Process

To study effectively for law school exams you must figure out a way to be actively engaged with the material. One way to do this is to "ERC" (*E*lementize, *R*ecognize, and *C*onceptualize) each legal principle covered in your casebooks and course outlines. *Elementizing* means reducing each legal theory and rule you learn to a concise, straightforward statement of its essential elements. Without knowledge of these elements, it's difficult to see all the issues as they arise. For example, if you are asked, "What is an excited utterance?" it is **not** enough to say, "An excited utterance is a statement a person makes while he or she is excited." This layperson description would leave a grader wondering if you had actually taken the Evidence course. An accurate statement of the excited utterance hearsay exception would be something like this: "To characterize an out-of-court statement as an excited utterance, the proponent must show that (1) there was a startling event, (2) the declarant made a statement relating to that event, (3) the declarant was under stress or excitement, and (4) the stress or excitement was caused by that startling event."

Recognizing means perceiving or anticipating which words or ideas within a legal principle are likely to be the source of issues and how those issues are likely to arise within a given hypothetical fact pattern. With respect to the excited utterance concept, there are four *potential* issues. Was there a startling event? Does the statement relate to that event? Was the declarant experiencing stress or excitement? Did the startling event cause that stress or excitement?

Conceptualizing means imagining situations in which each of the elements of a rule of law can give rise to factual issues. ***Unless you can imagine or construct an application of each element of a rule, you don't truly understand the legal principles behind the rule!*** In our opinion, the inability to conjure up hypothetical fact patterns or stories involving particular rules of law foretells a likelihood that you will miss issues involving those rules on an exam. It's ***crucial*** (1) to ***recognize*** that issues result from the interaction of facts with the words defining a rule of law and (2) to develop the ability to ***conceptualize*** or ***imagine*** fact patterns using the words or concepts within the rule.

For example, these facts illustrate how the "stress was caused by that startling event" element might be complicated:

> Husband A was walking on a street with his wife, and they were having a very severe argument. A became highly upset by various things his wife said about him, about politics, and about their children. A began to yell rejoinders at his wife. As they were arguing, they stopped to wait for a light to change so they could cross a street. Suddenly, a car ran a red light and collided with another car. A fire broke out and the drivers and passengers from both cars ran out into the street. A said to his wife, "That first driver ran the red light, just like you do when you're driving." In a lawsuit between the two drivers, should a court admit A's words as an excited utterance? Answering this question would depend on how the trial court decided to characterize A's state of mind when A made the statement. If he was upset because of the marital argument, the excited utterance exception would be wrong to use since the upset was about something different from the topic of the statement. On the other hand, if there was evidence that A was upset by the crash, the exception would cover the statement.

You should think of examples like this for every element of every rule you learn.

Issue-Spotting

One of the keys to doing well on an essay examination is issue-spotting. In fact, issue-spotting is ***the*** most important skill you will learn in law school. If you recognize a legal issue, you can find the applicable rule of law (if there is one) by researching the issue. But if you fail to see the issues, you won't learn the steps that lead to success or failure on exams or, for that matter, in the practice of law. It is important to remember that (1) an issue is a question to be decided by the judge or jury, and (2) a question is "in issue" when it can be disputed or argued about at trial. The bottom line is that *if you don't spot an issue, you can't discuss it.*

The key to issue-spotting is to learn to approach a problem in the same way an attorney does. Let's assume you've been admitted to practice and you expect to try a case on behalf of your client. You will have to consider (1) how each item of information you would like to present at the trial might be relevant, (2) whether it might be excluded as relevant but too prejudicial, (3) whether it is barred by any specialized relevance rules, (4) whether it presents hearsay issues, (4) whether it can satisfy various formal requirements like authentication and the original writing rule, (5) what arguments each side can make to persuade the court to resolve the issue in its favor; and finally, (6) what the *likely* outcome of each issue will be. *All the issues that can possibly arise at trial will be relevant to your answers.*

How to Discuss an Issue

Keep in mind that *rules of law are the guides to issues* (i.e., an issue arises where there is a question whether the facts do, or do not, satisfy an element of a rule); a rule of law *cannot dispose of an issue* unless the rule can reasonably be *applied to the facts.*

A good way to learn how to discuss an issue is to study the following mini-hypothetical and the two student responses that follow it.

Mini-Hypothetical

D is on trial for arson. The prosecution seeks to prove that he started a fire in a business building, with a motive to obtain a payment from an insurance company for the damage caused by that fire. The prosecution has information that about three years earlier, D had attempted to obtain a payment from another insurance company by making a false claim that his car had been damaged by a severe hailstorm. Discuss what use the prosecution might be allowed to make of D's past false claim if D testifies at the trial or if D declines to testify at the trial.

Pertinent Principles of Law:

1. If D testifies, the prosecution may seek to impeach him. When a witness has committed an act in the past that reflects on the witness's character for truthfulness, the opponent of that witness is permitted to ask the witness about the act on cross-examination but is not allowed to introduce extrinsic evidence of the act.

2. Whether or not D testifies, proof of past conduct that would be relevant *only* to show that D has character traits that are consistent with acting unlawfully would be barred. However, evidence that would support a finding of bad character traits may nonetheless be admitted if it could *also* support some legitimate finding, such as a finding that the defendant has some uncommon knowledge or skill.

3. Trial courts may exclude otherwise admissible evidence if its probative value is substantially outweighed by a risk of unfair prejudice.

First Student Answer

There are two possible uses of the information about the false insurance claim. One is to impeach D's credibility if D testifies, and the other is to provide substantive support for the prosecution's claim that D committed the arson. The credibility use is available to the prosecution only if D testifies. The substantive use may be available regardless of whether D testifies.

Impeachment Use. When someone testifies, the opponent may cross-examine him or her about past acts that could support a finding that the witness has a character trait of untruthfulness, under Federal Rule of Evidence 608(b). To apply this rule, the court would have to be persuaded that making a false claim to an insurance company is conduct that could rationally support a conclusion that the person who made the claim has bad character for credibility. A court would likely make that finding here since lying to an insurance company has a very strong relationship to a person's respect for truth and a person's willingness to make false statements.

It is important to note that the prosecution can ask D about this past conduct on cross-examination but may not do anything else with the information. For example, it may not introduce extrinsic evidence about it.

The trial court would consider whether there was a significant risk of unfair prejudice to D in allowing cross-examination on this topic. While there definitely is a risk that a jury will conclude that because D tried to defraud an insurance company once before, he likely committed the arson in this case for the same reason, the probative value of the past conduct on the issue of credibility is high. A court would likely be justified in allowing the questioning, particularly if the prosecution did not have other equivalent impeaching information available.

Substantive Use. FRE 404(b)(1) prohibits use of information about a person's past acts to show that the person has a character trait and that the person acted in conformity with that trait on a particular occasion. But FRE 404(b)(2) provides illustrations of circumstances in which this kind of evidence can be relevant for non-character purposes and would therefore be admissible. In this case, the past attempted insurance fraud would be treated as improper character evidence unless the prosecution could show that it had a relevant different form supporting a conclusion that D is a law-breaking kind of person. Could it show special knowledge? Could it show a special motive? The conduct does not show knowledge different from the knowledge most people have. The facts that insurance companies pay claims and that a beneficiary has to make a claim to be paid are well known by almost everyone. The motive to gain money by unlawful acts is also too general to be a basis for admitting this evidence. For these reasons, substantive use would likely be prohibited.

The risk of prejudice associated with admission of this information is high. A jury could conclude that because D once tried to defraud an insurance company he likely attempted to do it another time. Its probative value is low, so even if it were potentially admissible, a court would probably exclude it under Rule 403.

Second Student Answer

This question involves impeachment and substantive evidence. You can cross-examine a witness with information about their past acts. Here, the past act involves credibility, so proving it would be proper. The risk of prejudice is less than the probative value of the information, so it would be admissible.

Evidence about past acts is also admissible to show motive or knowledge or plan. The hailstorm fraud shows that D habitually seeks to defraud insurance companies and that D knows how to do that. He has a motive to gain money by unlawful acts. For these reasons, his prior conduct would be admitted.

The risk of prejudice associated with admission of this information is high. A jury could conclude that because D once tried to defraud an insurance company he likely attempted to do it another time. Its probative value is low, so even if it were potentially admissible, a court would probably exclude it under Rule 403.

Critique

The First Student Answer has a clear structure and discusses all the important issues. The question is a two-part question since it asks about use of certain evidence if D testifies and if D declines to testify. This answer reflects that structure and explains that one possible use is available only for impeachment and the other possible use is available regardless of whether or not D testifies.

The answer describes FRE 608(b) and then applies it in the context of the question's facts. This is an example or IRAC-style writing since it begins with a problem, states a rule, applies the rule, and then offers a conclusion.

The answer also explains that inquiry (but not anything else) is allowed. IRAC would not be useful for a concept such as this, but it is an aspect of the problem that a grader would probably like to know a student understands.

The answer also treats the risk of unfair prejudice in a straightforward way, with a fair amount of connection to the facts of the problem.

The answer has similar strengths for its discussion of substantive uses of the past fraud information. It suggests how both sides of the question could be raised and then makes and supports a choice.

In contrast, the Second Student Answer does not make the distinction between impeachment use and substantive use particularly clear. Also, it fails to describe the rules it applies. The first paragraph gives incomplete descriptions of the factors that are involved. When it refers to the balance of probative value and unfair prejudice, it is completely abstract, with no specification of what those values and risks might be in the particular facts of this question.

The second paragraph of the Second Student Answer is one-sided. It does not really dig into the facts of the question, and it does not justify its conclusion in terms of the applicable rule.

The last paragraph asserts that there is low probative value for this evidence, but it never explains why that might be true.

Structuring Your Answer

Graders will give high marks to a clearly written, well-structured answer. Each issue you discuss should follow a specific and consistent structure that a grader can easily follow.

One format for analyzing each issue is the *I-R-A-C format*. Here, the *I* stands for *Issue*, the *R* for *Rule of law*, the *A* for *Application of the facts to the rule of law*, and the *C* for *Conclusion*. *I-R-A-C* is a legitimate approach to the discussion of a particular issue within the time constraints imposed by the question. The *I-R-A-C format* must be applied to each issue in the question; it is not the solution to the entire answer. If there are six issues in a question, for example, you should offer six separate, independent *I-R-A-C* analyses. Another technique is the *I-R-A-A-O format*. In this format, the *I* stands for *Issue*, the *R* for *Rule of law*, the first *A* for *one side's Argument*, the second *A* for *the other party's rebuttal Argument*, and the *O* for your *Opinion as to how the issue would be resolved*. The *I-R-A-A-O* format emphasizes the importance of (1) discussing *both* sides of an issue and (2) communicating to the grader that, where an issue arises, an attorney can only advise his or her client as to the *probable* decision on that issue.

These are each worthwhile techniques to analyze and organize essay exam answers. Whatever format you choose, however, you should be consistent throughout the exam and remember the following rules:

First, *analyze all of the relevant facts*. Facts have significance in a particular case *only as they come under the applicable rules of law*. The facts presented must be analyzed and examined to see if they do or do not satisfy one element or another of the applicable rules, and the essential facts and rules must be stated and argued in your analysis.

Second, you must communicate to the grader the *precise rule of law* controlling the facts. In their eagerness to commence their arguments, students sometimes fail to state the applicable rule of law first. Remember, the *R* in either format stands for *Rule of law*. Defining the rule of law *before* an analysis of the facts is essential in order to allow the grader to follow your reasoning.

Third, it is important to treat *each side of an issue with equal detail*. Don't permit your personal viewpoint to affect your answer! A good lawyer never does! When discussing an issue, always state the arguments for each side.

Finally, remember to *state your opinion or conclusion* on each issue. Keep in mind, however, that your opinion or conclusion is probably the *least* important part of an exam answer. Why? Because your professor knows that no attorney can tell his or her client exactly how a judge or jury will decide a particular issue. By definition, an issue is a legal dispute that can go either way. An attorney, therefore, can offer the client only his or her best opinion about the likelihood of a ruling on an issue. Because the decision on any issue lies with the judge or jury, no attorney can ever be absolutely certain of the resolution.

Discuss All Possible Issues

As we've noted, a student should draw *some* type of conclusion or opinion for each issue raised. Whatever your conclusion on a particular issue, it is essential to anticipate and discuss *all of the issues* that would arise if the question were actually tried in court.

Let's assume that an evidence hypothetical involves issues pertaining to relevance, character evidence, and hearsay. If the party objecting to introduction of the evidence prevails on any one of these issues, the evidence will be excluded. Suppose you feel strongly that the evidence has no relevance. Should you also discuss character issues and hearsay? Yes. You *must* go on to discuss all of the other potential issues. If you were to terminate your answer after a discussion of the relevance question only, you'd receive an inferior grade.

Why should you have to discuss every possible issue if you are relatively certain that the outcome of a particular issue would be dispositive of admissibility of the evidence? Because you may be *wrong* in your analysis of that issue. We can state with confidence that every attorney with some degree of experience has won issues he or she thought he or she would lose and has lost issues on which victory seemed assured. Because one can never be absolutely certain how a trial judge will rule on any element of an evidence question, a good attorney (and exam writer) will consider *all* possible issues.

To understand the importance of discussing all of the potential issues, you should reflect on what you will do in the actual practice of law. If you represent the defendant, for example, it is your job to raise every possible defense. If there are five potential defenses and your pleadings rely on only three of them (because you're sure you will win on all three), and the plaintiff is somehow successful on all three issues, your client may well sue you for malpractice. Your client's contention would be that you should be liable because if you had only raised the two additional issues, you might have prevailed on at least one of them, and therefore liability would have been avoided. It is an attorney's duty to raise *all* legitimate issues. A similar philosophy should be followed when taking essay exams.

What exactly do you say when you've resolved the initial issue in favor of the defendant, and discussion of any additional issues would seem to be moot? The answer is simple. You begin the discussion of the next issue with something like, "Assuming, however, the plaintiff prevailed on the foregoing issue, the next issue would be . . . . " The grader will understand and appreciate what you have done.

The corollary to the importance of raising all potential issues is that you should avoid discussion of obvious nonissues. Raising nonissues is detrimental in three ways: First, you waste a lot of precious time; second, you usually receive absolutely no points for discussing an issue that the grader deems extraneous; and third, it suggests to the grader that you lack the ability to distinguish the significant from the irrelevant. The best guideline for avoiding the discussion of a nonissue is to ask yourself, "Would I, as an attorney, feel comfortable about raising that particular issue or objection in front of a judge?"

Delineate the Transition from One Issue to the Next

It's a good idea to make it easy for the grader to see the issues you've found. One way to accomplish this is to cover no more than one issue per paragraph. Another way is to underline each issue statement. Provided that time permits, we recommend that you use both techniques. The essay answers in this book contain numerous illustrations of these suggestions.

One frequent student error is to write two separate paragraphs in which all of the arguments for one side are made in the initial paragraph, and all of the rebuttal arguments by the other side are made in the next paragraph. This organization is *a bad idea*. It obliges the grader to reconstruct the exam answer in his or her mind several times to determine whether all possible issues have been discussed by both sides. It will also cause you to state the same rule of law more than once. A better-organized answer presents a given argument by one side and follows that immediately in the same paragraph with the other side's rebuttal to that argument.

Understanding the "Call" of a Question

The statement *at the end* of an essay question or of the fact pattern in a multiple-choice question is sometimes referred to as the "call" of the question. It usually asks something specific such as "is the evidence hearsay," "is the evidence admissible," or "which arguments for admissibility are strongest." The call of the question should be read carefully because it tells you exactly what you're expected to do. If a question asks, "Is the evidence relevant?" you should write only about relevance and should ignore other issues such as hearsay or authentication. You will usually receive no credit for discussing issues or facts that are not required by the call. On the other hand, if the call of an essay question is simply "discuss," then *all* foreseeable issues must be covered by your answer.

Students are often led astray by an essay question's call. For example, if you are asked to "discuss admissibility," you may think you may limit yourself to arguments *in favor of* admissibility. This is *not correct*! You cannot consider admissibility well unless you consider arguments in favor of admissibility and also arguments against admissibility. Although the call of the question may appear to focus on the point of view, a superior answer will cover all the issues and arguments that a lawyer might *encounter* (not just the arguments he or she would *make*) in attempting to pursue a particular position.

The Importance of Analyzing the Question Carefully Before Writing

The overriding *time pressure* of an essay exam is probably a major reason why many students fail to analyze a question carefully before writing. Five minutes into the allocated time for a particular question, you may notice that the person next to you is writing furiously. This thought then flashes through your mind: "Oh, my goodness, he's putting down more words on the paper than I am, and therefore he's bound to get a better grade." It can be stated *unequivocally* that there is no necessary correlation between the number of words on your exam paper and the grade you'll receive. Students who begin their answer after only five minutes of analysis have probably seen only the most obvious issues and missed many, if not most, of the subtle ones. They are also likely to be less well organized.

Opinions differ as to how much time you should spend analyzing and outlining a question before you actually write the answer. We believe that you should spend about 15 minutes analyzing, organizing, and outlining a one-hour question before writing your answer. This will usually provide sufficient time to analyze and organize the question thoroughly *and* enough time to write a relatively complete answer. Remember to scrutinize each word of the question to determine if it (1) suggests an issue under the operative rules of law or (2) can be used in making an argument for the resolution of an issue. Because you can't receive points for an issue you don't spot, it is usually wise to read a question *twice* before starting your outline.

When to Make an Assumption

The instructions for a question may tell you to *assume* facts that are necessary to the answer. Even when these instructions are *not* given, you may be obliged to make certain assumptions about missing facts in order to write a thorough answer. Assumptions should be made only when you are told or when you, as the attorney for one of the parties described in the question, would be obliged to solicit additional information from your client. On the other hand, assumptions should *never be used to change or alter the question*. Don't ever write something like "if the facts in the question were . . . , instead of . . . , then . . . would result." If you do this, you are wasting time on facts that are extraneous to the problem before you. Professors want you to deal with *their* fact patterns, not your own.

Students sometimes try to "write around" information they think is missing. They assume that their professor has failed to include every piece of data necessary for a thorough answer. This is generally *wrong*. The professor may have omitted some facts deliberately to see if the student *can figure out what to do* under the circumstances. However, in some instances, the professor may have omitted them inadvertently (even law professors are sometimes human).

The way to deal with the omission of essential information is to describe (1) what fact (or facts) appears to be missing and (2) why that information is important. As an example, go back to the "Mini-Hypothetical" about arson and insurance fraud we discussed before. In that fact pattern, there was no mention of additional impeachment evidence that might have been available to the prosecution. If other impeachment information had been available, that would have affected the FRE 403 balancing test. The "First Student Answer" handled this well with the simple statement "[a] court would likely be justified in allowing the questioning, particularly if the prosecution did not have other equivalent impeaching information available." This sentence shows that the student understood these subtleties and correctly supplied the essential missing facts and assumptions.

Assumptions should be made in a manner that keeps the other issues open (i.e., they lead to a discussion of all other possible issues). For example, if there are difficult aspects associated with one item of evidence, don't say something like "probably the party has other evidence on this issue, so it would be wise to avoid these complications by using that evidence instead."

Case Names and Rule Numbers

A law student is ordinarily *not* expected to recall case names on an exam. The professor knows that you have read many cases and that you would have to be a memory expert to have all of the names at your fingertips. If you confront a fact pattern that seems similar to a case you have reviewed (but you cannot recall its name), just write something like, "One case we've read held that . . ." or "It has been held that . . . ." In this manner, you have informed the grader that you are relying on a case that contained a fact pattern similar to the question at issue.

The only exception to this rule is in the case of a landmark decision (e.g., *Crawford v. Washington*). Landmark opinions are usually those that change or alter established law. These cases are usually easy to identify, because you will probably have spent an entire class period discussing each of them. In these special instances, you may be expected to recall the case by name, as well as the proposition of law it stands for. It would be impossible to discuss a Confrontation Clause problem without knowing the details of *Crawford*. For that reason, you might as well use the name of the case. But even in this situation, if you described the case without using its name, your answer could still receive a high grade.

When you answer a question in the context of the Federal Rules of Evidence, you should refer to rules by their numbers, if a copy of the rules has been made available for use during the exam. Otherwise, you should describe the rules clearly and use their numbers only if you're absolutely certain you remember them correctly.

How to Handle Time Pressures

What do you do when there are five minutes left in the exam and you have only written two-thirds of your answer? One thing ***not*** to do is write something like, "No time left!" or "Not enough time!" This gets you nothing but the satisfaction of knowing you have communicated your personal frustrations to the grader.

First of all, it is not necessarily a bad thing to be pressed for time. The person who finishes five minutes early has very possibly missed some important issues. The more proficient you become in knowing what is expected of you on an exam, the greater the difficulty you may experience in staying within the time limits. Second, remember that (at least to some extent) you're graded against your classmates' answers, and they're under exactly the same time pressure as you. In short, don't panic if you can't write the "perfect" answer in the allotted time. Nobody does!

The best hedge against misuse of time is to ***review as many old exams as possible***. These exercises will give you a familiarity with the process of organizing and writing an exam answer, which, in turn, should result in an enhanced ability to stay within the time boundaries. If you nevertheless find that you have about 15 minutes of writing to do and 5 minutes to do it in, write a paragraph that summarizes the remaining issues or arguments you would discuss if time permitted. As long as you've indicated that you're aware of the remaining legal issues, you'll probably receive some credit for naming them.

If you can add even a brief sketch of how those issues might matter or how you would discuss them, of course you'll earn even more credit.

Formatting Your Answer

Make sure that the way you write or type your answer presents your analysis in the best possible light. In other words, if you write, do so legibly. If you type, remember to use many paragraphs instead of just creating a document in which all of your ideas are merged into a single lengthy block of print. Remember, your professor may have a hundred or more exams to grade. If your answer is difficult to read, you will rarely be given the benefit of the doubt. On the other hand, an answer that is easy to read creates a very positive mental impact upon the professor.

The Importance of Reviewing Prior Exams

As we've mentioned, it is *extremely important to review old exams*. The transition from blackletter law to essay exam can be a difficult experience if the process has not been practiced. Although this book provides a large number of essay and multiple-choice questions, *don't stop here*! Most law schools have recent tests online or on file in the library, by course. If they are available only in the library, we strongly suggest that you make a copy of every old exam you can obtain (especially those given by your professors) at the beginning of each semester. The demand for these documents usually increases dramatically as "finals time" draws closer.

The exams for each course should be scrutinized *throughout the semester*. They should be reviewed as you complete each chapter in your casebook. Sometimes the order of exam questions follows the sequence of the materials in your casebook. Thus, the first question on a law school test may involve the initial three chapters of the casebook, the second question may pertain to the fourth and fifth chapters, and so forth. In any event, *don't wait* until the semester is nearly over to begin reviewing old exams.

Keep in mind that no one is born with the ability to analyze questions and write superior answers to law school exams. Like any other skill, it is developed and perfected only through application. If you don't take the time to analyze numerous examinations from prior years, this evolutionary process just won't occur. Don't just *think about* the answers to past exam questions; take the time to *write the answers down*. It's also wise to look back at an answer a day or two after you've written it. You will invariably see (1) ways to improve your organizational skills and (2) arguments you missed.

As you practice spotting issues on past exams, you will see how rules of law become the sources of issues on finals. As we've already noted, if you don't **understand** how rules of law translate into issues, you won't be able to achieve superior grades on your exams. Reviewing exams from prior years should also reveal that certain issues tend to be lumped together in the same question. For instance, where a fact pattern involves a defendant's past bad acts, two potential avenues to admissibility may be present—substantive use and impeachment use. You will need to see if either or both of these theories have application to the facts.

Finally, one of the best means of evaluating if you understand a subject (or a particular area within a subject) is to attempt to create a hypothetical exam for that subject. Your exam should contain as many issues as possible. If you can write an issue-packed exam, you probably know that subject well. If you can't, then you probably haven't yet acquired an adequate understanding of how the principles of law in that subject can spawn issues.

As Always, a Caveat

The suggestions and advice offered in this book represent the product of many years of experience in the field of legal education. We are confident that the techniques and concepts described in these pages will help you prepare for and succeed at your exams. Nevertheless, particular professors sometimes have a preference for exam-writing techniques that are not stressed in this book. Some instructors expect at least a nominal reference to every aspect of admissibility of evidence (even though one or more of those concerns are **not** placed into issue). Other professors want their students to emphasize public policy considerations in the arguments they make on a particular issue. This book does not stress these individualized preferences. The best way to find out whether your professor has a penchant for a particular writing approach is to ask him or her to provide you with a model answer to a previous exam. If a model answer is not available, speak to second- or third-year students who received a superior grade in that professor's class.

One final point. The rules of law stated in the answers to the questions in this book have been drawn from mainstream common law and the Federal Rules of Evidence. If your professor emphasizes one state's specific discrepancies from those sources, *follow the professor's choices!* Because your grade is determined by your professor, his or her views should always supersede the views contained in this book.

Essay
Questions

Question 1

Dan was tried for theft and burglary of the home of Mr. and Mrs. Charles in Central City. The crimes had been committed during the early morning hours of April 17. Dan's defense was that he had been 200 miles away at the time. Mrs. Charles testified to the losses, described the scene, and identified a half-eaten piece of cheese found in the kitchen following the burglary.

The court admitted the following evidence offered by the prosecution:

The testimony of Mr. Charles that while he and Mrs. Charles were sitting in a park a week following the burglary, Dan walked by and Mrs. Charles screamed, "You stole that jacket from our house," whereon Dan ran away without saying a word.

The testimony of Dr. Yank, a dentist, that, based on a comparison of legally obtained impressions of Dan's teeth and a cast of the piece of cheese identified by Mrs. Charles, the bite in the cheese was made by Dan's teeth.

The court then admitted the following evidence offered by the defense:

The testimony of Bob that on April 16, Dan told Bob that he wanted to use Bob's mountain cabin, which was 200 miles from Central City, for the next two days; that Bob consented and gave Dan the key to the cabin; that on April 18, Dan returned the key and said that the stove had exploded when the stovepipe was struck by lightning during the early morning hours of April 17; and that when Bob visited the cabin on the evening of April 18, the stove was as Dan had described.

The prosecution then offered, and the court admitted, Abel's testimony that Bob had told him that Bob had not seen Dan during the entire month of April.

Assuming that all appropriate objections were timely made, did the court err in admitting the testimony of Mr. Charles, Dr. Yank, Bob, and Abel? Discuss.

Question 2

Vince Victim was crossing a street near a college dormitory when a car driven by David Driver collided with Victim, injuring Victim. Victim is suing Driver for damages, alleging that Driver drove his car negligently.

An issue in dispute at trial is whether Driver had been driving too fast at the time of the incident. To show that Driver had been driving too fast, Victim seeks introduced testimony by a college security guard, Gary Guard. Guard testified that on the day of the accident, someone named Walter Watcher rushed into a dormitory where Guard was on duty and said that there'd just been an accident and a student had been hit by a car that came around a corner incredibly fast. Guard testified that as part of his work routine he kept notes in a notebook about anything unusual that happened and that he wrote down the details of what Watcher told him.

For the same purpose, Victim also introduced notes from Guard's notebook, stating that Watcher rushed into the dormitory, said that there'd just been an accident injuring a student, and said that the car came around the corner going at least 80 miles an hour.

On cross-examination of Guard, the trial court allowed these questions:

- "Were you convicted of assault with a concealed deadly weapon about five years ago?"
- "Did Watcher once falsely say he was older than 21 to get into a campus event where alcoholic beverages were available?"

Assuming proper objections were made, discuss (1) the admissibility of Guard's testimony, (2) admissibility of the notes from Guard's notebooks, and (3) the propriety of each of the cross-examination questions. Discuss also (4) whether Guard could have been permitted to testify about what Watcher said without satisfying the Original Writing Rule with regard to Guard's notebook.

Question 3

P, a pedestrian, received injuries in an automobile accident involving two vehicles driven by D and X. The cars collided at an intersection, and P was struck by D's vehicle. P brings suit against D for $15,000.

1. At the trial, P called Dr. Jones, who testified that P was brought to his office by D shortly after the accident and that D said, "I'll pay this man's bill."

2. P testified that prior to trial there had been extensive settlement negotiations between the parties and that D had offered to pay $5,000 in full settlement of P's claim. P also testified that, on one occasion during these negotiations, D had said to him, "I might have gone through the light a little late."

3. Mrs. D, D's wife, was called as a witness by P. She testified that one evening during dinner, and while the butler was present, D said to her, "I'm afraid that I'm at fault in that collision with X."

4. Bystander is called as a witness for D. Bystander testifies that, shortly after the accident, he heard X say, "I'm dying, I'm dying. The accident was all my fault. I'm glad I have insurance." Other evidence disclosed that X, although injured, was not in serious condition. However, X died shortly thereafter en route to the hospital when the ambulance into which he had been placed struck a tree.

Discuss the admissibility of the above items of evidence, assuming that all appropriate objections have been made.

Question 4

Dan Driver is being sued by the estate of Ed Egan, on the theory that negligent driving by Driver caused Egan's death. On September 18 last year,
Driver was driving an SUV on a busy street in the business district of a
large city. At a point in the middle of a block, Egan walked into the street
from between two parked cars. There was a collision between Egan and
Driver's vehicle. Egan was hospitalized after the incident for treatment of
serious internal injuries. Four days after the collision, Egan said to Frank
Friend in the hospital, "I don't know if I'm ever going to recover—and I'll
tell you another thing I don't know. I don't know why a person would drive
an SUV and try to read a newspaper at the same time. If that guy hadn't
been reading the paper, he probably wouldn't have hit me."

Evaluate the trial judge's rulings and the judge's reasons for those rulings
in each of these situations:

1. At trial, the estate sought to have Friend testify about the statement
   Egan made in the hospital to show that Driver had been reading a newspaper while driving. The trial judge overruled a hearsay objection. The
   judge said, "I don't think Egan believed he was dying, but maybe the
   jury would disagree with me, so I'm going to admit it, and I'll instruct
   the jury to disregard it unless they believe he said it while he anticipated
   his death."

2. To support a defense that Egan intentionally caused the collision
   because he had hoped to be killed, Driver sought to introduce testimony
   that Egan had a reputation for being suicidal and that Egan had twice
   attempted to commit suicide. The trial judge sustained objections to
   this evidence, saying, "All of this is inadmissible character evidence."

3. Driver testified that Egan darted out in front of the vehicle suddenly,
   without looking around to see if any vehicles were coming. To impeach
   Driver's testimony, the estate sought to introduce evidence that Driver
   had been convicted in four years earlier for a felony related to receiving
   stolen goods. The trial court sustained an objection to this evidence,
   saying, "I'm just not sure how relevant a stolen goods conviction is when
   he's testified about a driving situation. I'd be more inclined to admit it if
   he'd been convicted of driving under the influence, or vehicular homicide, or something closer to what's at issue here."

Question 5

Peter suffered a head injury when the car he was driving collided with a car owned by Moses and driven by Adams, Moses' chauffeur. Peter sued Moses, alleging that the accident was due to the negligence of Adams, who was driving on business for Moses. Moses denied that Adams was negligent and also alleged that, at the time of the accident, Adams was on his own business. He further asserted that the accident was due solely to Peter's negligence.

At trial, the following items of evidence were received on behalf of Peter, over Moses' objections:

1. Testimony of Officer Jones that when he arrived at the scene 20 minutes after the accident occurred, Adams said to him, "I was going to the drugstore on an errand for Moses when the accident happened."

2. Testimony of Officer Jones that, in his opinion, Moses' vehicle was traveling at least 70 mph. (Prior to this, Officer Jones testified that he had had 15 years experience as a police officer; that he had not seen the accident in question but had examined both cars on the day of the accident; and that he had investigated the skid marks of Moses' vehicle and the distance it traveled after the point of collision.)

3. Testimony of Dr. Medic that he first saw Peter the day before the trial; that he examined Peter solely to prepare himself to testify; and that, during the examination, Peter complained to him of a severe headache from which he was then suffering and had suffered ever since the accident.

4. On cross-examination of Dr. Medic, Moses asked, over Peter's objection, "Doctor, how much are you being paid for testifying in this case?" The doctor answered, "$500."

5. Peter then called Walter, who, after being properly qualified, stated over Moses' objections that he knew the doctor's reputation for truth and veracity and that it was good.

6. On cross-examination, over Peter's objection, Walter was asked whether he had heard that, two months prior to trial, Dr. Medic had been indicted for falsification of his income tax returns and for concealment of assets in a bankruptcy proceeding. Walter answered that he had not heard that.

Assuming all appropriate reasons for admission and exclusion were timely presented by counsel, did the court rule correctly on the various objections? Discuss.

Question 6

P sued D Bus Co. to recover for brain injuries he allegedly received when struck by D's bus at noon on January 15 of the previous year, at Front and Elm Streets, in C City. D filed an answer alleging that P's injuries were caused by a fall at his office. At trial, the following issues arose:

1. P testified that his head injuries had affected his memory so that he no longer remembered the accident. Counsel for P then called F, P's best friend, to testify that P had told him on January 14 of the previous year that he was meeting another friend for lunch at noon the next day, at Front and Elm. F also would testify that P had told him a week after the accident, before his memory began to fail, that the bus had struck him when it was driven onto the sidewalk to get past the right side of a car stopped in the street. Are F's statements admissible over objection?

2. L testified for P, as an eyewitness. He stated that at the time of the accident, he had been in C City on a short vacation and was staying at M Motel on the outskirts. Thereafter, counsel for D offered evidence to show that L had been prosecuted a few months before for letting the air out of bus tires, and further, that L had resided in C City all his life and had never stayed at M Motel. Counsel for P objects to this evidence. Is he correct?

3. In D's defense, counsel proposed to call X, an accountant who had known P for many years, to testify that P's memory problems and insane behavior were not caused by his injuries but stemmed from anxiety over his business, which was failing. May X so testify over objection?

4. Counsel for D also called Dr. Q, a brain specialist, who stated that he had examined P and that P's loss of memory and insane behavior were caused by worry and anxiety, not by any injury. On cross-examination, counsel for P showed Dr. Q a book and then read him its title, which indicated that it was a reference work on brain injuries. After Dr. Q admitted that he had heard of the book, counsel for P proposed to ask whether Dr. Q realized that the author had come to a conclusion directly contrary to Dr. Q's. The book was not offered or admitted into evidence. Should counsel for P be allowed to ask the questions over objection?

Question 7

Peter sued Dan for damages for breach of a written contract. Peter's attorney is Row. Dan's answer in the case denied that he ever signed or entered into any such contract.

At the trial, before a jury, Peter testified that after extensive negotiations, he and Dan executed a written contract. Peter identified a document, purportedly signed and acknowledged by Dan before a notary public, as the original of the contract that he and Dan had signed and acknowledged. That document was then offered in evidence by Row and was admitted.

Thereafter, the following took place:

1. Abel was called as a witness by Dan. Abel testified without objection that he was a teller in the bank where Dan had his commercial account and that he had seen Dan's signature hundreds of times. Abel was then asked whether, in his opinion, the signature on the contract was Dan's and, over objection, was permitted to answer that it was not.

2. On cross-examination, Abel was asked, "Is it not a fact that Peter is suing the bank that employs you?" Defendant's objection was sustained.

3. Dan testified on his own behalf that the signature on the contract was not his. On cross-examination, Dan admitted attending a meeting in Row's office at which Peter showed him the original of the contract. On further cross-examination, Dan was asked, "Didn't Peter then say to you, 'You know that's your signature' and didn't you then smile and shrug your shoulders?" After objection by Dan's attorney, Dan was required to answer the question. Dan answered, "No, that never took place."

4. In rebuttal, Row was sworn as a witness and, over objection, testified that Peter did say to Dan, "You know that's your signature" and that Dan then smiled and shrugged his shoulders.

5. At the close of the trial, at Row's request and over Dan's objection, the jury was instructed: "The signatures on a document bearing a certificate of acknowledgment are presumed to be genuine. You will therefore assume that the signature on the contract is that of Dan unless you are persuaded to the contrary by a preponderance of the evidence." The Evidence Code of the jurisdiction provides in part: "Presumptions affecting the burden of producing evidence: The signatures on a document bearing a certificate of acknowledgment are presumed to be genuine."

   A. For each objection, what might properly have been the grounds of the objection, and how should the court have ruled? Discuss.

   B. Should the court have given the requested instructions? Discuss.

Question 8

Don Defendant was tried for arson. In his direct examination, his lawyer asked, "Did you commit the crime you're charged with, burning down a gas station?" Defendant replied, "No, I did not. I was someplace else that night, and I'm not the type of person who would wreck somebody's business."

1. In cross-examination of Defendant, the prosecutor asked, "Isn't it true that four years ago, you were convicted of burning down a clothing store?" Defendant was ordered to answer that question.

2. After Defendant testified, the prosecution sought to introduce proof that he was convicted of a felony—specifically, stealing valuable jewelry from a store, three years prior to the date of the trial. The trial judge stated, "I think that this information has some risk of unfair prejudice to the defendant, but it does also have some probative value on the issue of his truthfulness. So, I'm going to allow it because I conclude that although its probative value is a little less than its risk of creating unfair prejudice, I don't think its probative value is *substantially* outweighed by the risk of unfair prejudice."

3. After Defendant testified, the trial court allowed the prosecution to introduce evidence that Defendant was once convicted of vandalizing a display in a museum, as relevant to his guilt of the charged arson.

Assuming that all appropriate objections were timely made, did the court err in admitting the testimony by each of these witnesses?

Question 9

P sued D for personal injuries. P claimed that D had negligently manufactured a wooden ladder that broke while being used by a man named Carpenter, causing Carpenter to fall on P. Carpenter died as a result of the injuries received.

1. A police officer was called as P's witness. He testified without objection that when he arrived at the scene, Carpenter, who could not move, was conscious but appeared dazed; and that when the ambulance arrived, it backed over the ladder and broke it into several pieces. Over D's objection, the police officer was allowed to testify that at the scene of the accident he asked Carpenter what happened, and Carpenter said, "The ladder broke and I fell. You don't think I'm going to die, do you?"

2. P offered in evidence a certified copy of Carpenter's death certificate, which stated, among other matters, "If caused by injury, describe how injury occurred: Rung of ladder broke and victim fell on head." The court sustained an objection thereto.

3. P called Dr. Abel. It was stipulated that he was an expert in the field of strength of materials and accident reconstruction. Over D's objection, Dr. Abel was permitted to testify that based on information obtained from the police report, wood fiber analysis reports from an independent laboratory, records of the company from which Carpenter rented the ladder, and his own inspection of the scene, it was his opinion that at least one of the breaks in the ladder preexisted the ladder's being smashed by the ambulance.

4. D called Hood as a witness. Hood refused to answer any questions about the falling of the ladder on the ground that his answers might tend to incriminate him. D then called Baker, who testified, over P's objection, that Hood told him that he, Hood, had kicked the ladder out from under Carpenter.

5. On cross-examination, Baker had difficulty remembering anything else that happened the day Hood made the statement to him, but the court sustained D's objection to the question, "How can you remember what Hood said so clearly when you can't remember anything else that happened that day?"

Assume that all appropriate objections were timely made. Were the court's rulings correct? Discuss.

Question 10

Paul and Dave were driving their respective cars when they collided at an intersection. In a suit brought by Paul to recover damages, Dave denied Paul's allegations, and also asserted that Paul was contributorily negligent. The critical issue was whether Dave had entered the intersection without stopping, in violation of a red traffic light. The trial court, over Dave's objection, permitted Paul to introduce the following evidence:

1. Testimony of the clerk of the criminal court, in which Dave was charged with violating the red traffic signal at the time of the accident, that Dave had initially filed a plea of guilty; but that later, with the permission of the court, he had withdrawn that plea.

2. Testimony of Oliver, in response to a question by Paul's attorney as to whether he saw the accident, and if so, what he saw, that he saw an accident; that Dave drove through the red light, which was against him; and that "it was impossible for Paul to avoid the accident." The trial court, on motion by Dave, refused to strike the portion of Oliver's testimony in quotations.

3. Testimony of White that Dave had confided in him that he had gone through the red light. On cross-examination of White, Dave's counsel asked only one question: namely, whether Paul was related to White.

4. Later, in presenting his own case, over objection by Paul, Dave introduced the testimony of Brown, who said that a week after the accident White told him that he was going to get even with Dave for barring his membership in a local downtown club. Brown gave no further testimony on direct.

5. Paul, over objection by Dave, asked Brown on cross-examination if he had seen the accident. Brown said he had but had forgotten the details. Paul, over objection by Dave, then showed Brown a newspaper account of the accident and asked him if that refreshed his memory. Brown said it did, and then proceeded to describe the accident in a manner similar to Oliver's testimony (except for the statement in quotations).

Discuss the propriety of the court's rulings.

Question 11

Olson and Jones executed a burglary together. As they were leaving the building, the police arrived. A chase ensued, and Jones was arrested. Jones told the police: "You never would have caught me if Olson had not been so slow in finishing the job." The police then found Olson at his home, told him he was suspected of the burglary, fully advised him of his rights, and asked him where he had been earlier that evening. Olson replied that he had been to see the movie *Hellcats* at a downtown theater.

Jones died a month before Olson's trial for burglary. At that trial, Wilson, the owner of the burglarized premises, was called as a witness. Olson objected to Wilson's competence to testify, charging that in a recent accident, Wilson had suffered brain injuries that had rendered him insane. The trial court ordered a psychiatric examination, to which both sides agreed. Following the examination, the psychiatrist testified (in the absence of the jury) that Wilson was not insane, but that he had suffered brain injuries and to some extent was unable to distinguish between his own independent recollection of events and what had been told him by others. The trial judge ruled that Wilson was competent as a witness, recalled the jury, and offered both counsel opportunity to examine the psychiatrist concerning Wilson's reliability. Thereafter, Wilson testified that his premises had been burglarized.

At the trial, the following evidence was also offered by the prosecution:

1. Officer Carlisle's testimony as to Jones's statement at the time of the latter's arrest;

2. Olson's statement to the police, along with evidence that the movie *Hellcats* had closed two days prior to the day on which Olson was questioned;

3. Testimony by a reporter who sat behind Olson, but whom Olson did not see, that during a recess after the offer of Jones's statement, she heard Olson say to his wife, "I should have known Jones would spill his guts";

4. Testimony by a police officer that, while searching Olson's house under a warrant authorizing the search, a map of the burglarized premises was found and seized by the police.

   A. Discuss the propriety of the court's rulings on Wilson's testimony.

   B. Assuming that all possible objections to the introduction of evidence items 1-4 were timely made, how should the trial judge have ruled? Discuss.

Question 12

Derek Defendant was tried for the murder of Ralph Rider. The prosecution alleged that Defendant was walking in a park when Rider approached him on a bicycle. The prosecution claimed that Defendant became angry at Rider, pushed him off the bicycle, and then beat him to death with a small tree limb that Defendant picked up from the ground. Defendant claimed self-defense but did not testify.

1. A witness for Defendant testified that he had lived in Rider's neighborhood for a long time and that Rider had a reputation for being violent.

2. The prosecution introduced testimony by a neighbor of Rider's, in which the neighbor said that Rider had a reputation in their neighborhood for being calm, gentle, and peaceful.

3. The prosecution introduced testimony by a neighbor of Defendant's, in which the neighbor said that Defendant had a reputation in their neighborhood for being violent and aggressive.

4. The prosecution introduced testimony by a coworker of Defendant's, in which the coworker said that in his opinion, Defendant was a violent and aggressive person.

5. The prosecution introduced testimony by a security guard who worked at a grocery store in Defendant's neighborhood, in which the guard said that he had seen Defendant punch someone during a dispute about who had gotten to a checkout counter first.

Assuming that all appropriate objections were timely made, did the court err in admitting the testimony by each of these witnesses?

Question 13

Peter sued Defenders Insurance Company for a loss that occurred in September of last year. Defenders' defense was that it had canceled the policy on August 15 of last year for nonpayment of premium. Peter denied receiving any notice of cancellation (a requisite for cancellation to be effective).

1. At the trial, Abner, an underwriter for Defenders Insurance Company, was allowed to testify for Defenders over objection that he had prepared a notice of cancellation addressed to Peter and that it must have been mailed because it was the invariable practice of Defenders to mail notices of cancellation on the day they were initiated.

2. Baker, a postal inspector, was allowed to testify for Defenders over objection that in December of last year, while investigating the conduct of a letter carrier, he said to Peter, "You actually did receive that notice of cancellation, didn't you?" In response, Baker testified, Peter turned and walked away without answering.

3. Charlie, an underwriter for an insurance company that was in no way connected with Defenders, as a witness for Defenders, was not allowed to testify that his company had on three occasions canceled policies that Peter had with Charlie's company for nonpayment of premiums.

4. After Peter's five-year-old daughter, Debbie, told the judge, "People who do not tell the truth get spanked," she was allowed to testify for Peter over objection that, on August 16 and 17 of last year, she got all the mail from the letter carrier and "took it directly to daddy."

5. Ethel, a neighbor of Peter, was allowed to testify for Peter over objection that the letter carrier who delivered mail to Peter's house, and who is now in prison in another state, told her that during the third week in August of last year, his back was hurting, and so he had destroyed several items of "junk" mail addressed to Peter and others.

Discuss the propriety of the court's rulings. Assume that all appropriate objections were timely made.

Question 14

You represent Don, the proprietor of a swimming-pool supply business. Patterson, an apartment-house owner, brought suit against Don, claiming injury to his respiratory system allegedly caused by Don's mislabeling a bottle of muriatic acid and selling it to Patterson as a chlorine compound.

1. At the trial, Patterson was allowed to testify, over your timely and appropriate objections, that he poured liquid from a bottle purchased from Don and labeled "SODIUM HYPOCHLORIDE, especially prepared by Don for use with any type of automatic pool filter dispenser," into the automatic dispenser on his swimming pool filter pump and was overcome by fumes; that when he recovered, he destroyed the bottle; and that he later heard his friend Jack tell Don he ought to be run out of business for putting the chlorine label on muriatic acid, but Don simply ignored him.

2. On cross-examination, Patterson admitted smoking two packs of cigarettes a day for over 30 years.

3. Dr. Walton, a specialist in internal medicine and environmental hygiene, was called by Patterson and allowed to testify, over your timely and appropriate objections, that Patterson has chronic bronchitis; that he, Dr. Walton, in his laboratory constructed a plastic reproduction of Patterson's pool filterhouse in which he poured muriatic acid into a metal receptacle containing a small amount of water and sodium hypochloride; that he measured the concentration of fumes that resulted; and that Patterson's chronic bronchitis could, and probably did, result from a similar exposure.

4. The court refused to allow you to cross-examine Dr. Walton about certain articles in the *Wall Street Journal* to the effect that cigarette smoking and air pollution are the principal causes of chronic bronchitis.

5. The court also denied your motion that the jury be taken to the pool filterhouse under court supervision and be allowed to inspect it.

Judgment was for Patterson. What points would you make on appeal in regard to the rulings of the trial court? How would you expect the appellate court to rule on them? Discuss.

Question 15

Desmond Defendant was on trial for the alleged rape of Violet Victim. The prosecution contended that Defendant met Victim at a bar, offered her a ride to her home, drove her to a secluded area, and then committed a sexual attack on her while they were in his car at that location. Defendant admitted having driven Victim in his car but denied having committed a sexual attack.

1. The prosecution introduced testimony showing that Defendant was convicted of robbery four years prior to trial, and that he committed that crime by meeting someone in a bar, offering the person a ride home, and then driving that person to a secluded area where he stole the person's money and other possessions of value.

2. The prosecution also introduced evidence that two years prior to trial, Defendant was convicted of sexual assault on a ten-year-old boy.

3. The trial court excluded evidence sought to be introduced by Defendant that would have shown that on two occasions prior to the alleged rape, Victim had met a man at the same bar where she met Defendant, and that in exchange for being given a ride to her home, Victim had engaged in voluntary sexual intercourse with each of those men.

Assuming that all appropriate objections were timely made, did the court err in admitting testimony about Defendant's robbery conviction and sexual assault conviction, and excluding Victim's prior voluntary sexual intercourse?

Question 16

Dan is on trial for the murder of Flora. The prosecution contends that Dan and Flora were lovers and that when Dan discovered Flora's involvement with another man, he intentionally pushed her from a pier into the ocean, where she drowned. The theory of the defense is that Dan had ended his and Flora's relationship and that Flora had committed suicide by jumping off the pier because she was despondent about the end of the relationship.

1. At the trial, the State offered the testimony of Nabor, who testified that the day after Flora's body was found, he witnessed a confrontation between Flora's father, Harvey (who is now deceased), and Dan, during which Flora's father stated to Dan: "You killed my daughter. I saw what you did to her," and that Dan made no reply.

2. Also at the trial, the State offered the testimony of Jack, a jailer, who testified that while Dan was in jail awaiting trial, he attempted suicide.

3. The defense called Rita, Flora's roommate, who testified that the day before Flora's death, she had read a crumpled-up piece of paper in the wastebasket in their apartment, on which Flora had written: "Dear Dan: I have nothing left to live for now that you have left me."

4. On rebuttal, the State called Dr. Slade, a licensed psychologist, who testified that Flora had been undergoing therapy for over a year, that he was well acquainted with her psychological problems, and that based on what Flora had related to him during therapy sessions, he was of the opinion that she was completely lacking in suicidal tendencies.

5. On cross-examination, defense counsel asked Dr. Slade: "Doctor, on at least three separate occasions in the past two years, have you committed acts of shoplifting?" Over objection, Dr. Slade was ordered to answer the question. He stated: "No, that is not so." Defense counsel then asked: "How do you expect us to believe that, Doctor, when I have the investigation reports of the stores right here?" An objection to this question was sustained.

Discuss the admissibility of items 1-4, assuming that all appropriate objections were timely made. As to item 5, discuss the propriety of the court's rulings on the objections.

Question 17

Paul brought a personal injury action against Helico, a helicopter manufacturer. The injury occurred when Paul attempted to board a Model Z helicopter manufactured by Helico. As he approached the helicopter from the rear, he was struck by the rotating tail rotor.

Two days after the accident, Al, the pilot of the helicopter, told Sam, an investigator of the National Transportation Safety Board ("Board"), that immediately after Paul was struck by the tail rotor, Paul exclaimed: "It's not anyone's fault. I just wasn't paying attention. I goofed."

Paul's complaint alleged Helico was negligent because the tail rotor was not marked so as to be conspicuous when operating under normal daylight ground conditions as required by a regulation of the Federal Aviation Administration ("FAA"), and that Helico was strictly liable because the helicopter was defectively designed.

At the trial before a jury, the following occurred:

1. Paul testified that, after his suit was brought, an officer of Helico not only offered to settle the action but also admitted during settlement negotiations that the company agreed with Paul that the helicopter was defectively designed.

2. After the jury had viewed the helicopter involved in the accident, Paul called Professor Jason, a recognized expert in the areas of engineering, navigation, and the operation of aircraft. Professor Jason testified that, based solely on his in-court examination of photographs of the Helico Model Z helicopter and photographs of other helicopters, in his expert opinion the tail rotors on Helico Model Z helicopters are not conspicuous when operating under normal daylight ground conditions as required by the FAA.

3. When called by the defense, Al testified, after repeated attempts to refresh his recollection, that he could not remember what Paul said. The court then admitted testimony by Sam in which Sam said Al had told him Paul admitted not paying attention.

Assuming that all appropriate objections were timely made, did the court properly admit the testimony of Paul, Professor Jason, and Sam? Discuss.

Question 18

Tim was tried in a State A court for possession of 1/10 gram of heroin, a felony. The government's only witness was Officer Jenks, an undercover police officer. Jenks testified that after Tim arranged to sell drugs to Jenks, Tim, in company with Sue, met Jenks on September 13 of last year. Jenks also testified that Tim refused to make the sale, and that Jenks then arrested Tim, searched him, and found a substance that Jenks believed to be heroin in Tim's jacket pocket.

1. The prosecutor then offered as an exhibit a document entitled "Official State A Forensic Laboratory Report," which states that the unknown substance found in the possession of Tim was tested and found to be heroin. The report concluded: "I certify that the above is a true and accurate statement of the findings of this state agency as made this date" and is signed by A. Smith, Executive Director and Custodian (seal).

2. As its first witness, the defense called the defendant, Tim, who testified on direct that he was in possession only of powdered milk and that he was being framed by Jenks. On cross-examination, Tim was asked, "Isn't it true that, two years ago, on May 1, you were in possession of 1/2 gram of heroin?" Over defense objection, Tim was instructed by the court to answer, and said, "Yes."

3. As its second witness, the defense called Sue, who testified that she had been dating the defendant for a year, that they had dined out prior to the offense on eight occasions, and that he always drank his coffee after adding powdered milk taken from a jacket pocket.

4. Sue then testified that Jenks once arrested her for prostitution and offered to release her on payment of a bribe; that, when she refused, Jenks said, "Just wait. I'll get you and all your friends."

5. In rebuttal, the prosecution called Dr. Walt, M.D., who testified that in September of last year he had examined Tim, who complained of insomnia and anxiety; that during the private examination Tim stated he was a narcotics addict in need of money to supply his habit; and that Tim asked Dr. Walt if he would like to buy drugs.

Assume that all appropriate objections were timely made. Were the items of evidence 1-5 properly admitted? Discuss.

In dealing with item 2, discuss only the cross-examination and ignore the defendant's privilege against self-incrimination.

Question 19

Bob was struck by an automobile owned by Owner and driven by Chauf, Owner's employee. After two weeks in a hospital, Bob died.

Chauf was convicted of involuntary vehicular manslaughter. He died in a prison knife fight one week after he was imprisoned.

Paula, Bob's wife, sued Owner for the wrongful death of Bob, alleging that Owner was liable, both under the doctrine of *respondeat superior* and because Owner was negligent in hiring Chauf.

At the trial before a jury, the following occurred:

1. Paula's first witness, Carl, a police officer, testified that when he arrived on the scene immediately after the accident, he asked Bob what had happened, but he does not remember what Bob said; however, he had immediately made a note of what Bob told him and incorporated it into his written report. Carl verified the accuracy of his report and read it aloud. The report stated that Bob told Carl that he, Bob, was crossing the street when a car crossed over the center line and hit him. On Paula's request, the report was introduced into evidence.

2. Paula next called Flo, who testified that she was on duty when Bob arrived at the hospital; that Bob complained of severe pain in his stomach and head; that Bob swore he would get even with the driver of the car that hit him; and that when asked what happened, Bob said he was hit by a speeding car driven by a drunken lunatic.

3. Paula next called Earl, the warden of the prison where Chauf died, who identified a writing made by Chauf a few hours before Chauf's death. The writing commenced with the statement, "I believe I am about to die and I make this statement with no hope of recovery." The writing recited that Chauf was intoxicated and was driving about 80 mph in a 25 mph speed zone at the time of the accident. The writing was admitted into evidence.

4. Paula next called Frank, who testified that he had known Bob for 30 years, that he had seen Bob on many occasions cross the intersection where the accident occurred, and that Bob always waited for the green light and looked both ways before crossing the street.

5. Paula called Owner as an adverse witness and asked Owner whether he
   had heard that Chauf had received five traffic citations over the last five
   years for driving under the influence of alcohol. Owner answered: "No,
   because Chauf never had a traffic citation."

Assume all appropriate objections were timely made. Were items of evidence 1-4 properly admitted, and were the question and answer in item 5 proper? Discuss.

Question 20

Paul brought an action against Dexter Labs, based on strict liability. Paul alleged that he had suffered permanent liver damage from using sleeping pills manufactured and marketed by Dexter. The answer to Paul's complaint denied that the pills did or could cause liver damage.

1. At trial, Paul testified he took Dexter's pills and subsequently developed symptoms of liver damage. On cross-examination, the court sustained an objection to the question, "Isn't it a fact that this is the fifth time you sued a food or drug manufacturer?"

2. Over defense objection, the court permitted the jury to view and hear a videotape of the deposition of Dr. Box, Paul's treating physician, consisting of Dr. Box's expert medical testimony supporting Paul's claim, and the cross-examination of Dr. Box by Dexter's attorney. A stenographic transcript of the deposition was available. Dr. Box refused to testify voluntarily at trial because Paul had refused to pay him a fee of $1,000 for each day of testimony in court. Dr. Box successfully avoided a subpoena requiring him to appear at trial. The only relevant statutory provisions (a) require that, on a deposition, the testimony be taken stenographically and be transcribed, and (b) permit such a deposition to "be used by any party for any purpose if the witness is deceased, out of the jurisdiction, or otherwise unavailable."

3. Over defense objection, the court received into evidence the testimony of an officer of Dexter that after Paul filed suit, Dexter changed its sleeping pill formula to remove a chemical that tended to accumulate in the liver, for the purpose of supporting Paul's claim that the prior formula was unreasonably dangerous.

4. Dr. Abel, a qualified expert, testified for the defense that nothing in the pills that Paul took could possibly have caused liver problems. Over defense objection, Paul's attorney was allowed to cross-examine Dr. Abel regarding the contents of a series of newspaper articles on the toxic effects of sleeping pills.

5. The court sustained Paul's objection and refused to allow the defense to introduce the testimony of attorney Carl, to the effect that Paul had previously consulted him concerning his claim against Dexter, Paul had told him that his liver was permanently damaged before Paul took the Dexter pills, and Carl had refused to represent Paul.

Assuming all appropriate objections were timely made, were the court's rulings correct? Discuss.

Question 21

Dick is brought to trial on an indictment charging him with larceny of a dangerous drug, a statutory offense. The prosecution's theory of the case, as revealed by its opening statement, is that Phil saw Dick enter Phil's Pharmacy, loiter about the prescription counter, reach behind the counter, grab two bottles, and flee by car. Phil called police officers, who arrested Dick after a lengthy high-speed chase.

At the trial before a jury, the following occurred:

1. The prosecution offers in evidence a properly authenticated transcript of testimony by Officer Oats given during a previous trial of Dick for reckless driving based on the high-speed chase from Phil's Pharmacy. Oats's testimony was that during the chase and while Dick's car was passing over a bridge, two objects were ejected from Dick's car into the river below. It is stipulated that Dick was represented by counsel at the earlier trial and that Oats is now deceased.

2. The prosecution offers the testimony of Phil that the bottles seized by Dick were labeled "DLD," that the bottles were the original labeled containers received from the supplier, and that the bottles had not been opened.

3. The prosecution requests the court to take judicial notice that DLD is a derivative of opium. The statute under which Dick is prosecuted does not list DLD as a "dangerous drug," but it does define dangerous drugs to include "any derivative of opium." In support of its request, the prosecution offers for the court's inspection a standard pharmacological dictionary, which defines DLD as an opium derivative.

4. The prosecution offers the testimony of Dick's divorced wife, Win, that during her marriage to Dick the latter frequently used narcotics but attempted to conceal that fact from Win.

Assuming that all appropriate objections were timely made by Dick, how should the court have ruled on each of the prosecution's offers and requests? Discuss.

Question 22

Plaintiffs as the parents and guardians *ad litem* of Peter, age four, brought suit for damages against the parents of David, age ten, alleging that defendants negligently entrusted David with an air rifle with which David shot Peter in the eye, causing serious personal injury. Among other things, defendants denied that David inflicted Peter's eye injury.

At the trial before a jury, the following occurred:

1. After Peter told the court that "good little boys always tell the truth," Peter testified that David shot him in the eye with the rifle.

2. Peter's father testified that the defendants had paid a substantial portion of Peter's medical bills and had offered to pay the rest.

3. Bill, a neighbor, testified that (a) David was "a vicious little bully with malicious tendencies"; and (b) that when Bill, Bill's wife Clara, and David's mother were all standing together in Bill's yard after the incident, Clara stated to Bill that David's mother had said to her about one week before the accident that "she had tried to get David's father to put the air rifle in the attic where David couldn't get to it, before someone got hurt" and that David's mother had said nothing in response to Clara's statement.

4. Wilbur, an eyewitness, corroborated Peter's description of the shooting. On cross-examination Wilbur was asked: "Aren't you addicted to heroin? Aren't you in fact now under the influence of a narcotic?" The court sustained plaintiff's objections to both questions.

In each instance, all appropriate objections were timely made, and in items 1-3, the court permitted the testimony over objection; in item 4, the court sustained the objections to both questions.

Were the rulings of the court correct? Discuss.

Question 23

About two years ago, Larry Landowner invited Carl Camper to camp on Landowner's land in a rural area and to swim in a small pond on the land. Camper spent about ten weeks there, camping and swimming. But Camper then became ill. Camper sued Landowner for damages associated with his illness. Camper claims that Landowner knew about toxic chemicals that were on the land and in the pond, and that therefore under the state's tort doctrines about landowners and land entrants, Landowner had a duty to disclose the presence of the invisible dangerous condition (the toxic chemicals). Landowner claims that he was ignorant of the presence of the chemicals.

1. At trial, to prove that Landowner knew about the presence of the chemicals, Camper introduced testimony by Bob Barkeep. Barkeep is a bartender in a small bar near Landowner's land. Barkeep testified that a frequent customer at the bar, Harry Handyman, had often spoken to him about Landowner. Barkeep testified that Handyman said about three years ago that Landowner had hired Handyman to dump large containers of chemicals into Landowner's pond and that Landowner had told Handyman that the chemicals were toxic and that dumping them was illegal. Handyman was not available to testify.

2. In cross-examination of Barkeep, counsel for Landowner asked, "Does Camper owe you several thousand dollars in unpaid debts?"

3. Counsel for Landowner introduced testimony by Nat Neighbor, who lived in Handyman's hometown, that Handyman had a reputation in their hometown for being a liar.

4. Counsel for Landowner introduced testimony by Nat Neighbor that Handyman once said to him, "Landowner is one of the most ethical people I've ever met."

Assuming that all appropriate objections were timely made, did the court err in admitting Barkeep's testimony, Landowner's cross-examination of Barkeep, and Neighbor's testimony?

Question 24

In a rape prosecution against Dan, the following occurred at the trial before a jury:

1. Adam, a neighbor of the victim, Tess, testified that, within five minutes after the rape was alleged to have occurred, Tess ran to his house sobbing and said that she had just been raped by a man with a large brown blemish on his left arm.

2. Detective Cable testified that, on receiving Tess's report, he examined the file of known sex offenders, and that Dan was described as having a blemish on his left arm.

3. Dan's wife voluntarily testified for the prosecution that Dan returned home on the night in question with scratches on his arm.

4. Dan testified in his defense and denied the act, saying that he had never been near Tess's house. In rebuttal, the prosecution offered one of Dan's shoes, seized in a search of Dan's house. The shoe was introduced together with expert testimony that a shoeprint identical to the shoeprint made by Dan's shoe had been located outside the window the rapist had used to enter Tess's house.

Assume all proper motions and objections were timely made.

Did the court err in admitting the testimony in items 1-3, or in admitting the shoe and testimony in item 4? Discuss.

Essay Answers

Answer to Question 1

Important aspects:
Consciousness of guilt, scientific evidence, plan as a state of mind, prior inconsistent statement to impeach, collateral topics.

1. *Testimony of Mr. Charles*

Dan ("D") could argue that the testimony of Mr. Charles ("C") is not relevant (i.e., does not tend to prove or disprove a material fact of consequence). He may have run away simply because he desired to avoid an altercation with someone who was erroneously charging him with having committed a crime. The prosecution ("P"), however, probably successfully argued in rebuttal that D's conduct does indicate a consciousness of guilt.

D could next assert that C's statement is hearsay. He is testifying as to what his wife stated and what D did in response. Hearsay statements are those made out-of-court that are offered to prove the truth of the matter asserted. As to D's conduct, P could contend that, in many states and under the Federal Rules of Evidence (FRE), nonassertive conduct is not hearsay at all. Even if it was, the party-opponent admission exception to the hearsay rule would apply (any statement by a party that is relevant is admissible if offered by the party's opponent).

Mrs. C's statement is arguably admissible as an adoptive admission (i.e., an out-of-court statement made in the party-opponent's presence that a reasonable person would have objected to or denied). P would contend that a reasonable person, hearing a false criminal accusation, would have protested his innocence to the speaker. D could argue in rebuttal, however, that a reasonable person confronted with a false accusation by a total stranger in a park would simply leave the area (as D did). However, P should prevail on this issue.

Mrs. C's statement would probably fall within the "excited utterance" exception to the hearsay rule. Such a statement ordinarily must be made about a startling event by someone who observed it, while the event is occurring (or while the declarant was still under the stress of the event). The "startling event" in this instance was seeing D wearing her jacket. Because Mrs. C's statement was made watching this startling event, this testimony should be admissible.

Thus, C's testimony was probably properly admitted.

2. The testimony of Dr. Yank ("Y")

D initially could have asserted that Y's testimony is not admissible because Y testified as an expert without any foundation having been laid that he had any specialized expert knowledge. Y is, apparently, an ordinary dentist. P could argue that any dentist who constantly analyzes teeth has sufficient specialized knowledge to give an expert opinion about dental impressions.

Assuming Y is qualified to testify as an expert, D could respond that no evidence was introduced to show that this type of comparison testing is scientifically valid. Because P apparently did not show that the comparison method used by Y is scientifically valid (which would be shown by factors such as error rate, peer review, general acceptance in the field, and whether the test can be reliably tested), the court erred in admitting Y's testimony.

3. Bob ("B")'s testimony

P could contend that B's testimony was hearsay because it described what D said out-of-court.

D could respond that D's desire to use the cabin for two days is admissible under the "present state of mind" exception to the hearsay rule because it describes what D indicated he would do in the future.

D's returning the key and commenting that the stove had exploded when the pipe was hit by lightning during the early morning hours of April 17 (when C's home was burglarized) is not hearsay because it is offered into evidence by D simply to show that he was aware that the cabin's stove had been damaged (rather than for the purpose of establishing that the item had, in fact, been damaged). D's knowledge of the damaged stove would tend to corroborate his assertion that he was 200 miles away when the crime occurred.

Thus, B's testimony was properly admitted.

The party-opponent exception to the hearsay rule would not be applicable to D's statements in this instance because B was D's witness.

4. Abel ("A")'s testimony

A's testimony appears to be offered for impeachment (the prosecution and D have each already presented the case-in-chief). Thus, a hearsay objection is not appropriate because A's statement was not offered to prove the truth of the matter (i.e., that B, in fact, had not seen D during the month of April), but rather to impair B's credibility by showing that he had made an earlier inconsistent statement. It is ordinarily proper to impeach a witness in this manner by extrinsic evidence (i.e., A's testimony), provided the impeachment does not go to a collateral matter. The "I was far away" alibi asserted by D is certainly *not* collateral to the case (it is the essence of D's defense).

In some jurisdictions, but not under the FRE, a foundation must be laid before impeachment by extrinsic evidence as to a prior inconsistent statement is admissible (i.e., P should have asked B, while he was on the stand, "Isn't it a fact that you told A that you had not seen D during the month of April?"). If such was the rule in this jurisdiction, A's testimony should not have been admitted.

In a few jurisdictions, prior inconsistent statements are not deemed to be hearsay. In that event, and assuming no foundation was necessary, A's testimony would have been admissible as substantive evidence on P's case-in-chief. Such is *not* the case, however, under the FRE unless the prior inconsistent statement was made under oath; FRE 801(d)(1)(A).

Answer to Question 2

Important aspects:

Relevance, excited utterance, business records, authentication, multiple levels of hearsay, inquiry into past acts regarding credibility, original writing rule.

1. Testimony by Guard ("G")

G's testimony was properly admitted for the following reasons. G's testimony is relevant to show Driver had been driving too fast because if it is believed, it supports a conclusion that Watcher ("W") reported excessive speed (assuming that Watcher's words are admissible for substantive use). G's testimony is based on G's personal knowledge since he saw W and heard W's statement to him.

G's testimony contains hearsay since it quotes W and since W's words have relevance only if their contents are taken as true. W said something like "incredibly fast," and that concept is the purpose for which Victim ("V") wants to introduce them. W's words may have been a present sense impression since it seems that they describe something immediately after W had seen those events. Also, W's words may be treated as excited utterances since he was likely upset (he "rushed" into the dormitory) and the words relate to the accident that may have caused his emotional stress. G's testimony about his practice of maintaining a notebook is relevant since it is the foundation for introduction of part of that notebook, and it is testimony within the scope of G's personal knowledge.

2. Notes from G's notebook.

The notes were properly admitted. They would need to be authenticated, which likely happened with testimony by G about the circumstances of making them and about whether the introduced portion actually were what V claimed them to be.

The notes represent two levels of hearsay. One declarant is W, and another declarant is G. W's words are admissible hearsay, as discussed before. G's written statement (his notes in the notebook) would qualify as a business record since he described the regular practice of maintaining the notebook in his work as a guard. The notebook could also be a present sense impression if the notes in it were made by G shortly after he perceived W's words and actions.

3. *Cross-examination questions.*

The first cross-examination question ("assault with a concealed deadly weapon") was wrongly allowed. To impeach the credibility of G, inquiry is permitted into past acts that shed light on credibility. In most jurisdictions, a crime of violence would not be considered an act that is relevant to the character trait of truthfulness, so a question about it would be prohibited.

The second cross-examination question is an attempt to impeach the credibility of a hearsay declarant (W). If W had testified, it would have been correct for that question to have been included in his cross-examination. However, W did not testify. The only method allowed for using this kind of information against someone is to ask that person about it when that person is subject to cross-examination. Substituting G for W, for this purpose, is outside the procedure authorized by the rules.

4. *G's testimony and the Original Writing Rule.*

G's testimony would have been properly admitted even if the notebook had not been available at trial. G was testifying about what G knew from personal knowledge. His testimony did not depend on the contents of any document, even though a document did exist that paralleled his knowledge. Had G testified in the style of "This is what my notes say," the Original Writing Rule would have applied. But the rule has no application when a witness only testifies about what the witness knows from personal observation independent of any writing.

Answer to Question 3

Important aspects:

Offers to pay medical expenses, statements made in settlement negotiations, spousal privilege, marital communications privilege, hearsay, dying declarations.

1. Dr. Jones ("J")'s testimony

D could have objected to J's testimony on the grounds that (1) it violated the physician-patient privilege; (2) it was irrelevant (i.e., did not tend to prove or disprove a fact of consequence) because D may have been motivated to take P to J's office from a humanitarian impulse, rather than as a result of feelings of culpability; (3) it was hearsay (J described what D said out-of-court); and (4) in nearly all states (as well as federal courts; FRE 409), offers to pay for medical assistance are not admissible to prove liability.

First, P could have argued that (1) the physician-patient privilege is not applicable because it pertains only to statements made for medical diagnosis and treatment, and D's instructions to J did not refer to these aspects; and (2) even if applicable, this privilege is held only by the person who received the diagnosis or treatment, P *not* D.

Second, P could have contended that D's conduct in taking him to a physician and promising to pay P's medical bills is relevant because it shows recognition of responsibility for P's condition (i.e., people don't ordinarily inconvenience themselves and incur liability for a stranger unless they feel responsible for the latter's situation).

Third, the hearsay objection would be overcome by the party-opponent admission exception to the hearsay rule.

Finally, in most states as well as the federal courts, an offer to pay medical expenses is not admissible to prove liability.

The evidence probably should not have been admitted because (1) the act of taking P to J's office is probably not relevant (any kindhearted person would have done this); and (2) the majority view is to exclude offers to pay medical expenses (the rationale being that aid to accident victims should not be discouraged).

2. P's testimony

D could have objected to this testimony on the grounds that (1) it is hearsay (P is describing what D said out-of-court); (2) settlement offers (D's offer to pay $5,000 in settlement of the action) are generally inadmissible; and (3) admissions of fact made during a settlement offer, although admissible under the common law, are inadmissible under the Federal Rules of Evidence (FRE 408).

The hearsay objection can be overcome by the party-opponent admission to the hearsay rule. The second objection is valid under the common law as well as the FRE. Evidence that a party has offered to settle a claim may not be admitted on the issue of the claim's validity. Therefore, D's promise to pay $5,000 for a release is inadmissible. Whether D's statement about "going through a red light" would be admissible depends on whether this jurisdiction adheres to the FRE view (excluding *all* statements made in the course of settlement negotiations). Assuming the FRE is followed in this state, P's entire testimony should not have been admitted.

3. Testimony of Mrs. D

D could have objected to this testimony as (1) violating the spousal privilege (in some states, one spouse can prevent the other from testifying against him); (2) violating the marital communications privilege; (3) being hearsay; and (4) offering an opinion pertaining to an ultimate issue of fact (i.e., that D's conduct fell below the applicable standard of care).

P could have argued in rebuttal, however, that (1) many jurisdictions apply the spousal privilege only to criminal cases; (2) the marital communications privilege is not applicable because D's statement was not "confidential" (i.e., it was made while the butler was present); (3) the party-opponent exception would overcome any hearsay objection; and (4) most jurisdictions permit lay witness opinion on an ultimate issue of fact. FRE 704 specifically provides that testimony in the form of an opinion that is otherwise admissible is not objectionable because it embraces an ultimate issue of fact.

Assuming this jurisdiction permits lay witness opinion on ultimate issues of fact and D was (or reasonably should have been) aware of the butler's presence, Mrs. D's testimony would be admissible.

4. Testimony of Bystander ("B")

D could have objected to B's testimony as (1) being hearsay (it reports the words that X said out-of-court); (2) containing a reference to insurance; and (3) including lay witness opinion (i.e., the portion of the testimony dealing with X's fault in the accident).

P could have contended in rebuttal that the statement is admissible under the dying declaration, statement against interest, excited utterance, or present sense impression exceptions to the hearsay rule.

Under the FRE, X's words fit the dying declaration exception. X is not available to testify, and the statement is about the cause or circumstances of what X believed to be his impending death. The "statement against interest" exception might not apply, if P could successfully contend that because X believed that death was imminent, the statement was actually *not* against his pecuniary interest. The excited utterance and present sense impression exceptions each would likely cover X's statement. X spoke about the accident while he was under stress caused by it. Also, it seems that X spoke about the accident immediately after it had happened.

Because X's statement is within the coverage of the dying declaration, present sense impression, and excited utterance exceptions, the hearsay objection should have been overcome.

The objection to the portion of B's testimony pertaining to X's statement about insurance should have been sustained. That portion is irrelevant because it doesn't tend to prove or disprove responsibility for P's injury. Also, public-policy grounds support its exclusion. A jury's decision-making might be affected by the fact that X's insurance could more easily compensate P for his injuries, and that would be an impermissible basis for decision.

Finally, the fact that X's statement expressed an opinion on an ultimate issue does not bar the testimony. FRE 704 expressly permits such ultimate issue testimony.

In summary, B's testimony was properly admitted. It should be noted that some states (but not the FRE) limit the dying declaration exception to cases involving homicide and may require a more detailed description of the cause or circumstances of death. Also, some states may prohibit ultimate issue statements.

Answer to Question 4

Important aspects:

Hearsay, dying declarations, judge's role in deciding admissibility, past acts for non-character uses, impeachment with felony convictions.

1. Hospital statement by Egan ("E")

If E made his statement while believing that his death was imminent, it would properly be admissible as a dying declaration. The proponent seeks to use it in a civil case, and it pertains to the circumstances of the cause of death. The trial judge may have reached the right result in admitting the statement, but the judge's rationale was seriously flawed. The judge, not the jury, is required to rule on the admissibility of evidence in every situation except "conditional relevance." There is nothing conditional about the relevance of E's words. Their admissibility depends only on the technical evidence issue of application of the dying declaration exception. That task is reserved for the judge.

2. E's suicidal reputation and acts

Evidence that is relevant only because it supports a conclusion about a person's character that would support a conclusion that the person acted in conformity with that character is prohibited. The evidence that E had a reputation for being suicidal would be introduced to show that he was a suicidal kind of person and would likely be barred by the anti-propensity rule. On the other hand, evidence that could support a conclusion about character is admissible if there is a non-character way in which a jury could use it. In this case, proof about past suicide attempts might be treated as admissible to show motive, or plan, or even knowledge if the circumstances of E's collision with the vehicle were ambiguous enough so that the trial judge could decide that extra information to characterize the event would seem useful to the jury.

3. Impeaching Driver (D) with felony

The trial judge properly excluded proof that D had been convicted of a felony for receiving stolen goods. The use of felonies for impeachment is controlled by FRE 609, which requires that the felony have probative value that is not substantially outweighed by the risk of prejudice. The risk of prejudice here is significant since jurors are likely to have extremely negative feelings about one who is involved in thefts and who traffics in stolen goods, and the probative value is relatively low since lying is probably not inherent in transactions such as those for which D was convicted.

The trial judge gave a very poor explanation for the ruling, however. If the past felony had been vehicular homicide, for example, its similarity to the conduct being litigated in the current trial should count *against* admissibility for impeachment since it increases the risk of prejudice without increasing the utility of the information for its proper purpose, assessing the credibility of the witness.

Answer to Question 5

Important aspects:

Statement by party-opponent, scientific evidence, statements for purpose of medical diagnosis or treatment, bias, rehabilitation for credibility, cross-examination of a character witness.

1. Officer Jones ("J")'s testimony

Moses ("M") probably contended that Jones ("J")'s testimony was hearsay (an out-of-court statement offered into evidence to prove the truth of the matter asserted therein) because J was testifying as to what Adams ("A") had told him. Peter ("P") probably argued in rebuttal that A's statement constituted an admission by the agent or servant of a party-opponent. Statements made by agents or servants in the course of their agency or employment are attributable to their principal if their subject is within the scope of their employment; FRE 801(d)(2)(D). The Federal Rule specifies that the contents of a statement may be considered by the court in ruling on whether the statement is an admission but that the contents of the statement may not be the *only* basis for concluding that the statement qualifies as an admission. If there was any proof in addition to A's own words that A was working for M, the statement was properly admitted.

2. J's testimony (opinion)

M probably objected to this testimony on the grounds that no foundation had been laid to the effect that (1) J had sufficient expertise to reconstruct an accident from skid marks; and (2) the process of interpreting a car's speed by skid marks is a scientifically valid basis for evaluating a vehicle's speed. The fact that J had been a police officer for 15 years would *not* necessarily establish that he had the special expertise presumably required to interpret skid marks. But, assuming that J was qualified to testify as an expert, the process by which skid marks are used to measure a vehicle's speed must be proven to be scientifically valid before it can be admitted into evidence. Scientific validity can be shown by factors such as error rate, peer review, general acceptance in the field, and whether the test can be reliably tested. Thus, unless additional evidence was presented by P's attorneys that addressed these objections, J probably should *not* have been permitted to offer an opinion as to the speed of M's vehicle.

3. Dr. Medic's testimony

M probably contended that Medic's testimony was hearsay (Medic is testifying as to what P told him).

FRE 803(4) provides an exception to the hearsay exclusion for statements for the purpose of medical diagnosis or treatment. The committee notes to FRE 803(4) say that statements made for the purpose of preparing the doctor to testify also qualify. This exception includes both past and present symptoms, such as P's complaints of headache. The testimony is admissible.

4. Cross-examination of Medic

Because bias in favor of a party is a proper basis for impeachment, the fact that Medic had received a substantial sum to testify on P's behalf was an appropriate subject of inquiry. Thus, the court correctly overruled P's objection.

5. Testimony of Walter ("W")

M probably objected to the rehabilitation of Medic's testimony by evidence of Medic's reputation for truth and veracity because Medic had been impeached only with respect to possible bias. Because there must ordinarily be some relationship between the area of impeachment and that which is being rehabilitated, M's objection should have been sustained.

6. The cross-examination of W

A witness who testifies as to another person's character for truthfulness or veracity in the community may ordinarily be questioned about specific acts of the latter that pertained to those qualities. Because the falsification of income tax returns and the concealment of assets would (if true) discredit W's testimony by suggesting that W was not well informed as to Medic's reputation in the community, the question was proper.

Answer to Question 6

Important aspects:

Plan as a state of mind, extrinsic evidence of past acts regarding credibility, lay opinion, expert opinion, learned treatises.

1. F's testimony

F's initial testimony (that P had told him he was meeting a friend for lunch on June 15 at Front and Elm) would be relevant (i.e., it tends to prove or disprove a material fact) because it would corroborate that P was at the scene of the accident.

D could have objected to this testimony, however, on the grounds that it was hearsay (an out-of-court statement offered into evidence to prove the truth of the matter asserted therein). However, P could successfully argue in rebuttal that F's statement was admissible under the hearsay exception covering statements of then-existing state of mind. Statements about a plan are covered by that exception.

D probably objected on hearsay grounds to F's second statement (that P had advised F that the bus had driven onto the sidewalk). Because P's statement was made one week after the accident, it would *not* qualify as an excited utterance or present sense impression. The state of mind exception would not apply because it does not cover statements of belief to prove the truth of the fact the declarant remembered or believed. The description of how the accident occurred should *not* have been admitted.

2. L's testimony

The substance of L's testimony is unclear. If L had corroborated P's version of the accident, it would be relevant. Otherwise, however, L's assertion that he was in C City for a vacation and was staying at M Motel would not appear to be pertinent to any issues of the case. In the latter instance, a relevancy objection to the testimony should have been sustained.

D's offer of evidence pertaining to L's prosecution, permanent residency, and failure to stay at the M Motel was apparently for the purpose of impeachment.

D's counsel could have contended that proof of the prosecution of L for letting air out of bus tires was proper impeachment because it tended to show bias by L against the defendant (if L's conduct had involved D's buses or even if it had just involved buses operated by other companies).

Extrinsic evidence showing that a witness is biased is properly admitted for impeachment. In some jurisdictions, a foundation must be laid prior to the admission of **extrinsic** (i.e., the facts indicate that counsel for D "offered evidence") evidence of bias (i.e., L should have been asked, while he was on the stand, if he had been prosecuted for letting the air out of bus tires). In those jurisdictions, the "evidence" would **not** be admissible. P could have responded that the proffered evidence was impeachment through prior bad acts. It is not clear from the facts whether the prosecution of L had resulted in a conviction. If it had not, L's "prior bad acts" would not be a proper basis of impeachment because (1) the acts complained of in this instance arguably do not pertain to truthfulness or veracity; and (2) impeachment with respect to prior bad acts not resulting in a conviction ordinarily cannot be accomplished by extrinsic evidence.

D could have contended that the evidence showing that L had resided in C City all his life and had never stayed at the M Motel was proper for impeaching L. P's attorney probably could have responded that one can never impeach by extrinsic evidence with respect to a collateral matter. Despite the fact that the location of L's lifelong residence has no connection with the material issues in the suit between P and D, the trial court could properly allow proof that L had testified that he was on "a short vacation" in his hometown. If an error about a "collateral" matter is one that no truthful witness would likely make, a trial court may allow that error to be proved to impeach the credibility of the witness.

3. X's testimony

P probably objected to X's testimony on the grounds that (1) it constitutes lay opinion pertaining to the causal relationship between P's injuries and his actions; and (2) it violated accountant-client privilege (assuming this privilege is recognized in this state). D could have argued in rebuttal that (1) lay opinion is often admissible if it is based on firsthand knowledge and helpful to a determination of the issues by the fact finder; and (2) the accountant-client privilege ordinarily extends only to communications (statements made by the client to the accountant), rather than the accountant's observations of the client's physical condition. However, X's testimony probably should not have been admitted because he does not have the expertise to offer an opinion as to the causal relationship between P's medical condition and his actions.

4. Dr. Q's testimony

P could have contended that Dr. Q's testimony violated the physician-patient privilege. However, this privilege is waived where the patient has placed his physical condition into issue. Because Dr. Q is a "brain specialist," there appears to be little doubt that he was qualified to testify as to the causes of P's memory lapse and insane behavior. Thus, Dr. Q's testimony was properly admitted.

D could have objected that P's cross-examination of Dr. Q was improper because (1) the work relied on by P was not established as a learned treatise; (2) Dr. Q did not rely on the work in giving his testimony; and (3) the statements in the book were hearsay. However, P could have successfully argued in rebuttal that (1) Dr. Q's own statement that the work was a reference book on brain injuries would establish the work as a learned treatise; (2) the modern rule is that an expert may be impeached by statements contained in a learned treatise regardless of whether he has relied on them; and (3) because the statements contained in the work are being offered to contradict Dr. Q (rather than for the truth of the matter contained therein), the hearsay rule is inapplicable. It therefore appears that the cross-examination of Dr. Q was appropriate. The Federal Rules recognize an exception to the hearsay rule for statements in a learned treatise; FRE 803(18).

Answer to Question 7

Important aspects:
Authentication, lay testimony on handwriting, bias, adoptive admissions, impeachment, production burden.

1. Abel ("A")'s testimony

Peter ("P") might properly have objected that A's testimony was opinion and therefore not admissible. However, a lay witness may ordinarily offer his opinion with respect to another's signature for the purpose of authenticating a document, as long as the witness possessed firsthand familiarity with the handwriting not acquired for the purpose of the litigation in which the lay witness testifies. Because A had seen Dan ("D")'s signature "hundreds of times" and his testimony is pertinent in proving that D had *not* signed the contract, the court correctly admitted this evidence.

2. The cross-examination of A

Assuming P's counsel had a good-faith basis for his question, the inquiry would appear to be proper because bias is a proper ground for impeachment. Although D could have objected on relevance grounds that P's lawsuit against A's employer would not necessarily cause bias on the part of A against P, actions that impair a business often affect its employees. If P's against the bank were successful, it might affect the bank substantially. Thus, D's objection should *not* have been sustained.

Although P's counsel asked a leading question, this mode of interrogation is ordinarily proper with adverse witnesses.

3. The cross-examination of D

D's counsel could have objected to this cross-examination on the grounds that (1) it was a leading question; (2) it was a compound question (D is being asked to answer two questions by a single inquiry—what P stated and how he responded); and (3) it calls for a hearsay response (i.e., for D to testify as to what P said out-of-court). P could have responded in rebuttal, however, that (1) leading questions are permissible on cross-examination; (2) the two inquiries were easily distinguishable (i.e., did P make a particular statement, and did D respond in a specific manner?); and (3) P's statement plus D's acquiescence constituted an adoptive admission by D.

Thus, the objection to D's cross-examination was properly overruled.

4. Row ("R")'s testimony

D could have objected to R's testimony on the grounds that (1) an attorney in a particular case should not be competent to testify because a jury would have a tendency to give too much weight to his statement; and (2) it is hearsay (R is testifying with respect to P's statement and D's lack of response). However, P could respond that (1) most jurisdictions permit anyone (other than a juror or the presiding judge) to testify; and (2) P's statement is an adoptive admission by D because a reasonable person would have denied P's allegation.

In any event, R's testimony would be admissible for impeachment purposes to contradict D (i.e., to show that D had previously behaved in a manner that contradicts his testimony).

There would be no difficulty in impeaching D through extrinsic evidence because this testimony was **not** collateral to the issues of the case (i.e., whether D signed the contract is a central issue in the litigation).

5. The judge's instruction

Where a presumption affects only the burden of producing evidence (as opposed to the burden of persuasion), the modern rule is that once the party against whom the presumption operates offers evidence sufficient to support a jury finding contrary to the presumption, the presumption is overcome. Consequently, the burden of proving the applicable fact is on the party attempting to establish it. Because A and D testified that the latter did not sign the contract, there was sufficient evidence for the fact finder to conclude that D had **not** executed the agreement. Thus, the court's instruction was erroneous. The judge should have instructed the jury that it should conclude that D signed the contract if it was persuaded of that fact by a preponderance of the evidence (rather than indicating that D had the burden of persuading the jury by a preponderance of the evidence that he had **not** signed the agreement).

Answer to Question 8

Important aspects:

Cross-examination of character witness, felony convictions for impeachment, extrinsic evidence of past acts for impeachment.

1. *Question about burning down a clothing store*

Defendant likely objected to this question as an improper character inquiry and also as an effort to introduce evidence of a specific past act to support a character inference.

The prosecution likely responded that character evidence would be proper once Defendant made a general statement about what kind of person he is. The prosecution would also have noted that its question was not proof of any kind.

The trial judge correctly allowed the question. Inquiry into a person's specific past acts is permitted on cross-examination of a witness who has testified about the character of that person (FRE 405(a)), and Defendant did provide testimony about his own character.

2. *Shoplifting conviction for impeachment*

Defendant would have objected that because the trial judge treated this evidence as relevant to impeachment, and because the judge said it had less probative value on that topic than prejudicial risk, the appropriate balancing test required exclusion of the evidence.

The prosecution might have responded that admission of this evidence was within the trial judge's discretion.

FRE 609(a)(1) permits use of a past felony conviction against a defendant for impeachment purposes *only* if its probative value outweighs the risk of prejudice. Because the trial judge used a different balancing test, one that was more favorable to the prosecution, the trial judge erred in admitting this evidence. The proper balancing test in this instance is different from the usual FRE 403 test that permits admission of evidence even if its probative value is outweighed (but not substantially outweighed) by the risk of prejudice.

3. *Defendant's museum vandalism*

Defendant would have objected to this evidence as improper character evidence, supporting a conclusion that he is a person who characteristically would be likely to set fire to someone's building. Defendant would also have argued that even if character evidence is permitted, the form of this evidence was improper.

The prosecution would have responded that Defendant opened the door to the character inquiry by saying about himself that he is not the type of person who would commit a crime like the charged crime.

The trial court erred in admitting the evidence. The prosecution is correct that it was entitled to rebut Defendant's own introduction of evidence about his character. However, the style of proof the prosecution used was the introduction of extrinsic evidence, not an inquiry on cross-examination. This kind of character evidence is prohibited. The prosecution could be permitted to rebut Defendant's evidence only with proof in the form of reputation or opinion.

Answer to Question 9

Important aspects:
Present sense impression, dying declarations, public records, basis for expert testimony, statements against interest, scope of cross-examination.

1. Testimony of the police officer

D probably objected to the officer's testimony on the grounds that it was hearsay (an out-of-court statement offered into evidence to prove the truth of the matter asserted). P could successfully contend that the statement by Carpenter ("C") constituted a present sense impression, a statement describing an event made while the declarant was perceiving the event or immediately thereafter.

P could also have contended that C's statement was a dying declaration (a statement made by an unavailable declarant who believed that his death was imminent and that concerned the cause of his impending death). Some jurisdictions limit this doctrine to homicide cases, but it applies to civil cases under the Federal Rules. Although it is unclear whether C actually believed that his death was imminent, his inquiry ("You don't . . . ") does suggest an awareness of that possibility.

2. The death certificate

D could have objected to this evidence on the grounds that it was hearsay and violated the Original Writing Rule. (No authentication objection appears to be appropriate because the document was certified.) The Original Writing Rule objection was probably overcome by the facts that (1) the original item was not removable from the public office in which it was deposited (i.e., the coroner's office); and (2) a duplicate is permissible to the same extent as an original, unless the circumstances indicate some question as to its genuineness; FRE 1003.

As to the hearsay objection, the initial statement ("If caused by injury . . . ") is admissible because it was offered not to show the truth of the matter asserted therein, but only to describe the directive to which the writer responded.

P might have contended that the public records exception to the hearsay rule is applicable to allow admissibility of the latter portion of the document ("Rung . . . "). Under this doctrine, factual findings resulting from an investigation are admissible, unless the circumstances indicate a lack of trustworthiness; FRE 803(8). Unless the court had a basis for concluding that there really was no "investigation," or that some aspect of the investigation was potentially untrustworthy, the court should have admitted this evidence.

3. Dr. Abel ("A")'s testimony

Because A is an expert in the field of accident reconstruction, he appears to be qualified to render an opinion that one of the breaks in the ladder existed before it was smashed by the ambulance.

D probably objected to this evidence on the grounds that A's opinion was based on unauthenticated hearsay (the police report, the wood fiber analysis report, and the ladder company's records). The Federal Rules (FRE 703) and many states permit an expert to base testimony on information that is reasonably relied on by experts in that particular field in formulating opinions, even if those facts or data are otherwise inadmissible in evidence. Because the items described above would seem to be the type of data on which an accident reconstructionist would rely in formulating an opinion, the testimony was properly admitted.

4. Baker ("B")'s testimony

P probably objected to B's testimony on the grounds that it was hearsay (B is testifying as to what Hood had told him out-of-court). However, the "statement against interest" exception to the hearsay rule was probably applicable. Under this doctrine, where an unavailable declarant made a statement that was contrary to her proprietary or penal interests, it may be quoted by another party; FRE 804(b)(3). At common law, the exception applies solely to statements against the declarant's financial interest; some states and the FRE have expanded the exception to cover statements against penal interest. Although P could have contended that Hood is not "unavailable" because he is in the courtroom, the latter's assertion of the Fifth Amendment privilege would satisfy the element of "unavailability"; FRE 804(a)(1). Thus, the court properly admitted B's testimony.

5. Cross-examination of B

Because the inability to recall is a proper basis of impeachment, P had the right to question B about B's recollection of events that occurred at approximately the same time as Hood's statement. The question to which D objected appears to be argumentative. Nevertheless, D's objection probably should *not* have been sustained because the cross-examiner was entitled to an explanation of why B could recall only a solitary event on the date about which he was testifying.

Answer to Question 10

Important aspects:

Withdrawn pleas, lay opinion, statement by party-opponent, bias, present memory refreshed, scope of cross-examination.

1. Clerk's testimony

FRE 410 explicitly covers this situation in both civil and criminal cases. It prohibits the introduction of a withdrawn guilty plea. Even in the absence of this rule, Dave ("D") could have objected to this testimony on the grounds that (1) it was not relevant (tending to prove or disprove a material fact) because people often file guilty pleas to minor traffic violations simply to avoid the expense and inconvenience of a trial; (2) the statement is hearsay (an out-of-court statement offered into evidence to prove the truth of the matter asserted) because the plea suggests that D, in fact, had driven through the red light; and (3) testimony about a withdrawn plea violates the presumption of innocence.

Paul ("P") could have replied that (1) the evidence is relevant because it tends to show a recognition of culpability; (2) the plea is admissible under the party-opponent admission exception to the hearsay rule; and (3) the plea's withdrawal does not negate the previous admission.

The argument that an accused who is allowed to withdraw a plea is entitled to the presumption of innocence would be highly persuasive. That notion is part of the policy basis for FRE 410.

2. Oliver ("O")'s testimony

D probably objected to O's testimony on the grounds that it was an opinion and lay witnesses are permitted to testify only to facts. P could argue in rebuttal that lay opinion is often permitted where the subject matter is otherwise difficult to describe (i.e., he was "drunk," "speeding," etc.). However, O's impressions could have been described without resorting to opinions (i.e., O could have testified that "D crossed P's line of sight at the intersection prior to the crash at a distance of only 10 feet"). Thus, this evidence should not have been admitted.

3. White ("W")'s testimony

(a) The initial statement (D confided to him that he had gone through the red light) might have been objected to as hearsay; but P would have successfully argued in rebuttal that it is admissible as a statement by a party-opponent.

(b) As long as D had a good-faith basis for asking the question ("Aren't you related to P?"), the cross-examination of W was proper because bias in favor of a party is a well-established mode of impeachment.

4. *Brown ("B")'s testimony*

B's testimony (that W said "he was going to get D for . . .") constitutes impeachment through extrinsic evidence of W's bias. The evidence is extrinsic because it is a form of proof other than a response to a question during examination of W. P might also have objected to B's testimony on the ground that no foundation had been laid while W testified earlier (i.e., W was never asked, "Didn't you tell B that . . ."). Some jurisdictions require this foundation for impeachment by extrinsic evidence with respect to bias. In such a jurisdiction, B's testimony should not have been admitted. It should be noted that no hearsay objection could be sustained because W's statement was not offered to prove the truth of what it asserted. It was offered only to demonstrate that W had made statements that showed bias.

5. *Cross-examination of B*

D might have objected to P's cross-examination of B on the grounds that (1) it exceeded the scope of the direct examination (B was asked only about W's statement pertaining to "getting even" with D); and (2) the description of the accident in the newspaper would constitute hearsay (and possibly opinion, depending on how the story itself was phrased). The FRE 611(b) and the majority view limit cross-examination to the subject matter of direct (subject to the judge's discretion to expand the allowable topics), although a minority position permits cross-examination pertaining to any relevant matter. Thus, in most courts, B's testimony would ***not*** have been admissible. As to the hearsay objection, most courts permit a witness's recollection to be refreshed by any type of material. Because the item is not actually offered into evidence, it is not subject to an objection on grounds of hearsay or opinion.

Answer to Question 11

Important aspects:

Competency, confrontation, hearsay, commercial publications, required confidentiality for privilege, original writing rule.

A. Wilson ("W")'s testimony

Traditionally, a witness was incompetent to testify if insane or otherwise incapable of accurately relating what he had seen or heard on a particular occasion. Today, however, a witness is competent if he understands the obligation to testify truthfully, has firsthand knowledge of the incident, and has the ability to communicate.

Although Olson ("O") probably objected to W's testimony on the grounds that a psychiatrist had testified that W was sometimes unable to distinguish between his independent recollection and what others had described to him, the court's decision to permit W to testify was probably appropriate. W's shortcomings as a witness could be brought to the attention of the jury by O's counsel. The jury could then evaluate from W's demeanor whether he had a clear recollection of the incident in question or seemed to be parroting the statements of others. Thus, W's mental handicap affects merely the weight of his testimony, rather than his competency to testify. The mental impairment could be used to impeach W's testimony if there was evidence that the defect impaired the accuracy of his observation, recall, or narration.

B. (1) Jones ("J")'s statement

It should initially be noted that Olson ("O") would have no standing to assert any Fifth Amendment rights that Jones might be able to assert (i.e., that he had not received his Miranda rights).

Officer Carlisle's testimony violates O's rights under the confrontation clause. *Crawford v. Washington* held that the confrontation clause bars use of "testimonial" hearsay statements against a criminal defendant unless the declarant is unavailable and the defendant had a previous opportunity to cross-examine the declarant. The statements by Jones were very likely "testimonial" because Jones made them to the police in what could be called the course of an investigation. O did not cross-examine J when J spoke to the police, and O cannot cross-examine J at trial because J has died. Testimony about J's statement should therefore have been excluded.

(2) O's statement and other evidence

O's statement is relevant (tends to prove a material fact) because his whereabouts on the date of the crime are crucial.

It is unclear from the facts what "other evidence" was offered to prove that *Hellcats* was not playing on the date he asserted. If O had identified a particular theater, the prosecution ("P") could have had the manager of that establishment testify that *Hellcats* was not playing on that date.

If P simply introduced, after proper authentication, the "movie" page of the local newspaper on that date, a hearsay objection could have been raised by O. However, the "commercial publications" exception to the hearsay rule followed in some states and in federal courts (FRE 803(17)) appears to apply because movie information contained in a newspaper is generally relied on by the public. If this exception was not applicable, P would have been obliged to bring in the managers and operators of every movie theater in the downtown area to testify that *Hellcats* was not playing on the evening in question.

Finally, although O might have contended that his statement (*Hellcats*) was hearsay, it was an admission, which is "nonhearsay" under the FRE and similarly admissible in state courts. Unlike "statements against interest," admissions need not be inconsistent with a party's interests.

(3) The reporter's testimony

O could have objected to the reporter's testimony on the grounds that it (1) was hearsay; (2) was irrelevant (i.e., it does not tend to show that O was a participant in the burglary); and (3) violated the marital communications privilege. However, P could have contended in rebuttal that (1) the party-opponent admission exception to the hearsay rule is applicable in this instance; (2) the evidence does tend to show that O was a participant in the crime (why else would he express disgust with J's statement?); and (3) the statement was apparently not "confidential" because the reporter could overhear it. Although O did not actually see the reporter, there is no indication that she attempted to hide her presence from him. Thus, even if this was a jurisdiction that precludes the testimony of a concealed eavesdropper, the evidence was admissible because O's personal carelessness permitted the statement to be overheard.

(4) Police officer's testimony and map

The facts of this question do not suggest any basis for an objection by O to testimony about the map on the grounds that it was illegally obtained.

O could have contended that testimony about the map of W's premises was inadmissible because (1) it was not authenticated (the facts do not show how the police officer knew that the map depicted W's premises); (2) it is hearsay; and (3) it violates the Original Writing Rule (in the absence of production of the map itself). However, P could have argued in rebuttal that (1) if the testifying police officer had viewed W's premises, he would have had sufficient firsthand knowledge to verify that the map described the burglarized premises; (2) the map did not constitute a "statement" for purposes of the hearsay rule (rather, it was merely a picture of another's premises); and (3) the map was a collateral document because it was offered to show only motivation and opportunity on the part of O. However, because (1) the map is a significant piece of evidence in establishing O's culpability and (2) there is no indication that the map itself is unavailable, the court probably erred in permitting testimony about the map without requiring introduction of the map (or a copy of the map or a reasonable excuse for failure to produce the map or a copy).

Answer to Question 12

Important aspects:
Victim's character, defendant's character in self-defense case, form for character evidence.

1. *Rider's reputation as violent*

The prosecution would likely have argued that this testimony was too vague and that it was therefore improper character evidence.

Defendant would have argued that at common law and under the Federal Rules, the defendant is permitted to introduce character evidence supporting a contention that the victim of a physical assault was the first aggressor.

The trial judge acted correctly, because violent character is a relevant trait in support of a defendant's claim that the victim was the first aggressor. FRE 404(a)(2)(B) provides for admissibility of this kind of evidence.

2. *Rider's reputation as peaceful*

Defendant would have argued that this testimony did not properly rebut the evidence that Rider had a reputation for violence, but the prosecution could persuasively point out that once a defendant introduces evidence about a victim's character, the prosecution is entitled to respond with opposite evidence about the same general character trait. Because FRE 404(a)(2) explicitly permits this, the trial judge ruled properly in admitting the evidence.

3. *Defendant's reputation as violent and aggressive*

Defendant might have objected that character evidence about himself could not be admitted unless he first introduced character evidence in his favor.

The prosecution might have responded that usually it is true that a defendant's character is off-limits unless the defendant raises it first. It would also have pointed out that cases in which a defendant introduces character evidence about an alleged victim are treated differently with respect to the prosecution's right to introduce character evidence about the defendant.

The trial judge properly admitted this evidence. Under FRE 404(a)(2)(B)(ii), if a defendant introduces character evidence about an alleged victim, the prosecution is then allowed to introduce character evidence about the defendant that refers to the same trait of character. In this case, Defendant introduced evidence about Rider's aggressive nature, and therefore, the prosecution was entitled to introduce evidence about Defendant's possession of that same character trait.

4. Opinion evidence about Defendant's character

As in part 3 of this question, Defendant might have argued that character evidence about a defendant may be introduced only by the defendant or by the prosecution to rebut character evidence that the defendant has introduced about himself. Defendant might also have argued that the form of this evidence was improper because it is opinion and not reputation evidence.

The prosecution would rely on FRE 404(a)(1) to support admissibility of character evidence in general. With regard to the form of this evidence, under FRE 405, when character evidence is permissible, either evidence of a person's reputation or evidence of someone's opinion about that person is allowed, provided that a witness who gives an opinion has an adequate basis for forming that opinion.

The trial court properly admitted this evidence because a coworker would ordinarily have a basis for forming an opinion about a fellow worker's character traits.

5. Evidence that Defendant punched someone

Defendant likely objected to this evidence, as relevant only if it supported an inference about his character for violence, to support a conclusion that he acted in accordance with that character on the charged occasion and that the form of the evidence was improper because reputation and opinion evidence are the only two styles of proof permitted for this kind of character inquiry.

The prosecution would likely have responded that because Defendant introduced evidence about the alleged victim, the prosecution could properly introduce character evidence about Defendant. With regard to the form of this character evidence, the prosecution would not likely have a reasonable response.

The trial judge erred in allowing proof of a past specific act when its only relevance was to support a conclusion about Defendant's character traits.

Answer to Question 13

Important aspects:
Original writing rule, adoptive admissions, habit, competency, statements against interest.

1. *Abner ("A")'s testimony*

Peter ("P") could initially have objected to A's testimony on the grounds that (1) it violated the Original Writing Rule because A testified about the contents of a writing (the notice of cancellation); (2) it was irrelevant (did not tend to prove or disprove a material fact) because (a) the fact that it was the practice of Defenders ("D") to mail cancellation notices on the date they were written does not prove that this particular notice was actually sent, and (b) even if the notice was sent, this fact would not prove that it had actually been received by P (the insured had to actually receive the notice that his policy had been canceled); and (3) A's statement that "it [the notice] must have been mailed" constitutes only his opinion as to what occurred because he does not have firsthand knowledge.

With respect to the initial objection, D might have responded that it could not produce the original document because it had been mailed to P (who is now, apparently, denying receipt of the notice). However, the Original Writing Rule requires production of a duplicate where the original is not available. If D did not produce a copy or have an acceptable explanation for failure to have a copy, the testimony would violate the Original Writing Rule.

As to the second objection, D could have argued in rebuttal that (1) evidence of a routine business practice is ordinarily admissible to prove conduct in conformity therewith on a particular occasion; and (2) a fact finder could infer from the fact of mailing that the notice had actually reached its destination. However, P could have successfully responded that an insufficient foundation for establishing the existence of a business custom existed in this instance because (1) A, an insurance agent, never testified that he was familiar with the day-to-day practices of D (i.e., that it is the practice of the particular office *at which he works* to send out such notices); and (2) the business practice itself has not been described with sufficient specificity (presumably, the letters must be placed in a particular receptacle, from which they are later removed and mailed by an identifiable person).

Finally, D does not appear to have a successful response to P's "opinion" objection.

Thus, the court was probably incorrect in admitting A's testimony.

2. Baker ("B")'s testimony

P might have objected to B's testimony on the grounds that it was irrelevant, in that the failure to answer B does not tend to prove or disprove that P had received D's cancellation notice.

D could have responded that (1) D's silence does tend to prove that the letter was actually received because most persons would assist a governmental employee in carrying out his functions (although a reasonable person could arguably choose to avoid gratuitous involvement in a criminal investigation of another individual); and (2) P's nonresponse to B's statement is an adoptive or tacit admission (i.e., P, in effect, answered B's inquiry in a positive manner by not denying B's insinuation when a reasonable person in P's position would have done so).

The court was probably correct in admitting B's testimony.

3. Charlie ("C")'s testimony

P could have objected to C's testimony on the grounds that it was irrelevant because P's permitting insurance policies to lapse with another company for nonpayment of premiums would **not** indicate that the policy in question had been canceled for the same reason. Additionally, evidence of prior conduct to prove conformity therewith on a particular occasion is ordinarily inadmissible. Although D might have argued in rebuttal to the second objection that P's conduct in permitting other insurance policies to lapse rises to the level of a habit (a person's regular response to a particular type of situation) and is therefore admissible, it is unlikely that permitting insurance to lapse on three separate occasions over an individual's lifetime would constitute sufficient regularity to be characterized as a habit. Thus, the court was correct in refusing to permit C to testify.

4. Debbie's testimony

There is no minimum age that a witness must have attained to be competent to testify. The judge, however, must believe that a potential witness (1) has sufficient maturity to be capable of receiving correct impressions through his or her senses; and (2) understands the necessity of telling the truth in the context of a legal proceeding. The facts are unclear as to Debbie's age at the time she purportedly transferred the mail from the mailperson to P. (The facts state only that she is **now** five years old.) However, assuming this matter came to trial in a relatively prompt period of time (i.e., within one year), the judge could have concluded that Debbie was capable of testifying as to an act that she had undertaken one year before. Additionally, her statement that untruthful persons "get spanked" tends to show a recognition of the importance of being honest. Thus, the court's decision that Debbie was competent was probably correct.

5. Ethel ("E")'s testimony

D probably objected to this testimony on the grounds that it was (1) irrelevant, because E has not adequately described how Harvey ("H") determined what was "junk" mail (D's letter should not have been viewed as being in that category); and (2) hearsay, because E has testified as to the out-of-court statement of another.

P probably argued in rebuttal to the first objection that regardless of the selection process used by H to discard letters, D's item *might* have been in the portion viewed as "junk" mail. As to the hearsay objection, the portion of H's statement pertaining to his back is probably admissible under the "existing physical condition" exception to the hearsay rule. His statement pertaining to destroying items of "junk" mail is arguably admissible under the "statement against interest" exception to the hearsay rule because he could presumably be terminated from his job and imprisoned for such conduct. However, the latter doctrine is applicable only where the declarant is unavailable. The facts are silent as to whether H could have been compelled to appear at the trial. If not, this element would be satisfied. The Federal Rules include statements against penal interest in the exception covering statements against interest, although some jurisdictions limit the coverage of that exception to statements against pecuniary and proprietary interest. Assuming that this jurisdiction extends the "statements against interest" doctrine to comments that would expose the speaker to criminal sanctions, the court was correct in permitting E's testimony.

Finally, E's testimony pertaining to H's being in prison is arguably pertinent to the factual determination whether the declarant was "unavailable."

Answer to Question 14

Important aspects:
Authentication, adoptive admissions, relevance, scientific evidence, experts, jury views.

1. Patterson ("P")'s testimony
(a) Label on bottle

Don ("D") could have contended that testimony as to the writing on the bottle was not admissible because (1) it was hearsay (an out-of-court statement offered into evidence to prove the truth of the matter asserted); and (2) the bottle was not authenticated (i.e., no evidence was introduced, other than testimony as to the bottle label itself, to prove that D produced the item).

P could have argued in rebuttal, however, that (1) the label is an admission, "nonhearsay" under the FRE, and an exception to the hearsay rule in other jurisdictions; (2) many jurisdictions and the FRE view "trade inscriptions" (i.e., statements on items sold in commerce) to be self-authenticating. Assuming trade inscriptions are self-authenticating, P's testimony with respect to the bottle label was properly admitted.

(b) Jack ("J")'s statement

D probably objected to P's testimony about J's statement on the grounds that (1) it was hearsay; and (2) the portion asserting that D should be "run out of business" was opinion. P could contend that J's statement was admissible under the "adoptive admission" exception to the hearsay rule. Under this doctrine, a statement made in the presence of the party-opponent is admissible if it contains assertions that a reasonable person would deny. If J simply accosted D and made the statement without D's having prior knowledge of the incident involving P, D's nonresponse would be perfectly understandable.

2. Cross-examination of P

Impeachment of P by inquiring about his smoking habits was probably proper because, given the well-known correlation between smoking and respiratory difficulties, the evidence would tend to contradict P's assertion that muriatic acid was the cause of his physical disability.

3. Dr. Walton ("W")'s testimony
(a) P has chronic bronchitis

This testimony appears to be pertinent because it pertains to the extent and nature of P's injury. Although it is not a fact but W's opinion, because he is a specialist in internal medicine, this form of testimony would be admissible.

(b) The laboratory experiment and opinion based on it

D probably objected to this evidence on the grounds that there was no proof that (1) there was a substantial similarity of conditions (i.e., that the amounts of water, sodium hypochloride, and muriatic acid used in W's experiment were proportionately equivalent to the amount of these substances in P's swimming pool at the time he was purportedly injured); and (2) the methodology itself was "scientifically valid" (i.e., that the test can be reliably tested; that it was subject to peer review; that it has a low error rate; and that this method is generally accepted in the field). Because P does not appear to have an adequate rebuttal to these objections, W's experiment and his opinion that P's condition resulted from exposure to muriatic acid probably should **not** have been admitted by the court.

4. Cross-examination of W

It is assumed that this jurisdiction follows the modern view, which permits cross-examination of an expert by a scholarly writing whether or not she relied on it in rendering an opinion.

P probably objected to the cross-examination on the ground that articles appearing in the *Wall Street Journal* cannot be characterized as scholarly works and therefore could not be utilized to impeach W through contradiction. Because the accuracy of articles appearing in newspapers is probably not independently verified by persons with expertise in a particular field, the court's refusal to permit cross-examination of W in this manner was probably correct.

5. Viewing of the pool

It is in the discretion of the court whether the time-consuming and disruptive nature of a viewing is justified by the likelihood of obtaining highly probative evidence that could not feasibly be reproduced in the courtroom. Because little evidentiary light could be shed on whether D had mislabeled a bottle of muriatic acid as sodium hypochloride by visiting the pool, the court's denial of P's motion to inspect the filterhouse was probably appropriate.

Answer to Question 15

Important aspects:
Propensity inference for non-sexual conduct, propensity inference for prohibited sexual conduct, rape shield rule.

1. Defendant's robbery conviction

Defendant would have objected that the only way in which the jury could have used information about his past robbery conviction would have entailed the prohibited propensity inference. Evidence of bad character to show action in conformity with that character on a charged occasion is prohibited.

The prosecution would have responded that this evidence did not require a jury conclusion about Defendant's character. Rather, it showed that he had a specific method of committing crimes (i.e., luring individuals into his car and then taking them to a secluded place to commit a crime), and that this distinctive "signature" establishes his identity or his knowledge of how to commit such crimes.

The trial court erred in admitting this evidence. Identity was not disputed by Defendant, so the "identity" rationale for admission would not have been proper. The other rationale, "knowledge," was weak. Characteristics of a past crime can support a conclusion that the perpetrator has special knowledge that might link him with a different crime only if those characteristics are highly specific and not typical aspects of crime. Finding a secluded place to commit a crime is hardly unusual. Similarly, using a car to take the target of a crime from one place to another is also likely commonplace. Because these aspects of the past and charged crimes are so typical of crimes in general, the argument that they represent distinctive knowledge is weak.

2. Defendant's sexual assault conviction

Defendant would have argued that admission of this conviction violated the rule against character evidence, because it is highly prejudicial and provides little information as to the guilt of the charged offense. There were significant differences between the past offense and the charged crime, because the past crime was committed against a young male and the charged offense involved an adult female.

The prosecution would respond that sex crimes are typically marked by recidivism and that a specific provision of the Federal Rules of Evidence authorizes admission of this evidence.

The trial judge acted properly in admitting this evidence, because FRE 413 specifies that past sexual assault convictions are admissible in sexual assault trials.

3. Victim's past sexual conduct

The prosecution would have argued that the "rape shield" provision in the Federal Rules (FRE 412) barred use of this evidence.

Defendant would have argued that admitting evidence of his past conduct while excluding evidence of Victim's past conduct would mislead the jury and would violate his constitutional rights.

The trial court ruled properly. FRE 412 prohibits the evidence Defendant sought to introduce, as the evidence does not fit within any of the Rule's exceptions. It does not show that the source of any physical evidence was someone other than Defendant, it does not show that because of prior relations between Defendant and Victim there was consent on the charged occasion, and it does not violate the constitutional rights of Defendant. The excluded evidence did not deny Defendant a fair trial because its probative value was low. The conduct it described was not highly unique, nor did it contradict the prosecution's contention that nonconsensual sexual relations had taken place between Defendant and Victim.

Answer to Question 16

Important aspects:

Adoptive admission, consciousness of guilt, original writing rule, impeachment.

1. Nabor ("N")'s statement

Dan ("D") probably objected to N's testimony on the grounds that it was (1) irrelevant (did not tend to prove or disprove a material fact) because Harvey could have been speaking emotionally instead of from personal knowledge; and (2) hearsay (an out-of-court statement offered into evidence to prove the truth of the matter asserted) because N is testifying as to what H said.

The prosecution ("P") could have contended that N's statement and D's failure to reply were relevant because an innocent person would have objected to even an ambiguous accusation of murder. As to the hearsay objection, D's nonresponse constituted an adoptive admission (a statement which, if untrue, the hearer would be expected to deny). By failing to refute the statement made to him, D, in effect, adopted it.

2. Jack ("J")'s testimony

D could have objected to this testimony on the grounds that (1) it was irrelevant because D may have attempted to take his life as a consequence of the depression and despair that follow an arrest for murder; (2) it was hearsay (i.e., D's conduct is being offered into evidence as a statement that he killed F); and (3) its probative value was outweighed by the highly prejudicial impact this evidence might make on a jury.

P probably contended in rebuttal, however, that (1) it is relevant because one may infer a consciousness of guilt from the fact of attempted suicide; (2) an action like a suicide attempt is not a statement and therefore is not hearsay under both the Federal Rules and most jurisdictions; and (3) because there were apparently no eyewitnesses to the crime, the probative value of this evidence outweighs its possible prejudicial impact.

J's testimony should be admissible.

3. Rita ("R")'s testimony

P probably objected to this testimony on the grounds (1) that it violated the Original Writing Rule because R is testifying about the contents of a writing; (2) the writing was not authenticated (i.e., no showing was apparently made that R was familiar with Flora ("F")'s handwriting); and (3) the testimony was hearsay (i.e., F's alleged statement is being offered into evidence for the purpose of proving that she committed suicide). D could overcome the Original Writing Rule objection if the crumpled-up letter was discarded in good faith. The authentication objection could be overcome by having R testify that she was familiar with F's handwriting. Finally, the hearsay objection could probably be overcome as follows: (1) the initial phrase of the statement ("I have nothing to live for . . .") is probably admissible under the present state of mind exception to the hearsay rule; and (2) the balance of the writing need not be admitted for its truth since there is other evidence of the break-up of the relationship.

Assuming the letter is no longer in existence, the testimony should be admitted by the court.

4. Dr. Slade ("S")'s testimony

D could have objected to S's testimony on the grounds that (1) it violated the psychotherapist-patient privilege; and (2) it was hearsay because S's testimony was based on what F had told him. P could initially argue in rebuttal that, even assuming this jurisdiction extends the patient-client privilege to psychologists in criminal cases, the privilege must be asserted by the patient.

The hearsay objection would probably also be unavailing because in most jurisdictions, an expert may base an opinion on data that would otherwise not be admissible if the information is of the type that is "reasonably relied on" by experts in that particular field.

Thus, S's testimony should be admissible.

5. Cross-examination of S

A witness's credibility can sometimes be attacked by questioning about acts of misconduct not resulting in conviction. The acts must be relevant to truth-telling, and their probativeness must not be substantially outweighed by any unfair prejudice associated with them; FRE 608(b).

Defense counsel's second question was improper because impeachment as to prior bad acts that have not resulted in a conviction may not be accomplished by extrinsic evidence. The reference to the investigative report was therefore inappropriate. Additionally, the second question was argumentative (phrased in a manner that would compel a response that takes issue with the inquiry).

Answer to Question 17

Important aspects:

Settlement offers and settlement statements, expert testimony, statement by party-opponent, excited utterance.

1. The statements by Helico ("H")'s officer

H's officer made two separate statements (the offer to settle and the admission).

(a) The offer to settle

H probably contended that the offer to settle was inadmissible because (1) it is irrelevant (does not tend to prove or disprove a material fact), in that H may have just proposed the settlement offer to avoid the expense and inconvenience of litigation (rather than out of a belief of legal responsibility for the incident); (2) most states and the Federal Rules preclude such evidence; and (3) it is hearsay (an out-of-court statement offered into evidence to prove the truth of the matter asserted therein). Paul ("P") probably argued in rebuttal that (1) settlement offers (which in this instance were probably substantial) are not usually made unless the offeror believes that he was legally culpable; and (2) the party-opponent exception to the hearsay rule is applicable (statements made by a party to the litigation, other than the party introducing the evidence, are ordinarily admissible as an exception to the hearsay rule).

Both the common law and the FRE hold that the fact that a party has offered to settle a claim may not be admitted on the issue of the claim's validity. Admission of such settlement offers would give the parties a strong disincentive to pursue settlement negotiations.

The evidence was wrongly admitted.

(b) The admission of defective design

Under the FRE, evidence of statements made in settlement negotiations is not admissible to prove liability for the underlying claim. In a minority of jurisdictions, *any* statement made within the course of settlement negotiations is admissible. In one of those minority jurisdictions, H's initial argument was probably that the statements made by the corporate officer were hearsay and did not constitute a party-opponent admission because he was not authorized to comment on H's liability. Additionally, H probably contended that the officer's statement was an opinion as to an ultimate fact by a layperson (ordinarily, only the opinions of experts are admissible). P probably argued in rebuttal that in some states, statements by corporate employees are admissible against the employer so long as they are "within the course and scope of their employment." In addition, most courts have abandoned the rule barring opinion testimony on ultimate issues. Therefore, under the minority view, the second part of the officer's statement should have been admitted.

2. Are the statements of Jason ("J") admissible?

We'll assume that (1) the photographs were properly authenticated (i.e., that the proponent of the evidence testified that the pictures were, in fact, what they purported to be); and (2) J was actually qualified as an expert witness by the court (i.e., the judge determined and advised the jury that J was to be considered an expert).

H probably contended that J should *not* have been qualified as an expert because (1) whether the tail rotor was conspicuous or not is not a matter on which special expertise is needed; and (2) although J may have been knowledgeable about aircraft engineering, navigation, and operation, the matter about which he testified involved aircraft design and construction. P could have argued in rebuttal, however, that (1) whether the rotor was "conspicuous" within the FAA rules is a matter of expert opinion; and (2) aircraft engineering, navigation, and operation are sufficiently related to aircraft design and construction so that opinion evidence by J was proper. Experts can give their opinions on ultimate facts. The testimony of J was proper.

Assuming the pictures were authenticated, H could have argued that there was not a sufficient basis for J's opinion that the tail rotor was not conspicuous under the FAA regulations ("regs") because (1) the photographs of other helicopters were irrelevant for purposes of determining if H's helicopter failed to meet FAA regs; and (2) there was no showing that J was familiar with the FAA regs. P probably argued in rebuttal, however, that (1) J's opinion that the helicopter rotor was not conspicuous within the FAA rules wasn't necessarily predicated on the pictures of other helicopters; and (2) an expert can usually give an opinion without describing his basis for it (the foundation can be dealt with on cross-examination).

In summary, J's testimony was properly admitted.

3. Sam ("S")'s testimony

H could have objected that S's testimony is inadmissible as double hearsay (S is testifying as to what Al said that P said). P's statement would be a statement by a party-opponent. (It might also be an excited utterance because it occurred "immediately" after P was struck and described the event that had caused the declarant's excited state.) This leaves for analysis only the issue of whether there is admissible proof that P actually made that statement. Al's out-of-court statement is itself hearsay on that topic (the fact that P did say certain words). S can testify that Al made an out-of-court statement, but there is no hearsay exception that would allow the court to admit Al's statement for the truth of what it asserts (it asserts that P said certain words).

P could have also contended that S's first and third sentences are layperson conclusions of law and therefore inadmissible. However, many states permit a lay witness to give an opinion where she has personal knowledge of the occurrence and the opinion would be helpful to the fact finder.

Because of the hearsay problem, it therefore appears that S's testimony was wrongly admitted.

Answer to Question 18

Important aspects:
Confrontation Clause, business records, past acts for impeachment, habit, bias, impeachment by contradiction.

1. Lab report

Tim ("T") probably contended that admitting the lab report violated T's Sixth Amendment right of confrontation (because Smith was not present at trial). Tim could also have argued that (1) it was not properly authenticated (there was no chain of continuous custody that satisfactorily established that the substance tested was the same item that was taken from T; nor was there adequate proof that the report itself was genuine); (2) it was hearsay (an out-of-court statement offered to prove the truth of the matter stated therein or inferable thereby); (3) no proof was introduced that the process by which the substance was tested was "scientifically valid."

With regard to the Confrontation Clause objection, a lab report of this type is "testimonial." The prosecution may introduce it only if the author of the report is available to testify and be cross-examined at trial or is unavailable at trial but was earlier subject to cross-examination by Tim. With regard to Tim's other objections, the prosecution ("P") probably argued in rebuttal that (1) implicit in the report is that Officer Jenks ("J") gave the substance directly to Smith because the latter stated that he had tested the substance taken by J, and the seal (plus signature) on a document by the officer who was the custodian thereof ordinarily establishes a writing's genuineness; (2) the hearsay objection is overcome by the (a) "public records" (i.e., a document that sets forth matters observed pursuant to a duty imposed by law), *or* (b) "business records" (a matter observed in the course of a regularly conducted activity whose regular practice is to make such a report) exception to the hearsay rule; and (3) the process of determining if a substance is heroin may be so well established that evidence of its scientific validity was unnecessary.

Separate from the disposition of the hearsay and Confrontation Clause issues, because the chain of custody with respect to the substance tested by Smith was *not* established, the report should *not* have been admitted.

2. The cross-examination of T

It is assumed that P had a good-faith belief that T was in possession of heroin on the date mentioned (if this were not the case, a mistrial could have been ordered).

At common law, courts generally allowed impeachment by bad acts that did not lead to conviction. However, FRE 608(b) and the majority of states limit bad-act evidence to bad ,acts that pertain to **truthfulness**. Because the incident about which T was cross-examined did not pertain directly to truthfulness (i.e., the fact that one possessed heroin on a particular occasion would not necessarily suggest that she would lie under oath), most jurisdictions would probably disallow the question on that ground. Also, there is a great potential for prejudice here, especially in view of the similarity between the bad act and the act charged on the present occasion. (That is, the jury might desire to punish T for his previous act, rather than for the act with which he is now charged; also, the jurors may reason that because T possessed heroin in the past, he's likely to be guilty of the same thing now.) Therefore, P's question should **not** have been permitted.

3. Sue ("S")'s initial testimony

P could have objected to S's initial testimony on the grounds that (1) it was irrelevant (did not tend to prove or disprove a fact of material consequence) because the fact that T had used powdered milk during the eight times she and T had dined out would not tend to disprove that T had heroin in his possession on the occasion in question (especially because S did not testify that she and T intended to dine out after meeting with J); and (2) prior conduct is inadmissible to prove conduct in conformity therewith on a particular occasion. T might have contended, in rebuttal, that (1) having powdered milk with him on prior occasions does tend to indicate that the substance taken by J was not heroin (the relatively small number of times S had seen T use powdered milk goes to the weight of her testimony, rather than its admissibility); and (2) carrying powdered milk was a habit (a routine response to a particular set of conditions) and therefore is evidence admissible in most jurisdictions. It is unlikely that possession of powdered milk eight times over a one-year period is sufficient to establish a habit. Thus, S's initial testimony should **not** have been admitted as direct evidence.

Alternatively, T might have argued that S's testimony was given for the purpose of impeaching J by contradiction (in which event, no relevancy objection could be successfully made). However, P could have argued in rebuttal that (1) T had already contradicted J, and so this additional impeachment was superfluous; and (2) S's testimony would not necessarily contradict J (the fact that T brought his own powdered milk when he dined out with S on prior occasions would not directly contradict J's testimony that T had possession of heroin on September 13). Again, P should have prevailed.

Finally, T might have asserted that S's initial testimony was rehabilitation (because P had tried to impeach T's prior testimony). The fact that T sometimes carried powdered milk would tend to corroborate his earlier testimony that the substance that was taken from him on the date in question was *not* heroin. However, because S had *not* testified that they were going out to dinner after meeting with J, and she cited only eight occasions over a one-year period, her testimony probably would *not* sufficiently corroborate T's assertion that he had powdered milk with him on the occasion in question.

Thus, S's initial testimony should *not* have been admitted.

4. S's testimony about J

Assuming that T offered J's statements as impeachment, P probably contended that (1) the first statement (J's offer to release S in return for a bribe) is not admissible because impeachment through prior bad acts cannot be accomplished by extrinsic evidence (i.e., S's testimony). The impeachment effort, however, was proper. While the bribe attempt is a past act that may not shed light on character for truthfulness, the overall transaction provides strong evidence of bias. Bias on the part of a witness may always be shown by extrinsic evidence. Here, J has announced that he has a bias against T and some others. His statement would not be hearsay since it is covered by the exception for statements about a declarant's state of mind or plans.

5. Dr. Walt ("W")'s testimony

Because P had already put on its case-in-chief, the testimony in question is apparently an attempt to impeach T by contradiction. Thus, no hearsay objection can successfully be made because W's testimony is offered only for the purpose of contradicting T's earlier statement that he possessed only powdered milk when arrested.

T probably objected to this testimony on the grounds that (1) it possessed too great a potential to prejudice the jury; and (2) it violated the physician-patient privilege. P probably responded that (1) the potentially prejudicial impact is outweighed by the fact that this statement was made only with respect to impeachment of T's earlier testimony; and (2) in many states, the physician-patient privilege is not extended to criminal proceedings in which the patient is the accused. Additionally, the privilege pertains only to statements relating to diagnosis or treatment. Although the initial statement (that T was a drug addict) might arguably be pertinent to treatment of his insomnia and anxiety, T's second statement ("would W like to buy drugs?") is not. Assuming that impeachment by contradiction does **not** require a foundation in this jurisdiction, W's testimony was probably properly admitted.

Answer to Question 19

Important aspects:
Multi-level hearsay, business records, excited utterance, dying declaration, statements for medical diagnosis or treatment, authentication, statements against interest, habit, non-propensity use of evidence of character.

1. Carl ("C")'s report

Owner ("O") could have objected to this evidence on the grounds that it is multiple hearsay because Bob ("B")'s statement to C and C's statement were both made out-of-court.

Paula ("P") could have contended that C's declaration (i.e., the report) is admissible under either the "past recollection recorded" or "business records" exception to the hearsay rule. However, O could have argued in rebuttal that (1) the "past recollection recorded" exception is inapplicable because the declarant must have firsthand knowledge of the event he reported, and C wrote only what B had told him (i.e., C had not seen the accident himself); and (2) the "business records" exception is not appropriate because the source of the information must be "trustworthy," and B was hardly an unbiased party.

Assuming, however, P prevailed on either of the above theories, B's statement to C must also come within an exception to the hearsay rule. The "excited utterance" doctrine might not apply, because the facts do not indicate that B was under the emotional stress of the accident at the time he made his statement to C, especially because B's description of the incident was made in response to C's question. The "dying declaration" exception also appears to be inapplicable because the facts do not indicate that B believed death was imminent. However, the "present sense impression" exception would likely apply. It covers statements describing an event made immediately after the declarant perceived the event.

Thus, C was properly permitted to read the report into evidence.

2. Flo ("F")'s testimony

O probably objected to the initial portion of B's statement about stomach and head pains as being irrelevant (not tending to prove or disprove a fact of consequence) because any mental anguish suffered by B prior to his death would not be recoverable by P. Thus, this portion of F's testimony should ***not*** have been admitted. Although the same objection was probably made by O with respect to B's second statement ("getting even"), this comment has relevance because it tends to show that B did not consider the accident to be his fault.

O probably also made a hearsay objection to F's testimony (F testified as to what B told her). B's statement about head and stomach pains, if relevant, would probably be admissible under the "present sensation" or "medical diagnosis or treatment" exceptions to the hearsay rule. The portion of B's comments pertaining to "getting even" with the driver are probably admissible under the "existing mental condition" exception. The part pertaining to being "hit by a speeding car" is probably also admissible under the "medical diagnosis and treatment exception" (especially because it was made in response to F's question as to "what happened"). Although B's use of the word "speeding" is lay opinion, many jurisdictions permit such descriptions if they are based on firsthand knowledge and helpful to the fact finder's understanding of factual circumstances. However, B's contention that the car was driven by a "drunken lunatic" should not have been admitted because it (1) was hearsay not pertaining to B's medical diagnosis or treatment; and (2) was opinion that was not based on B's visual perception of Chauf.

Thus, only B's promise of revenge and his comment that he was hit by a speeding car should have been admitted.

3. Chauf's writing

This evidence was probably objected to by O on the grounds that (1) it was not properly authenticated (how did Earl know that the signature on the document was Chauf's?); (2) it was hearsay (the writing is an out-of-court statement); and (3) it contained opinion ("intoxication" is an opinion because Chauf did not know if he was legally intoxicated or not).

P probably contended in rebuttal, however, that (1) Earl may have seen Chauf's handwriting on other writings, and thus may have gained sufficient familiarity with it (we'll assume that Earl had not actually seen Chauf write the statement in question); and (2) the writing comes within the "dying declaration" or "statement against interest" exceptions to the hearsay rule. However, the "dying declaration" doctrine would probably **not** be applicable because Chauf's statement was **not** about the cause of his death (i.e., the knifing). O would also contend that the statement was not against Chauf's pecuniary interest because Chauf was about to die (and therefore he had no apprehension of legal liability). However, if C left an estate of any significance, P should have prevailed on the hearsay question on the basis of the "statement against interest" exception.

Assuming the authentication problem can be overcome, Chauf's written statement was properly admitted.

4. Frank's testimony

O probably objected to Frank's testimony on the grounds that it was (1) character evidence (which is ordinarily not admissible to prove conduct in conformity therewith on a particular occasion); and (2) hearsay (Frank was testifying about what B did out-of-court for the purpose of permitting the inference that B acted in a safe manner on the occasion in question). P probably contended in rebuttal, however, that (1) Frank's testimony described a habit (a consistently repeated response to a particular situation), and such evidence is ordinarily admissible. With regard to the hearsay objection (2), B's conduct in crossing that street was not hearsay because only statements or assertive conduct can be hearsay. Crossing a street is not a means of asserting anything. Because Frank's testimony did not include any hearsay and probably pertained to a habit, it was properly admitted.

5. P's question and O's response

(It will be assumed that P had some reason to believe that Chauf had, in fact, received traffic citations for driving under the influence of alcohol. If P had no basis for his inquiry, it would have been improper, and a mistrial could have been declared.)

O might have contended that P's question was not proper because it pertained to prior specific acts of misconduct by Chauf, and prior misconduct is not admissible to prove that Chauf was driving in a similar manner on the occasion in question. P probably argued in rebuttal, however, that the prior traffic citations are admissible to show that O was negligent in not having learned about Chauf's prior misconduct (and therefore the evidence is **not** being offered to show that Chauf drove negligently on the occasion in question). For this reason, the question was proper.

P probably complained to the court that O's answer was nonresponsive (O was asked only for a "yes" or "no" answer, but volunteered that the basis of the question was false). This objection was probably proper, and so the judge should have (1) admonished O to answer the precise question that was asked; and (2) advised the jury that it should disregard the portion of O's response that followed his "no."

Answer to Question 20

Important aspects:
Impeachment with inquiry about past acts, former testimony, subsequent remedial measures, cross-examination based on learned treatises, attorney-client privilege.

1. *Paul ("P")'s prior lawsuits*

P probably contended that Dexter ("D")'s cross-examination was not proper because it did not ask about any conduct relevant to P's character for truthfulness (the fact that a witness has filed previous actions against food or drug manufacturers does not tend to show that these actions were undertaken fraudulently, and therefore that the witness is untrustworthy). Although D probably argued in rebuttal that it is unlikely that an "honest" person would bring that many lawsuits against food and drug manufacturers (and therefore an inference of untrustworthiness could be drawn), the objection to D's question was correctly sustained.

2. *Deposition of Dr. Box*

We'll assume the videotape was properly authenticated.

D probably contended initially that the statute permits only transcriptions, not a videotape. However, P could have argued in rebuttal that (1) the statute should not be viewed as being restrictive; and (2) a videotape should be preferred over a transcript because it permits the jury to actually observe the declarant's demeanor. P properly prevailed.

D could have argued that Box was not "unavailable" within the meaning of the statute because he would have appeared if P had paid the required fee. However, because Box deliberately avoided P's attempt at service, P properly prevailed on this issue too; FRE 804.

Finally, D probably contended that the videotape was hearsay (the videotape is reproducing what Box said). Hearsay is an out-of-court statement offered into evidence for the purpose of proving the truth of the matter asserted therein. P would initially argue that the statute says that testimony within its parameters is usable "for any purpose," and so Box's statements were admissible, even though the hearsay rule would otherwise be applicable. Second, if the hearsay rule is applicable to Box's statements, P could contend that the evidence is admissible under the "prior testimony" exception to the hearsay rule (i.e., a statement made under oath by an unavailable declarant, provided the party against whom it is offered had a motive and opportunity to cross-examine the declarant). This exception is often applied to statements that have been memorialized in a writing (usually a transcript), and it can also apply to videotaped testimony because the jury has the benefit of observing the declarant's demeanor.

In summary, the videotape was properly admitted.

3. Modification of the pill

D probably argued that this testimony was (1) irrelevant (i.e., did **not** tend to prove or disprove a material fact) because the fact that D recently removed a particular chemical that often accumulated in the liver does not necessarily mean that the initial pill was defective; and (2) inadmissible on public-policy grounds (FRE 407 prohibits evidence of subsequent remedial measures because defendants would be discouraged from making their products safer if their efforts could be introduced into evidence against them).

P probably argued in rebuttal, however, that the testimony is relevant because business entities rarely improve nondefective products. The rule against evidence of subsequent remedial measures to prove defectiveness has clear application here, and the evidence should **not** have been admitted.

4. Dr. Abel ("A")'s testimony

D probably contended that the cross-examination was improper because (1) it exceeded the scope of direct (A testified about D's pills, not sleeping pills in general); and (2) although cross-examination of an expert by reference to a **learned treatise** is permissible, newspaper articles are not learned treatises (because they are not extensively checked for accuracy and are usually written with a view toward being interesting rather than authoritative). Although P probably contended that A's knowledge (or lack of it) about sleeping pills does pertain to his ability to testify that D's pills were **not** defective, there doesn't appear to be an adequate response to D's second objection. Thus, D's objection should have been sustained.

5. Carl ("C")'s testimony

P probably contended that C's testimony is hearsay (C was repeating P's out-of-court statement) and was privileged (i.e., a confidential statement made for the purpose of obtaining legal services). D could have argued in rebuttal, however, that (1) P's statements were admissible as statements of a party-opponent (they were sought to be introduced by P's opponent);

(2) because P never retained C, the privilege never accrued; and (3) the privilege is not applicable, in any event, if legal counsel was sought for the purpose of perpetuating a fraud. D will prevail on issue (1). With respect to (2), P probably responded that so long as legal services were being solicited, the privilege applies (even if the attorney involved was not retained). With respect to (3), P probably argued that no foundation was laid that P's suit was fraudulent because P's remark to C could have been intended to imply only that, although P had previously suffered liver damage, he had suffered a new, but similar type of disability as a consequence of D's pills. The court's ruling was correct.

Answer to Question 21

Important aspects:

Former testimony, Confrontation Clause, original writing rule, judicial notice, marital communications privilege.

1. The transcript of Oats's testimony

The transcript is relevant because it would tend to prove Dick ("D") took two bottles from Phil's store.

D can be expected to contend that the transcript was hearsay (an out-of-court statement offered to prove the truth of the matter asserted). The prosecution will argue in rebuttal that Oats's testimony satisfies the "former testimony" exception to the hearsay rule (i.e., an unavailable declarant gave testimony, under oath, against the party against whom the testimony is being offered, and the latter party had an opportunity and similar motive to question the declarant): Oats is dead, his testimony was under oath, and D had the same motivation to question Oats because throwing objects out of a window supports the contention that D was driving recklessly (i.e., it evidences a desire to hide the reason or cause of the allegedly reckless driving). D could contend that in his reckless driving case there was no reason to question Oats's testimony because throwing objects out of a car could have been viewed as irrelevant (i.e., not tending to prove or disprove that he was driving recklessly). This hearsay is "testimonial," for Confrontation Clause purposes, but it may be properly admitted because D had an opportunity to cross-examine the declarant.

In summary, the transcript was properly admitted.

2. Phil ("P")'s testimony

D could have objected to P's testimony on the grounds that (1) it violates the Original Writing Rule; (2) there was no authentication of the DLD label (proof that the bottle actually did contain DLD); and (3) the DLD label was hearsay. In rebuttal, P would have contended that (1) the Original Writing Rule is satisfied because D had thrown away the bottles in good faith; (2) the FRE and most states treat trade inscriptions as self-authenticating, absent any evidence of forgery; and (3) the "business records" exception to hearsay is applicable (the DLD label was printed in the ordinary course of the manufacturer's business).

P's testimony was properly admitted.

3. Judicial notice

A court may take judicial notice of facts that are easily verifiable from indisputable sources. The "standard" pharmacological dictionary, if well researched and written by persons prominent in the pharmaceutical field, would satisfy this standard. Generally, the judge is not required to give advance notice to the parties that he plans to take judicial notice of a fact.

However, D could argue that the court should not take judicial notice of facts essential to conviction in a criminal case. Although the explicit language of FRE 201 would permit this, many courts would hold that because identifying DLD as an opium derivative is central to D's criminal conviction, the prosecution should be required to prove that fact in conventional ways and should be barred from establishing it through judicial notice.

4. Win ("W")'s testimony

D would have argued that W's testimony comes within the "marital communications" privilege. The prosecution could have responded, however, that conduct is not a "communication" and, even if it were, it was not "confidential" in this instance (D attempted to *conceal* his drug use from W, rather than confide in her about it). The prosecution properly prevailed on this issue.

A witness may ordinarily testify only as to facts observed and not to opinions based on those facts. However, where lay witness opinion is based on personal observation and is helpful to a clear understanding of the relevant testimony, it is often admitted. D probably argued that W's testimony that D "concealed" his drug use constituted an opinion. However, the prosecution could have contended in rebuttal that W's testimony described her impressions in the most practical way. The prosecution properly prevailed.

Answer to Question 22

Important aspects:

Competency, payments of medical expenses, character evidence in the context of negligent entrustment, adoptive admissions, drug use for impeachment.

1. Peter ("P")'s testimony

Presumably, the defendants ("Defs") objected to P's testimony on the grounds that a four-year-old boy is not competent to testify. However, a child is usually considered able to testify so long as he understands the nature of his obligation to tell the truth. Because P stated that "good little boys tell the truth," the judge's determination that P was competent would be proper.

2. P's father's testimony

The Defs probably objected to this testimony on the grounds that (1) the offer of future payments and the prior payment are irrelevant (do not tend to prove or disprove a material fact) because these gestures could have been made out of humanitarian reasons (rather than as an acknowledgment of culpability); (2) the offer of future payments was a compromise, and in most states and under the FRE such offers are **not** admissible; and (3) FRE 409 specifically bars admission of evidence of payment or offer to pay medical expenses related to an injury to prove liability for that injury. Plaintiffs ("Pls") could have contended that as a matter of logic, the evidence was relevant, but that argument cannot prevail against the explicit rule prohibiting admission of medical payment information in circumstances such as the ones in this case. The evidence was wrongly admitted.

3. Bill ("B")'s testimony

B's testimony is relevant because it tends to prove that D's mother was aware of the risk posed by the firearm, which in turn permits an inference that Defs failed to act reasonably in not taking affirmative measures to extinguish the risk.

(a) That David ("D") was a bully

Although character evidence is ordinarily not admissible to prove conduct in conformity therewith on a particular occasion, it may be admitted for any other relevant purpose. Pls probably argued that proof of D's character is appropriate to show that Defs knew, or should have known, of his dangerous tendencies (and therefore they acted negligently in permitting him to gain possession of an air rifle).

Defs, however, might also have contended that B's statement reflects his personal opinion of D, rather than the community's view of him. The FRE and some states permit opinion testimony as to character. Thus, B's testimony as to his opinion of D probably should have been admissible.

(b) Clara ("C")'s statement
Defs probably attacked this statement as double hearsay (B was testifying as to what C told him D's mother had said). But D's mother arguably "adopted" C's statement by not objecting to it (where a reasonable person in the party-opponent's position would have denied an assertion made in her presence, she is deemed to have adopted the statement).

4. Impeachment of Wilbur ("W")

Pls could have contended that the initial question was *not* proper impeachment because W's prior bad act (possession of an illegal drug) has no bearing on whether he would be likely to be truthful or not under oath. Although Defs probably argued that one who would engage in criminal conduct is likely to lie, the court was probably correct in sustaining the objection.

Pls probably made the same objection to the second question. However, one who is under the influence of a drug while testifying might *not* be able to (1) recall an incident that occurred some time before; and (2) coherently relate what had occurred. Assuming Defs had a good-faith basis for their question, this objection probably should *not* have been sustained.

Answer to Question 23

Important aspects:

Multi-level hearsay, impeachment of hearsay declarants, bias, prior inconsistent statements.

1. Barkeep's testimony

Landowner would have made two objections to Barkeep's testimony: relevancy and hearsay. With regard to relevancy, Landowner would have argued that there was no proof that Handyman actually did dump the chemicals and that Landowner's belief that they were toxic does not actually prove that they were toxic. With regard to hearsay, Landowner would argue that Barkeep's testimony presented hearsay within hearsay. One declarant was Landowner, whose words had to be true in order for Barkeep's testimony to have any relevance. The second declarant was Handyman. His statements (that Landowner had hired him and had said the chemicals were toxic) also had to be true in order for Barkeep's testimony to be relevant.

Camper would have replied that Barkeep's testimony passes the minimal requirements for relevance. It has some tendency to make a material fact more likely to be true than it would be without the evidence. It sheds some light on whether Landowner knew that toxic chemicals were on the land. Issues about whether the dumping actually took place or about whether the materials really were toxic would go to the weight, not admissibility, of the testimony.

The hearsay objection is partially correct. Landowner's words could be considered hearsay, or might be legally operative words (an offer of employment) and circumstantial evidence of knowledge of the chemicals' toxicity. Regardless of whether Landowner's words are hearsay, they are admissible. Landowner's words are admissions, because they are a party's words introduced by the party's opponent. Handyman's words are definitely hearsay because the events they describe (he dumped chemicals and Landowner made certain statements) must be true in order for his testimony to have relevance. They would be covered by the exception for statements against penal interest. They exposed him to potential liability for illegally dumping chemicals. The facts state that Handyman is unavailable, which is among the requirements for using the "statement against interest" exception. Another theory for admitting all of the out-of-court statements would be that they were statements of co-conspirators, treating Landowner and Handyman as conspirators in a plot to dump illegal chemicals.

Admission of Barkeep's testimony was therefore proper.

2. Cross-examination of Barkeep

Camper would have argued that this topic of cross-examination was outside the scope of direct examination and was not relevant. Landowner would have replied that examination with regard to bias is always proper. The questioning was permitted properly. If Camper owed Barkeep money, Barkeep had a motive to shade his testimony in favor of Camper and against Landowner. Proof of this kind of bias is properly admitted.

3. Handyman's reputation

Camper would have argued that character evidence about Handyman is prohibited and that opinion evidence about it is additionally improper.

Landowner would have replied that a hearsay declarant is subject to impeachment in most of the ways that would be proper if the declarant testified in person. Impeachment of a witness's credibility by showing that person's reputation for untruthfulness is proper impeachment and is not a violation of the rules against character evidence.

The trial court properly admitted this evidence. FRE 806 permits impeachment of a hearsay declarant, and FRE 608 allows impeachment by means of evidence of the witness's reputation with regard to truth-telling.

4. Handyman's prior statement

Camper would have argued that this impeachment effort was an attempted use of a prior inconsistent statement and that it was improper because the statement was not brought to the attention of Handyman before it was introduced.

Landowner would have replied that there was no way to bring it to the attention of Handyman, because Handyman was not available at trial, and therefore, the impeachment was proper.

The trial court properly allowed the impeachment. FRE 806 expressly provides that inconsistent statements by hearsay declarants may be introduced without regard to when they were made and without any requirement that the declarant be given an opportunity to deny or explain the statement.

Answer to Question 24

Important aspects:
Excited utterances, original writing rule, confidential marital communications privilege, spousal incompetency, scientific expert testimony.

1. Adam ("A")'s testimony

Dan ("D") probably contended that A's testimony about Tess ("T")'s statements is not admissible because it is hearsay (an out-of-court statement introduced into evidence to prove the truth of the matter asserted). The State ("St.") could argue that the statement is admissible under the "excited utterance" exception to the hearsay rule. In some jurisdictions, the statement must have been made while the event was occurring; but in others (including federal courts), the statement must have been made only while "under the stress" of the startling event. Even if the latter rule is followed in this state, five minutes is probably *not* so long a period of time as to suggest that the stress of the alleged event had dissipated. The court correctly admitted A's statement.

2. Cable ("C")'s testimony

D probably contended that C's testimony was not admissible because (1) it violated the Original Writing Rule (to prove the contents of a writing—the police file—the original is required); (2) the testimony is hearsay and outside the coverage of the exception for public records; (3) the file was not authenticated (no foundation was laid that the writing was what it purported to be); (4) the portion of the file showing that D had previously been convicted of rape is inadmissible because evidence of prior criminal convictions to show action in conformity therewith on a subsequent occasion is usually not admissible; and (5) admission violated the Confrontation Clause.

The St. might have argued in rebuttal that (1) the file was authenticated by C's testimony that he obtained it from the location where the file of known sex offenders was supposed to be located (i.e., testimony of a witness with knowledge); (2) the "business records" (writings kept in the ordinary course of the profession) and "public records" (writings compiled by public officers about matters observed pursuant to a duty imposed by law) exceptions to the hearsay rule are applicable; (3) the prior convictions tend to identify D as T's assailant and thus fall within the rule that other-crimes evidence may be used for identification purposes; and (4) the evidence is not too prejudicial in light of its crucial probative value. However, there appears to be no satisfactory response to the Original Writing Rule objection, the public records hearsay exception does not cover records of matters observed by law enforcement personnel if sought to be introduced in criminal trials, and there was no showing that the prior rape convictions involved attributes similar enough to attributes of the charged crime to support a showing of proof of D's identity. Additionally, the Confrontation Clause issue might be decided against the state, depending on the source of the data in the file. Therefore, C's testimony should **not** have been admitted.

3. *Testimony of D's wife*

D probably contended that the adverse testimony privilege permits him to prevent his wife from testifying. In federal courts and under the law in many states, this privilege belongs to the testifying spouse. If this state adheres to this modern view, D's wife should have been permitted to testify.

Confidential communications made during a marriage can be precluded by a spouse. The St. probably contended that actions (D's agitated appearance and the scratches on his arm) are not communications; and even if they are deemed to be communications, a party's physical appearance is ordinarily not deemed to be "confidential" in nature (because persons other than his spouse could presumably observe him and his condition).

If the adverse testimony privilege applies, D's wife's testimony should have been excluded. If there is no privilege against adverse spousal testimony under the law of the state where the trial takes place, then the testimony would have been properly admitted because the confidential communications privilege does not preclude it.

4. *D's testimony*

D probably contended that the St. did not provide adequate foundation for admission of the expert's testimony. Where a procedure or test is used, there usually must be a foundation showing that the process is scientifically valid. The facts fail to indicate that the expert gave any testimony about the scientific validity of the shoeprint comparison procedure. Thus, this portion of the evidence probably should not have been admitted.

5. *Prosecutor's request and closing argument*

A witness may be impeached by extrinsic evidence showing a contradiction in his testimony provided such impeachment does not pertain to a collateral matter. Although D's arm is extrinsic evidence, the blemish on it would tend to contradict D's statement that he did not rape T. This is not a collateral matter because it pertains to the essence of the St.'s case against D.

Although no comment may be made on a criminal defendant's refusal to testify on his own behalf, once an accused takes the stand, any legitimate comment about his testimony may be made. Thus, the prosecutor's comment was proper.

Multiple-Choice Questions

1. There had recently been complaints about the price of gasoline. Exton Corporation was accused of price-gouging by the State of Utopia's Department of Commerce. Exton retained Gibelco & Bunn to defend it. Gibelco's attorney requested that Exton send her all pertinent records, so that the documents could be carefully reviewed. The Utopia Department of Commerce commenced an action against Exton to recover the millions of dollars that it claimed had been overcharged to citizens of that state.

   During the discovery stage of the case, the Utopia Department of Justice made a request for certain relevant documents. Gibelco's attorney responded that the documents requested were in its possession and therefore privileged. The Utopia Department of Justice disagreed with this assertion.

   It is most likely that

   A. The records are discoverable because they are not within the attorney-client privilege.

   B. The records are discoverable because any purported attorney-client privilege must be asserted by Exton at trial.

   C. The records are not discoverable because they are now in Gibelco's possession.

   D. The records are not discoverable because, if reviewed by Gibelco, the records now constitute Gibelco's work product.

2. Bill Sacamore and Joe Schmoe were two ex-convicts. Joe asked Bill to help him in "knocking over" a grocery store. When Bill vacillated, Joe promised that he would give Bill at least $1,000 for his participation. Bill then agreed. They agreed that Bill would drive the getaway car, and Joe would actually steal the money from the grocer. On the prearranged date, Bill and Joe drove to the grocery store. Joe went inside, while Bill waited in the car. Joe pulled a gun on the Owner, and removed $5,000 from the safe. However, as he was about to exit, a security guard at the store shot Joe in the leg. Joe was captured and arrested.

   When the paramedics arrived, Joe said to one of them, "Give Bill Sacamore this $1,000. If he doesn't get his money, his friends will get me in the slammer." Joe subsequently confessed, and Bill was arrested and charged with conspiracy to commit armed robbery. At Bill's trial, the paramedic is called to testify about Joe's statement to him. However, Bill's attorney objects to this testimony. (Assume the testimony is not hearsay.)

It is most likely that the statement is

A. Inadmissible because it is not relevant.

B. Inadmissible because it is within the physician-patient privilege.

C. Inadmissible because a paramedic is not a physician.

D. Admissible because Bill's participation in the robbery could arguably be inferred from Joe's statement.

3. Post sued Dean for personal injuries allegedly caused by Dean's negligence. A major issue at trial was whether Post's disability was caused solely by trauma or by a preexisting condition of osteoarthritis. Post called Dr. Cox, who testified that the disability was caused by trauma. On cross-examination, Dr. Cox testified that a medical textbook entitled *Diseases of the Joints* was authoritative and that she agreed with the substance of passages from the textbook that she was directed to look at. But Dr. Cox contended that the passages were inapplicable to Post's condition because they dealt with rheumatoid arthritis rather than with the osteoarthritis that had been diagnosed in Post. Dean then called his expert, Dr. Freed, who testified that, with reference to the issue being litigated, there is no difference between the two kinds of arthritis. Dean's counsel then asks permission to read to the jury the textbook passages earlier shown to Dr. Cox. The judge should rule that the textbook passages are

A. Admissible only for the purpose of impeaching Cox.

B. Admissible as substantive evidence if the judge determines that the passages are relevant.

C. Inadmissible because they are hearsay and do not fall within any exception.

D. Inadmissible, if Cox contended that they are not relevant to Post's condition.

4. Bill and Harry are accused of conspiring to commit a bank robbery. Bill was apprehended immediately after leaving the bank and confessed to the crime. Under questioning, he advised police that Harry had supplied the gun and was to meet him afterward to receive one-third of the cash proceeds. Bill subsequently gave the police a note written by Harry, which stated: "Don't forget my share. If you get lost, I'll find you, and it won't be pretty." When the prosecution attempts to introduce this note at Harry's trial, Harry's attorney objects. (Assume the note is not hearsay.)

It is most likely that the note is

A. Admissible, but only if a handwriting expert corroborates the validity of Harry's signature.

B. Admissible, if the court determines there is adequate evidence of the letter's authenticity.

C. Inadmissible because the letter is not relevant to whether Harry was a co-conspirator.

D. Inadmissible because the letter was confidential in nature.

5. Darryl and Paul were motorists. As Paul was driving to work one day, his car was struck by a vehicle driven by Darryl. Paul immediately got out of his car and, after getting Darryl's driver's license and other data, began asking people in the area if they had seen what had occurred. Although somewhat reluctant to "get involved," Martha told Paul that she had seen the accident, and that Darryl's vehicle was over the center line when the crash occurred. Three days later, an adjuster employed by Paul's insurer also asked Martha what had occurred and received the same response. Paul sued Darryl (who claimed that Paul's vehicle was over the center line). At trial, when Paul's attorney attempts to have the insurance adjuster testify as to what Martha had said to him, Darryl's attorney objects.

It is most likely that the testimony will be

A. Admissible because it is an admission.

B. Admissible because Martha's statement was an excited utterance.

C. Inadmissible because there is no indication that Martha is unavailable.

D. Inadmissible because Martha's statement is hearsay.

6. Jack was shot and killed by someone with a pistol. Michael is accused of the murder. The prosecution's case is premised on the argument that Michael was greatly angered by Jack's constant taunting and reacted in a murderous manner. At the criminal trial, the prosecution seeks to introduce testimony by Pete to the effect that he had heard Jack call Michael a "sissy" and "scaredy cat" on numerous occasions, and that Michael had objected to these characterizations. However, Michael's attorney objects to this testimony.

It is most likely that Pete's testimony is

A. Admissible, if it is offered to show Michael's alleged motivation.

B. Admissible, if Michael asserts his Fifth Amendment right against self-incrimination and there is no other means of admitting this evidence.

   C. Inadmissible because it is hearsay.

   D. Inadmissible because it is a statement pertaining to Michael's character.

7. Dick and Paul were motorists in the State of Utopia. One day, as Paul was backing out of his driveway onto the street, his car was struck by a vehicle driven by Dick. Paul was immediately taken by paramedics to a local hospital. Paul subsequently sued Dick. Dick denied liability, contending that Paul had illegally backed into the street. Dick also contested the extent of Paul's asserted injuries.

In presenting Paul's case, his attorney called one of the paramedics, Mike, who attended to Paul in the ambulance that brought him to the hospital. Mike was asked to testify about the seriousness of Paul's injuries. However, before Mike testified, he reviewed the report of the patient's condition that he is required by law to complete in such instances. This report was given to him by Paul's attorney. The report had not been admitted into evidence, and Dick's attorney objected to Mike's testimony.

It is most likely that Mike's testimony is

   A. Admissible, under the doctrine of present recollection refreshed.

   B. Admissible because it constitutes past recollection recorded.

   C. Inadmissible because it is based on a document that is hearsay.

   D. Inadmissible, if the report has not been authenticated.

8. Pam owned a large house on Marlborough Street in the City of Alacon. She entered into a written agreement with Deborah whereby the latter agreed to add a second story onto Pam's home. The specific work that Deborah was to perform was described in detail in the written agreement. After the work was completed, Pam refused to pay the last installment, claiming that there were numerous deficiencies in Deborah's work. In fact, Pam sued Deborah for the sum of money that she paid to another entity to perform the work in question "correctly." At the trial, Deborah sought to personally testify as to the detailed provisions of the contract, to show that her performance satisfied the precise requirements set out in the contract. Pam's attorney objected to this testimony.

Deborah's testimony about matters described in the written contract is

   A. Admissible because the "business records" exception to the hearsay rule is applicable.

B. Admissible because Deborah's testimony is based on firsthand knowledge.

C. Inadmissible because the Original Writing Rule is applicable to this situation.

D. Inadmissible because the parol evidence rule is applicable in this situation.

9. Dora, an elderly woman, was walking down a city street toward a corner. Paul was jogging toward the corner along the intersecting sidewalk. Paul and Dora arrived at the street corner at the same time, and Paul inadvertently brushed against Dora. Dora, because of her age, fell to the ground (breaking her left arm). Paul did not believe he was at fault, but advised Dora that he would "take care of her doctor bills, and that he was sorry the incident had occurred." George, a passerby, heard Paul's statements. When Paul failed to pay Dora's higher-than-expected medical bills, she sued him. At the trial, Dora's attorney attempted to have George testify about Paul's statements to Dora. Paul's attorney vigorously objected to this testimony.

It is most likely that George's testimony about Paul's statements is

A. Admissible, as a party-opponent admission.

B. Admissible because it is relevant on the question of Paul's failure to act reasonably.

C. Inadmissible because Paul promised to pay Dora's medical bills.

D. Inadmissible because Paul did not intend for his statement to constitute an acknowledgment of culpability.

10. Paul was injured when the brakes on his six-month-old Fordico Company ("Fordico") automobile abruptly failed to work. Paul commenced a products liability action against Fordico, contending that the latter had manufactured a defective vehicle. However, Paul was injured while driving on a rain-soaked street. In its defense, Fordico attempted to introduce evidence that, despite the poor weather, Paul was negligently exceeding the speed limit by at least 15 mph when he was injured. Fordico would like to call a witness, Rob, who witnessed the accident to testify as to the foregoing.

If Paul's attorney objects to the introduction of this evidence, it is most likely that

A. The objection will be sustained because the evidence is not relevant.

B. The objection will be sustained because the evidence is hearsay.

C. The objection will be overruled because the evidence is relevant.

D. The objection will be overruled, because Paul's conduct, though hearsay, will be treated as an admission.

11. On the way home from school one day, Dan's stepdaughter, Amy, failed to stop at a red light and crashed into Patricia's car. Under the applicable law, a vehicle "owner" is vicariously liable for its negligent operation by members of her household. Case law has defined a vehicle "owner" as the legal owner or person "in control" of the automobile. Patricia sued Dan and the legal owner (i.e., the person in whose name the vehicle was registered) of the car, Dan's second wife, Carol. In rebuttal, Dan claimed that the vehicle belonged to Carol, and therefore he has no personal liability to Patricia. At trial, Patricia attempts to introduce evidence that Dan had purchased liability insurance for the car that Amy was driving when the collision occurred.

   If Dan objects to the introduction of this evidence, it is most likely that

   A. The objection will be overruled because Dan's purchase of insurance tends to show that it was more likely than not that Amy was at fault.

   B. The objection will be overruled because Dan's purchase of liability insurance tends to show that he is the "owner" of the vehicle.

   C. The objection will be sustained because the existence of insurance is irrelevant to who was at fault.

   D. The objection will be sustained because the availability of insurance tends to bias a fact finder against the insured party.

12. Margaret was shopping at Frank's Market when she fell after slipping on some liquid spilled in one of the aisles. Mr. Jamison, the manager of Frank's Market, heard Margaret's fall and the ensuing commotion. He did not see the incident, however. Sensing what had occurred, Jamison walked over to Margaret and immediately said to her, "Frank's Market will pay you $5,000 to forget any claim." Margaret angrily refused this offer, and told Jamison that she was going to "Sue, sue, sue!" Soon afterward, Margaret did commence litigation against Frank's Market, which denied liability in its answer.

   At trial, Margaret tries to introduce evidence that, immediately after her slip-and-fall, Jamison offered, on behalf of Frank's Market, to pay her $5,000 in settlement of her claim.

If counsel for Frank's Market objects to the introduction of this evidence, it is most likely that

A. The objection will be sustained because Jamison's statement was a compromise offer.

B. The objection will be sustained because Jamison's statement is hearsay and not relevant (i.e., he hadn't even observed the incident).

C. The objection will not be sustained because Jamison's statement is pertinent to a determination of the culpability of Frank's Market.

D. The objection will not be sustained because Jamison's statement was not made in the course of formal settlement negotiations.

13. After Karen purchased her new white car, she immediately drove it to a local shopping mall. Because the car was brand new, Karen parked it at the very end of the parking lot, far from any other vehicles. In this manner, she hoped to avoid its being "nicked" by a careless driver. After she had finished her shopping, Karen returned to her car. She observed that a black van was parked next to it. As Karen walked to the driver's side of her car, she noticed a large black stripe on the rear portion of her car and some white paint on the right front fender of the van. Karen, understandably upset, took down the van's license plate number and sued the owner for damage to her vehicle.

At trial, Karen attempts to introduce testimony from the owner of the van that he had his vehicle painted only two days after the alleged incident.

If counsel for the defendant objects to this testimony, it is most likely that

A. The objection will be overruled because the testimony shows that the van owner had attempted to conceal evidence.

B. The objection will be overruled because in negligence cases evidence of remedial measures is ordinarily admissible.

C. The objection will be sustained because evidence of remedial measures is not admissible.

D. The objection will be sustained because the evidence fails to show that the defendant was the driver of the vehicle at the time in question.

14. Alice and her friend Pam were walking downtown on their way to a restaurant. They passed by a building that was under construction. As Alice and Pam were staring at the new masonry, they heard an ugly "scraping" sound. Immediately thereafter, a piece of masonry fell from the building, directly onto Alice's shoulder. Alice sued Mr. Moneybags, the owner of the building, and Cosgrove, Inc., the construction company working on the building. In his answer, Moneybags claimed that Cosgrove was an independent contractor and that the building was completely under Cosgrove's control when the incident occurred. Thus, Moneybags argued, he had no liability. Moneybags further contended that he exercised no control over the construction at the time of the accident.

At trial, Alice attempts to introduce evidence that, one day after the incident, Moneybags ordered Cosgrove to erect a screen on the portion of the roof overlooking the street, and that Cosgrove complied.

If counsel for Moneybags objects to the introduction of this evidence, it is most likely that

A. The objection will be sustained because evidence of remedial measures is inadmissible.

B. The objection will be sustained because the evidence has no bearing on Moneybags's alleged negligence.

C. The objection will be overruled because the evidence shows Cosgrove's control of the construction.

D. The objection will be overruled because (with a limiting instruction) the evidence could be used to show that Moneybags retained control over the building's construction.

15. Marla wanted to buy some new diamond earrings. Accordingly, she drove down to Ripoff's, a store recommended to her by a friend. Clyde Ripoff, the owner, showed her several pairs of beautiful earrings. He eventually sold Marla a pair of what appeared to be diamond studs. Ripoff told Marla that the earrings were "very" valuable and that he was "giving her an excellent bargain." Later, when Marla attempted to insure the items, she was emphatically informed by her insurance agent that the earrings were merely cubic zirconia. They were therefore of only minimal worth. Marla commenced an action against Ripoff for "grossly" misrepresenting the value of the earrings.

At trial, Marla's counsel seeks to introduce evidence that Ripoff had a well-deserved reputation for being "unsavory and unethical" in his business dealings.

If counsel for Ripoff objects to the introduction of this evidence, it is most likely that

A. The objection will be sustained because the reputation evidence is hearsay.

B. The objection will be sustained because the evidence is being offered to show that Ripoff acted in conformity with his usual character on the occasion in question.

C. The objection will be overruled because the evidence tends to show that Ripoff deceived Marla.

D. The objection will be overruled, if Ripoff offers evidence of his character for honesty.

16. One Sunday afternoon, James was driving on a public street. Unfortunately, he was injured when a car driven by Paul went through a stop sign and crashed into the passenger side of James's car. James sued Paul's parents under a negligent entrustment theory, contending that they carelessly permitted Paul to borrow their car. Paul had been in several car accidents during the prior two years. In these incidents, Paul had been adjudged as either "negligent" or "reckless."

At trial, counsel for James attempts to introduce evidence of those past findings that Paul had been "negligent" and "reckless." If counsel for Paul's parents objects to the introduction of this evidence, it is most likely that

A. The objection will be overruled, if the evidence is offered to show that Paul's parents knew (or should have known) about his reckless or negligent tendencies.

B. The objection will be overruled, if the evidence is offered to show that Paul had acted unreasonably.

C. The objection will be sustained because proof of the past adjudications would be hearsay.

D. The objection will be sustained because Paul's prior "negligent" or "reckless" conduct has no logical connection to the likelihood that he was negligent when he hit James's car.

17. Theresa was charged with the attempted robbery of a beauty-supply store. Theresa was a "make-up junkie" who had two prior convictions for robbing beauty-supply and cosmetics stores at gunpoint. Theresa had worked previously as an Avon representative, until the company discovered that Theresa was often keeping, rather than selling, its products. Theresa was arrested at the scene. She admits committing

the crime, but claims that she was coerced into participating in it by her boyfriend, who threatened to "give her a thrashing" if she didn't "come through with some money."

At trial, the prosecution attempts to introduce evidence that Theresa had two prior convictions for the robbery of other beauty-supply stores.

If Theresa's attorney objects to the introduction of this evidence, it is most likely that

- A. The objection will be sustained because prior convictions ordinarily are not admissible.
- B. The objection will be sustained because Theresa's prior convictions are not relevant.
- C. The objection will be overruled because Theresa's prior convictions are admissible character evidence in this situation.
- D. The objection will be overruled because the prior convictions are relevant to prove that Theresa (as opposed to anyone else) committed the crime in question.

18. Magda was shopping at Nordstrom's Department Store. She saw a lovely silk scarf and tied it around her neck to see how it looked. After doing this, Magda saw some leather gloves and walked over to them. Then other items caught her attention while she continued to shop. Suddenly, Magda remembered that she was supposed to meet a friend for lunch at noon. She hurried out of the store, still wearing the scarf. However, as soon as she left Nordstrom's, Magda was arrested by security personnel for shoplifting. At trial, Magda contended that she had simply forgotten about the scarf she had tied around her neck.

At trial, the prosecution sought to introduce evidence that, on a prior occasion, Magda was stopped outside of a different store for neglecting to purchase an item that she was wearing (jeans she had purportedly "tried on" at a Gap store). However, no charges against Magda had been filed in that instance.

If Magda's attorney objects to the introduction of this evidence, it is most likely that

- A. The objection will be overruled because the evidence rebuts Magda's assertion that she had made an innocent mistake.
- B. The objection will be overruled because prior similar conduct is generally admissible to prove conduct in conformity therewith on the occasion in question.

C. The objection will be sustained because the Gap store incident is irrelevant to Magda's conduct on this particular occasion.

D. The objection will be sustained because prior conduct is not admissible.

19. On July 1, John Adams executed a deed conveying a life estate in Blackacre to Charles Baker. Thereafter, Baker brought an action against Adams for reformation of the deed, contending that it was the intention of the parties that Blackacre be conveyed to Baker in fee.

Evans, a witness for Baker, testified that she worked as a secretary in the office of Ladd, an attorney who represented Adams in many of his business dealings. Evans was shown a document that bore the printed letterhead, "John Adams, Bigtown." The document was dated June 12, and it read: "Dear Mr. Ladd: I have decided to sell Blackacre outright to Baker. In a few days, I'll call you about preparing the deed." At the bottom in longhand was written, "John Adams."

Evans, on examining the document, stated that it was a photocopy of a letter that Ladd had received through the mail about the middle of June, that she had seen the letter at that time, and that the letterhead on it was the same as that which appeared in Ladd's office file of correspondence with Adams, who lived in Bigtown. Baker then offered the document into evidence.

The ***best*** objection that Adams should make against the introduction of this evidence is that it is

A. Irrelevant.

B. Violative of the Best Evidence Rule.

C. Hearsay.

D. Violative of the attorney-client privilege.

20. Bill Bungler was on trial for attempting to extort money from Harvey Hardin. Harvey owned a large hardware store in Centerville. The prosecution introduced into evidence Bungler's telephone registry, which showed a call to a particular phone number on the day a demand for $50,000 was telephonically made on Harvey. The prosecution sought to introduce into evidence a properly authenticated copy of the Centerville telephone book. This book contained a listing for Harvey's store at that number. The evidence is

A. Inadmissible because it is hearsay.

B. Inadmissible because it is entirely possible that Bungler called Harvey's store for a business purpose.

    C. Inadmissible because of the Best Evidence Rule.

    D. Admissible because it is relevant to show that Bungler might have been the extortionist.

21. In an extortion trial, to show that the intended victim reasonably felt threatened with imminent harm, the prosecution sought to introduce into evidence an unsigned, hand-printed note received by the victim reading "Deliver $50,000 to the phone booth on Main and Grand at 8:00 P.M. tomorrow, or you'll be out of business within a week." This evidence is

    A. Inadmissible because it was unsigned.

    B. Inadmissible because it is hearsay.

    C. Admissible because it is not hearsay.

    D. Admissible because it is a party-opponent admission.

22. Bob Barker was arrested for burglary. At the trial, Barker testified in his defense that he was playing cards with Jack on the night of the burglary. Defense counsel also called Joseph Blow as a witness on the defendant's behalf. Blow testified that he lived in the same community as Barker and that the latter had an excellent reputation for honesty and integrity. On cross-examination, the prosecution asked Blow if he was aware that Barker had been fired from his job as a supermarket cashier two years before for taking money from the cash register. The question is

    A. Proper because Blow testified as to Barker's character.

    B. Proper because a witness may always be cross-examined with respect to prior acts of misconduct committed by him.

    C. Improper because the prior misconduct was different from burglary.

    D. Improper because Barker was never asked about the supermarket incident.

23. Bob Brown had been employed as a miner for the ABC Mining Corp. for 12 years. He was recently killed when there was an explosion in the underground area in which he was working. His executor brought a wrongful death action against ABC, claiming the latter negligently permitted unsafe working conditions to exist, as a consequence of which Brown was killed. The executor called Jock as a witness. He testified that earlier on the day of the explosion, Brown had commented to him, "I could swear that I smell gas down here." Brown's statement, quoted in Jock's testimony, is

A. Admissible, as a statement against interest.

B. Admissible, as a dying declaration.

C. Admissible, as a present sense impression.

D. Admissible, as an excited utterance.

24. Arlene parked her relatively new car facing downward on a steep hill, turned her tires toward the curb, and set the parking brake. She then exited the vehicle. When Arlene returned approximately one hour later, the vehicle had moved forward and hit the vehicle in front of her. While Arlene was surveying the damage, Clyde, the owner of the other vehicle, arrived. He subsequently sued Arlene, claiming that her negligence caused the damage to his vehicle. Arlene filed an indemnity action against the manufacturer of her car, alleging that the parking brake was defective.

At trial, Arlene attempts to testify that, whenever she parks her car, she invariably sets the parking brake.

If Clyde's attorney objects to the introduction of this evidence, it is most likely that

A. The objection will be sustained because prior conduct to prove action in conformity therewith is inadmissible.

B. The objection will be sustained because it is inconsistent with Arlene's claim against the manufacturer.

C. The objection will be overruled because evidence of habit is admissible.

D. The objection will be overruled because prior conduct is admissible to prove action in conformity therewith on the occasion in question.

25. Mary is a 72-year-old retired junior high school teacher. She commenced an action against Matthew, a licensed stockbroker, claiming that he had deceived her into investing her life savings by fraudulently claiming that he would greatly enrich her via a series of stock transactions. Matthew has no history of disciplinary action or lawsuits against him with respect to stock transactions initiated by him. Matthew is generally known as an "honest" person by his friends, colleagues, and clients.

At trial, Matthew's counsel attempts to introduce evidence, via the testimony of another stockbroker who works closely with Matthew, that Matthew "has an excellent reputation for honesty in the business community."

If Mary's attorney objects to the introduction of this evidence, it is most likely that

A. The objection will be overruled because character evidence is admissible in civil cases.

B. The objection will be overruled because Matthew's character is directly in issue in this case.

C. The objection will be sustained because the testimony is hearsay.

D. The objection will be sustained because evidence of Matthew's character is not admissible.

26. Carlyle always had a very fond relationship with his children. Prior to his death, Carlyle (a wealthy 72-year-old man who resided in a nursing home) changed his will to leave everything to his neighbor and friend, Jojo. After the will was read, Carlyle's two children, Maggie and April, claimed that the modification was invalid because Carlyle was not mentally competent when the will was changed.

At trial, Maggie and April attempt to introduce evidence of specific acts of Carlyle's that occurred about the time that his will was modified (e.g., neighbors will testify that Carlyle sometimes dressed as a cowboy and pretended to shoot outlaws with a toy pistol).

If counsel for the executor of Carlyle's estate vigorously objects to the introduction of this evidence, it is most likely that

A. The objection will be overruled because Carlyle's character is in issue.

B. The objection will be overruled because character evidence is ordinarily admissible.

C. The objection will be sustained because the evidence pertains to prior specific acts (rather than general character traits).

D. The objection will be sustained because character evidence is generally inadmissible.

27. Charley and Bill were oil rig workers. Over time, they developed an intense hatred of each other. They recently got into a barroom brawl. In the midst of the fight, Bill pulled a switchblade from his hip pocket, and slashed Charley across the throat. This cut ultimately caused Charley to bleed to death. Bill has been charged with Charley's murder. Bill claims that Charley had initiated the altercation and that he had acted in self-defense.

At trial, Bill's attorney seeks to introduce evidence to the effect that Bill had an excellent reputation for "honesty and dealing fairly with people."

If the prosecution objects to this evidence, it is most likely that

A. The objection will be sustained because Bill cannot initially introduce evidence of his own good character.

B. The objection will be sustained because this evidence does not tend to rebut the commission of the crime for which Bill has been charged.

C. The objection will be overruled because a defendant may initially introduce evidence of his own positive character traits in a homicide case.

D. The objection will be overruled because character evidence pertaining to a defendant is admissible in criminal cases.

28. Jamie and Sharon have been college roommates for two years. One afternoon, Sharon stole one of Jamie's personal checks and went to a store. She used the check to purchase several sweaters. At the time of purchase, Sharon forged Jamie's name on the check. As her roommate, Sharon was very familiar with Jamie's signature. Jamie eventually found out about the forged check and pressed forgery charges against Sharon. Sharon has claimed that she neither took the check nor forged Jamie's name.

At trial, Sharon's attorney attempts to introduce evidence that Sharon had an excellent reputation for honesty and truthfulness.

If the prosecution objects to this evidence, it is most likely that

A. The objection will be overruled because evidence of Sharon's character for honesty is pertinent to the crime for which she is charged.

B. The objection will be overruled because positive character traits pertaining to a defendant are admissible in criminal trials.

C. The objection will be sustained because only evidence of prior specific acts by Sharon is admissible.

D. The objection will be sustained because evidence of an accused's character must be initiated by the prosecution.

29. Kellie and Shawna were dancers at a striptease bar. While performing a duet on stage, Shawna grabbed at Kellie's costume and Kellie then punched Shawna. Kellie's punch knocked out Shawna and caused

serious injury. Shawna sued Kellie for battery. Kellie claimed that she had acted in self-defense and that the amount of force she used was proper because she was genuinely afraid that Shawna would harm her seriously.

At trial, Kellie's attorney attempts to introduce testimony that Shawna had a reputation for being "an aggressive bully."

If Shawna's counsel objects to this evidence, it is most likely that

A. The objection will be sustained because this is a civil case.

B. The objection will be sustained because it is not relevant to whether Kellie committed the torts asserted.

C. The objection will be overruled because the case involves conduct that was arguably criminal in nature.

D. The objection will be overruled if there is also evidence that Kellie knew of that reputation at the time when she punched Shawna.

30. Jimmy is a macho-type guy who lives in a "rough" neighborhood. One day, while standing at the window of his apartment, Jimmy saw Slash slicing the tires of his car with a knife. Jimmy ran out of his house with a baseball bat. He swung the bat and hit Slash several times, breaking Slash's arms and legs. Jimmy was taken into custody and charged with aggravated battery. In his defense, Jimmy claims Slash threatened him with the knife, resulting in his actually striking the latter with the bat.

At the criminal trial, Jimmy's counsel attempts to introduce evidence to show that he is "peaceable in nature."

If the prosecution objects to this evidence, it is most likely that

A. The objection will be sustained because character evidence is not admissible.

B. The objection will be sustained because this is mere opinion evidence.

C. The objection will be overruled because this type of character evidence is admissible in this situation.

D. The objection will be overruled because only specific instances of Jimmy's peaceable character are admissible.

31. Tanya recently became a member of the Roses, a female gang at her high school. Although Tanya is in high school, she was held back one year and is now 18 years old. As a manifestation of allegiance to her new gang, Tanya was told that she must "slash" a member of a rival

gang. Tanya was mistakenly informed that Rita, another girl at the high school, is a member of the Orchids. In fact, Rita had no gang ties whatsoever. One day after school, Tanya pulled out a razor blade and slashed at Rita's arm. Rita attempted to avoid being cut by ducking. As a consequence, Tanya accidentally slashed Rita's neck, wounding her fatally. Tanya is arrested and charged with murder.

At the criminal trial, Tanya testifies that (1) she acted in self-defense (i.e., Rita had initially attacked her with a switchblade), and alternatively (2) Rita provoked the situation by insulting Tanya. In response, the prosecution attempts to introduce character evidence of Rita's peaceable, nonviolent nature.

If Tanya's attorney objects to the introduction of this evidence, it is most likely that

A. The objection will be overruled because evidence of Rita's character is admissible to disprove Tanya's assertions.

B. The objection will be overruled because pertinent character evidence concerning the victim is always admissible in criminal cases.

C. The objection will be sustained, if the prosecution failed to introduce evidence pertaining to Tanya's character during its case-in-chief.

D. The objection will be sustained because the prosecution may introduce evidence only pertaining to Tanya's character. *stopped here*

32. Mark and Rick were both chefs at a restaurant. One night, while preparing dinner for customers of the restaurant, Rick and Mark started to argue about how much soy sauce to put in a particular type of dish. Mark lost his temper, picked up a knife, and stabbed Rick in the hand, wounding (but not killing) him. Rick pressed charges against Mark, and Mark was arrested.

At the criminal trial, Mark asserts that he acted in self-defense. The prosecution, as part of its case-in-chief, attempts to introduce evidence of Rick's peaceful character to rebut Mark's assertion.

If Mark's attorney objects to this evidence, it is most likely that

A. The objection will be sustained because Mark did not commit homicide.

B. The objection will be sustained because, although any type of character evidence is admissible, it must initially be offered by Mark.

    C. The objection will be overruled because Rick's character is pertinent to the question of Mark's guilt.

    D. The objection will be overruled because only evidence of specific instances of peaceful character is admissible in this situation.

33. Betty is an 18-year-old college student. At a fraternity party, she met Alan. After a couple of hours of dancing, Alan asked Betty if she'd like to "come upstairs" with him. Betty, naive to the sexual connotation inherent in Alan's invitation and having never been at a fraternity house, agreed. In Alan's room, Alan and Betty had sexual intercourse. Although Betty seemed to protest, Alan assumed that she wasn't really serious. Betty pressed charges against Alan. Alan admitted having sexual relations with Betty but claimed that she had impliedly consented to the act.

At the criminal trial, Alan's attorney attempts to introduce evidence that Betty had a well-known reputation on campus for sexual promiscuity.

If the prosecution objects to this evidence, it is most likely that

    A. The objection will be sustained because Betty's past sexual behavior is not admissible through reputation or opinion evidence.

    B. The objection will be sustained because Betty's past sexual behavior is admissible, but only through evidence of specific past acts.

    C. The objection will be overruled because Betty's past sexual behavior is relevant to the issue of her alleged consent.

    D. The objection will be overruled because Betty had voluntarily gone into Alan's room.

34. Steve and Cindy have been "dating" for over three years. They have had sexual relations together on numerous occasions. Although Cindy had always assured Steve that she "couldn't get pregnant" and was having sexual relations with him alone, Steve had suspicions to the contrary. One day, Cindy informed Steve that she was pregnant with his child. Steve said he did not believe Cindy.

In the paternity civil suit subsequently filed by Cindy against Steve, Steve attempts to introduce the testimony of several witnesses to the effect that Cindy bragged to them about sexual behavior with other men.

If Cindy's counsel objects to the introduction of this evidence, it is most likely that

A. The objection will be overruled because evidence of Cindy's prior sexual behavior with other men directly pertains to the issue of whether Steve is the child's father.

B. The objection will be overruled because evidence of Cindy's prior sexual behavior with other men is pertinent to the issue of Cindy's consent.

C. The objection will be sustained because Cindy's past sexual encounters are not admissible.

D. The objection will be sustained, unless the evidence is limited to Cindy's sexual behavior with men during the time period during which she could have become pregnant.

35. Brenda, owner of Brenda's Bridal Registry Shop, ordered and paid for 14 dozen glasses from Bill's House of Glass ("Bill's"). Before the glasses were shipped, Bud, an employee of Bill's, examined the glasses. After the glasses arrived, Brenda complained to Bill's that many of them had cracks. She asked for a refund of her purchase price, but Bill's refused. Brenda has sued Bill's for that refund.

At trial, Bill's attorney called Terry, Bud's supervisor, to testify that when Brenda complained, Bud told him that "the glasses were in perfect condition when I examined them."

If Brenda's counsel objects to the introduction of this testimony, it is most likely that

A. The objection will be sustained because it is irrelevant if Terry personally inspected the glasses or not.

B. The objection will be sustained because Bud's statement to Terry is hearsay.

C. The objection will be overruled because Bud's statement to Terry is an admission of a party-opponent.

D. The objection will be overruled because Bud's statement to Terry is not offered to prove the truth of the matter asserted.

36. Lou and Jack were both farmers. They had been next-door neighbors for years. One day, Jack, who was not married and had no children, walked over to Lou's house, handed a completed deed to Lou, and said, "Here, old friend, the farm is yours." The next day, Jack suffered a heart attack and died shortly thereafter. Lou subsequently took the deed to be recorded. At the Recorder's Office, however, he learned that it had been improperly executed. Although Jack had signed the deed, he had forgotten to notarize it (as required by state law to record a deed). Lou has never recorded the deed.

At the quiet title action commenced by Lou concerning his ownership of the farm, Lou's counsel attempted to introduce into evidence Jack's manual delivery of the deed and statement, "Here, old friend, the farm is yours." This would be relevant in proving that Jack had intended the transfer to be "immediately operative," and therefore a conveyance had occurred.

If the executor of Jack's estate objects to the introduction of this evidence, it is most likely that

A. The objection will be sustained because the evidence is hearsay.

B. The objection will be sustained because the evidence is irrelevant (unless the executor has contended that Jack was not competent).

C. The objection will be overruled because the testimony is admissible to show that Jack intended the conveyance to Lou to be immediately operative.

D. The objection will be overruled because the evidence constituted a dying declaration.

37. Carol works as a teller at Hometown Bank in Boise, Idaho. One day, while she was sitting behind the counter, Miss Gribbins, a wealthy, well-known eccentric, stormed up to Carol's window and shouted, "Your boss is a big crook." Miss Gribbins then promptly turned and left the bank. Several customers standing at the windows of the other tellers overheard Miss Gribbins's statement and knowingly smiled. Mr. Revered, the owner of Hometown Bank and Carol's boss, subsequently learned of Miss Gribbins's statement. He commenced an action for slander against Miss Gribbins, seeking damages of $1,000,000.

At trial, Mr. Revered's counsel called Carol to the stand to testify that Miss Gribbins had said to her, "Your boss is a big crook."

If counsel for Miss Gribbins objects to the introduction of this testimony, it is most likely that

A. The objection will be overruled because Carol's testimony is not hearsay.

B. The objection will be overruled because Carol's testimony is hearsay but constitutes present state of mind.

C. The objection will be sustained because Miss Gribbins's statement was mere opinion (rather than fact).

D. The objection will be sustained, unless Mr. Revered's counsel has already proved that Miss Gribbins was competent.

38. Claire was watching television when a friend (Penny) told her that Susan, Claire's neighbor, had hit Claire's daughter Amy for no apparent reason. This incident had supposedly occurred while Amy was playing on the sidewalk outside of Susan's house the day before. Claire immediately went to Susan's house to confront her. Their disagreement escalated until they got into a physical altercation. During the struggle, Claire kicked Susan. Susan subsequently filed a tort action (alleging assault, battery, and false imprisonment) against Claire. Claire counterclaimed.

At trial, Claire's counsel attempted to have Jane testify that the day before the fight between Claire and Susan, she (Jane) heard Penny tell Claire that Susan had hit Amy.

If Susan's attorney objects to the introduction of this testimony, it is most likely that

A. The objection will be overruled because this testimony shows that Claire had a motive for accosting Susan.

B. The objection will be sustained because this testimony is irrelevant (i.e., it doesn't pertain to who actually commenced the altercation).

C. The objection will be sustained because it probably has too great a likelihood of prejudicing the jury against Susan.

D. The objection will be sustained because Jane's testimony is hearsay.

39. Conrad, Donald, and Peter golfed together each Wednesday afternoon. Conrad and Peter were medical students, and Donald worked for MegaBank. One Wednesday while on the links, Donald casually mentioned to Peter and Conrad that "MegaBank always has megabucks in it on Fridays because Friday afternoon it takes its cash to the Feds." That Friday, someone robbed MegaBank at gunpoint. Peter was arrested and charged with that crime. Peter contended that his arrest was a case of mistaken identity and that he's not "into" bank robbery.

At trial, the prosecution called Conrad to testify that he overheard Donald tell Peter that "MegaBank always has megabucks in it on Fridays." Donald was unavailable to testify.

If Peter's counsel objects to the introduction of this testimony, it is most likely that

A. The objection will be overruled, because Donald is "unavailable" under FRE 804(a)(5).

B. The objection will be overruled because the evidence shows Peter's belief that MegaBank had a large amount of cash money in it when the robbery occurred.

C. The objection will be sustained because Conrad's testimony is hearsay.

D. The objection will be sustained because the testimony is irrelevant in that it does not pertain to whether Peter robbed MegaBank.

40. Winona was reading a book one evening. Harry, her husband, suddenly entered their home in a hasty manner. He was sweaty and out of breath. He walked past Winona, into the bathroom. Winona then heard the water running. She later noticed that Harry had put small bandages in several places on his arms. Soon afterward, Winona and Harry were divorced. One month later, Harry was charged with raping Cindy on the night in question. At the trial, the prosecution called Winona to testify about what she had seen that evening. (Assume that Winona was willing to testify.)

If Harry's attorney objects to the introduction of this evidence, it is most likely that

A. Her testimony is inadmissible under the spousal privilege.

B. Her testimony is inadmissible under the marital communications privilege.

C. Her testimony is admissible because the marital communications privilege does not apply to statements made for the commission of a crime.

D. Her testimony is admissible because only Winona holds the privilege of testifying or not (and she is willing to do so).

41. Three years ago, Jack and Tina were involved in a car accident. Bob, who was standing on the sidewalk when the cars driven by Jack and Tina collided, was the only eyewitness. Jack sued Tina for the numerous injuries that he sustained in the incident, and Tina counterclaimed.

At trial, Bob testified on behalf of Jack that Tina ran a stop sign and crashed into Jack's car. During the cross-examination, Tina's attorney asked Bob if he and Jack had recently become partners in a business venture. Bob answered, "Yes." After Bob left the witness stand, Jack's attorney called Morgan, who had come on the scene moments after the accident occurred. Morgan testified that Bob told him (Morgan) then that Tina had driven right past the stop sign.

If Tina's attorney objects to the introduction of Morgan's testimony, it is most likely that

A. The objection will be sustained because the testimony is excluded by the hearsay rule.

B. The objection will be sustained because the testimony is an improper means of rehabilitation.

C. The objection will be overruled because Morgan's testimony is admissible as rehabilitation evidence.

D. The objection will be overruled because Morgan's testimony is proper rehabilitation and substantively relevant to Jack's contention that Tina was negligent.

42. Paul, the plaintiff in a personal injury action, called Wes as a witness to testify that Dan's car, in which Paul had been riding, ran a red light. Wes, however, testified that Dan's car did not run the light. Paul then called another witness, Vic, to testify that Dan's car ran the light.

The trial judge should rule that Vic's testimony is

A. Admissible as impeachment because Paul was surprised by Wes's testimony.

B. Admissible as evidence of Paul's case-in-chief because Vic's testimony was relevant to material issues.

C. Inadmissible because Paul cannot impeach his own witness.

D. Inadmissible because Paul is bound by the testimony of his own witness.

43. Tom Talker testified for the plaintiff in a personal injury case. On cross-examination, the defendant's attorney asked Talker if he was drunk at the time he witnessed the accident that he had testified about in direct examination. Talker responded, "No, I have never in my life been drunk." The defendant's attorney then sought to prove by Friend's testimony that Talker was drunk on New Year's Eve two years ago. The trial judge should rule that Friend's testimony is

A. Admissible to impeach Talker by showing that he had an imperfect recollection of recent events.

B. Admissible to show that Talker is not a truthful individual.

C. Inadmissible because a witness cannot be impeached by proof of specific acts of misconduct.

D. Inadmissible because the question of whether Talker has ever been drunk is a collateral matter.

44. Observer testified for the plaintiff in a contract case. The defendant called Zemo as a witness and asked him if he knew Observer's reputation for veracity in the community where Observer resided. The trial judge should rule that this question is

  A. Objectionable because it is collateral to the issues on trial.

  B. Objectionable because character cannot be proven by reputation.

  C. Proper because Observer may be impeached.

  D. Proper because Zemo's personal knowledge of Observer can be inferred if Observer knows his reputation.

45. The bus in which Pat was riding was struck from the rear by a taxi. Pat sued Cab Company for a claimed neck injury. Cab Company claimed the impact was too slight to have caused the claimed injury and introduced testimony that all passengers had refused medical attention at the time of the accident. Pat called a doctor from City Hospital to testify that three persons (otherwise proved to have been on the bus) were admitted to the Hospital for treatment within a week after the accident complaining about severe neck pains. The trial judge should rule the doctor's testimony

  A. Admissible because a doctor is properly qualified as an expert in medical matters.

  B. Admissible if other testimony establishes a causal connection between the other passengers' pain and the accident.

  C. Inadmissible because the testimony as to the neck pain complained about by the other three passengers is hearsay, not within any exception.

  D. Inadmissible because the testimony cannot be introduced without also introducing the medical records that contain reports of the other passengers' pain.

46. Tim and Samantha were involved in a serious traffic accident. After settlement efforts failed, Tim sued Samantha for the injuries that he sustained as a result of the incident. During discovery, Beth testified at a deposition called by Tim's attorney. At the deposition, Beth stated that she saw the accident and that Samantha had failed to come to a complete halt at a red light.

At trial, when asked by Tim's attorney whether Samantha had completely halted at the red light, Beth answered, "Yes." Tim's attorney then attempted to introduce the portion of Beth's deposition that was inconsistent with her trial testimony. (Assume that it was authenticated.)

If Samantha's attorney objects to the introduction of the deposition testimony, it is most likely that

A. The objection will be overruled, and Beth's deposition testimony can be utilized by the fact finder as substantive evidence (as well as for impeachment).

B. The objection will be overruled because Beth's deposition testimony is admissible for impeachment (but not as substantive evidence).

C. The objection will be sustained, assuming Samantha's attorney was present and also had the opportunity to question Beth at the deposition.

D. The objection will be sustained because Beth's prior deposition is hearsay.

47. Gina sued Exico Company, a Delaware corporation that operates a toxic waste disposal plant. Gina claimed that fumes emitted from the plant had caused her to become sterile. At the trial, Exico's attorney called Dr. Evans, a medical expert, who testified that, in his opinion, Gina's sterility was an inherited condition. On cross-examination, Dr. Evans was shown a voluminous book written by Dr. Frank. Dr. Evans candidly acknowledged that Dr. Frank was considered an expert with respect to sterility by many in the medical field. Gina's attorney then attempted to read into the record a portion of Dr. Frank's book that indicated that, based on his extensive research, sterility occasionally resulted from emissions emanating from toxic waste disposal plants.

If Exico's attorney objects to the introduction of this evidence, it is most likely that

A. The objection will be overruled, if Dr. Frank's book is a learned treatise.

B. The objection will be overruled because authenticated writings can be read into evidence for impeachment purposes only.

C. The objection will be sustained because Dr. Frank's book constitutes hearsay.

D. The objection will be sustained, if Dr. Frank is available to testify.

48. Justin sued William for negligently causing a collision that occurred on a highway, in which Justin was injured and his car damaged. William had received several drunk-driving citations before this accident.

At the trial, Justin's attorney attempts to introduce a guilty plea for drunken driving entered against William pertaining to the incident in question as proof of William's unreasonable behavior. In this jurisdiction, driving under the influence is punishable by a maximum term of five years in prison and a $50,000 fine.

If William's attorney objects to the introduction of this evidence, it is most likely that

A. The objection will be overruled because there is an exception to the hearsay rule for prior, serious criminal convictions.

B. The objection will be overruled, if William's guilty plea was made under oath.

C. The objection will be sustained, if the guilty plea was properly authenticated.

D. The objection will be sustained because the guilty plea constitutes hearsay.

49. An armed robbery occurred at the Abco Bank. The crime was accomplished by three men. Later, Mel was arrested and successfully tried for conspiracy to commit, and committing, an armed robbery at the Abco Bank. Subsequently, Duane was apprehended and prosecuted for the same crimes. As part of its case-in-chief against Duane, the prosecution offered evidence of its successful prosecution of Mel for conspiring with Duane and Ralph to rob the Abco Bank. Duane chose to assert his Fifth Amendment right to refrain from testifying at his trial. (Armed robbery is punishable in this jurisdiction by imprisonment for up to ten years.)

If Duane's attorney objects to the introduction of this evidence, it is most likely that

A. The objection will be sustained because the judgment against Mel is irrelevant to Duane's culpability for the crime charged.

B. The objection will be sustained because the judgment against Mel is inadmissible hearsay.

C. The objection will be overruled because a prior criminal conviction constitutes an exception to the hearsay rule.

D. The objection will be overruled because prior criminal convictions are a proper basis for impeachment.

50. Alvin was stabbed by Mitch during a fight at a local bar. Perceiving that he had been mortally wounded, Alvin told Carl, another patron at the bar, "I owe Jim a thousand dollars." Alvin then died. Jim had previously sued Alvin to recover the $1,000. However, in his answer to that complaint, Alvin had contended that the $1,000 was actually a gift. This action was subsequently dismissed without prejudice before trial.

Jim has now filed another action, this time against Alvin's estate, for recovery of the $1,000. At trial, Jim's attorney called Carl to testify about Alvin's statement.

If the attorney for Alvin's executor objects to the introduction of this testimony, it is most likely that

A. The objection will be sustained because Carl's testimony constitutes hearsay.

B. The objection will be overruled because Alvin's remark constitutes a dying declaration.

C. The objection will be overruled because Alvin's remark constitutes a declaration against interest.

D. The objection will be overruled because Alvin's remark evidences his present state of mind.

51. Tim (who was insolvent) was driving his friend Todd's car when he struck Mary, a pedestrian who was lawfully using a crosswalk at an intersection when injured. Two days after the accident, Tim told his friend Jeff that he had imbibed eight shots of tequila prior to driving Todd's car. Tim recently relocated to India.

Mary sued Todd, but not Tim, pursuant to a statute that made the owner of a vehicle vicariously liable for the negligent driving of persons using it with his permission. Todd is an extremely wealthy individual. Assume that persons convicted of driving under the influence are subject to imprisonment for a maximum term of six months.

At the trial, Todd's attorney sought to have Jeff testify about Tim's statement to him.

If Todd's attorney objects to the introduction of this testimony, it is most likely that

A. The objection will be overruled because Tim's statement is admissible under the "statement against interest" exception to the hearsay rule.

B. The objection will be overruled because Tim's statement is an admission.

C. The objection will be sustained because there is no direct proof that Tim was intoxicated at the time of the incident.

D. The objection will be sustained because Jeff's testimony constitutes hearsay.

52. Daniel and his wife Margaret had been having marital problems for some time. One evening, while Daniel was supposedly working late, Margaret was stabbed to death. After an extensive investigation, the police arrested and charged Daniel with killing Margaret. At the trial, Daniel's counsel attempted to support a theory that Daniel's and Margaret's neighbor Kerry had a motive to murder Margaret. Counsel sought to have Ben, Daniel's neighbor, testify that his wife, Kerry, had told him (Ben) that she was in love with Daniel and had feelings of hatred toward Margaret. Although aware of the trial, Kerry had decided to remain at home.

    If the prosecution objects to Ben's testimony, it is most likely that

    A. The objection will be sustained because Kerry's statement to her husband was privileged.

    B. The objection will be sustained because the testimony contained hearsay within hearsay.

    C. The objection will be overruled because Kerry's confession to Ben constitutes an admission.

    D. The objection will be overruled because Ben's testimony is relevant and does not violate the hearsay rule.

53. Megan sued MedCo, which manufactures breast implants. She claims that she contracted an unusual disease from a breast implant produced by MedCo, which she received several years earlier. At the trial, MedCo attempted to introduce a transcript recording the testimony of Dr. Peters, a recognized expert, which was given in a previous lawsuit against MedCo by Jane. Jane is another MedCo breast implant recipient, who had contracted a disease similar to that of Megan. Dr. Peters, who has long since died, had testified at that trial (in which MedCo prevailed) that MedCo's breast implants did not cause the disease contracted by Jane.

    If Megan's attorney objects to the introduction of Dr. Peters's authenticated transcript, it is most likely that

    A. The objection will be sustained because Dr. Peters's transcript is hearsay.

    B. The objection will be overruled because Jane's counsel had opportunity and similar motive to cross-examine Dr. Peters.

    C. The objection will be overruled because Dr. Peters's transcript was properly authenticated.

    D. The objection will be overruled, if Dr. Peters was an expert with respect to matters about which he testified.

54. Jimmy was a passenger in a car being driven by Martin. The automobile was struck at an intersection by a vehicle driven by Trish. Jimmy sued Trish under a negligence theory. However, Trish answered that Martin had "run a red light." At the trial, Jimmy's attorney called Martin to the stand to testify that Trish went through a yellow light and "was clearly speeding" when the collision occurred.

If Trish's attorney objects to this testimony, it is most likely that

A. The objection will be overruled because Martin's opinion testimony is admissible (assuming he saw Trish coming toward their vehicle).

B. The objection will be overruled because testimony regarding Trish's conduct (though hearsay) constitutes an admission.

C. The objection will be sustained because layperson "opinion" testimony is inadmissible.

D. The objection will be sustained because there is no independent means (e.g., a radar gun) of verifying Martin's opinion.

55. Angie was injured in a car accident. While crossing a street, she was struck by a car driven by Bill. After the accident, Angie was examined by Dr. Martin. He ordered a lab technician to take X-rays. The lab technician who took the X-rays subsequently advised Dr. Martin that the X-rays "clearly demonstrated" that Angie's back injuries were permanent in nature. Angie sued Bill under a negligence theory to recover for her extensive, painful injuries. At the trial, Angie's attorney attempted to have Dr. Martin testify that, based on the evaluation of the X-rays as related to him by the lab technician, Angie's back injuries were permanent in nature. However, the X-rays had not been introduced into evidence.

If Bill's attorney objects to Dr. Martin's testimony, it is most likely that

A. The objection will be overruled because Dr. Martin may base his opinion on data perceived by him prior to or at the hearing.

B. The objection will be overruled, assuming Dr. Martin is also testifying from his personal knowledge (i.e., he had personally examined Angie).

C. The objection will be sustained because the X-rays had not been authenticated and admitted into evidence.

D. The objection will be sustained because Dr. Martin's testimony is based on hearsay.

56. Margaret was driving down Paramount Boulevard when her car was struck by a vehicle driven by Dennis. She sued Dennis under a negligence theory for the personal injuries that she sustained in the incident. William was a passenger in Dennis's vehicle at the time of the incident, but suffered no physical injuries.

At trial, William was called as a witness for Margaret. Surprisingly, he testified that Margaret "ran a red light." Margaret's attorney then called Jason to testify that William had, prior to the trial, told him (Jason) that "Dennis failed to see the red light."

If Dennis's attorney objects to Jason's testimony, it is most likely that

A. The objection will be sustained because Jason's testimony is hearsay.

B. The objection will be sustained because Margaret cannot impeach her own witness.

C. The objection will be overruled, if William was given the opportunity of explaining his statement to Jason and was available for redirect examination.

D. The objection will be overruled because Jason's testimony was a proper mode of impeachment (whether or not William was available for redirect examination).

57. Karen was injured when a car being driven by Stacey struck her car. Tom, an eyewitness to the accident, testified at trial that Stacey "ran a red light" and collided with Karen's car. After Tom concluded his testimony, Stacey's attorney called Bob to testify. Bob attempted to testify that he lived near Tom and that Tom had a reputation for having an "aggressive, impetuous nature."

If Karen's attorney objects to Bob's testimony, it is most likely that

A. The objection will be sustained because Bob's testimony is hearsay.

B. The objection will be sustained because Bob's testimony doesn't pertain to truthfulness or veracity.

C. The objection will be sustained because no foundation for Bob's testimony was laid (i.e., Bob did not state that he was personally familiar with Tom's character).

D. The objection will be overruled because Bob's testimony impairs Tom's credibility.

58. Potts sued Dobbs on a products liability claim. Louis testified for Potts. On cross-examination, which of the following questions is the trial judge most likely to rule improper?

  A. "Isn't it a fact that you are Potts's close friend?"

  B. "Isn't it true that you are known in the community as 'Louie the Lush' because of your addiction to alcohol?"

  C. "Didn't you deliberately fail to report some income on your tax return last year?"

  D. "Weren't you convicted seven years ago of obtaining money under false pretenses?"

59. In an action to recover for personal injuries arising out of an automobile accident, Plaintiff calls Bystander to testify. Claiming the privilege against self-incrimination, Bystander refuses to answer the question as to whether she was at the scene of the accident. Plaintiff moves that Bystander be ordered to answer the question. The judge should allow Bystander to remain silent only if

  A. The judge is convinced that she will incriminate herself.

  B. There is clear and convincing evidence that she will incriminate herself.

  C. There is a preponderance of evidence that she will incriminate herself.

  D. The judge believes that there is some reasonable possibility that she will incriminate herself.

60. In a products liability suit against a manufacturer of thermal underwear, Paul Phillips testified that he purchased a suit of thermal underwear manufactured by the defendant. While he was attempting to stamp out a fire, the underwear caught fire and burned Phillips. He suffered a heart attack a half-hour later. Dr. Jones, a physician specializing in cardiovascular difficulties, having listened to Phillips's testimony, was called by Phillips and asked whether, assuming the truth of such testimony, Phillips's subsequent heart attack could have resulted from the burns. His opinion is

  A. Admissible because he is an expert.

  B. Admissible because the physician's expertise enables him to judge the credibility of Phillips's testimony.

  C. Inadmissible because a hypothetical question may not be based on prior testimony.

  D. Inadmissible because an expert's opinion may not be based solely on information provided by laypersons.

61. Dr. Black, a physician specializing in internal medicine, was called by the plaintiff in a personal injury case. She testified that, on the basis of her examination of the plaintiff and blood analysis reports by an independent laboratory, reports that were not introduced in evidence, she believes that the plaintiff has a permanent disability. This testimony is

   A. Admissible because such laboratory reports are business records.

   B. Admissible if such reports are reasonably relied on in medical practice.

   C. Inadmissible unless Dr. Black has been shown to be qualified to conduct laboratory blood analyses.

   D. Inadmissible because Dr. Black's testimony cannot be based on tests performed by persons not under her supervision.

62. Penny sued Dion for personal injuries that she sustained when a car being driven by Dion struck her vehicle. At trial, on behalf of Penny, Walter testified that Dion "ran a red light." On cross-examination, Walter was asked, "Why were you standing on Second and Maple?" (the viewpoint from which Walter purportedly observed the incident). Walter responded that he had gone "to the corner store to buy a paper." Dion's attorney then called Shirley, Walter's friend, to testify that Walter was at the corner waiting to meet her for lunch.

   If Penny's attorney objects to Shirley's testimony, it is most likely that

   A. The objection will be overruled because Shirley's testimony impeaches Walter's veracity.

   B. The objection will be overruled because Shirley's testimony undermines Walter's memory.

   C. The objection will be sustained because Shirley's testimony is irrelevant to the issue of fault.

   D. The objection will be sustained because Shirley's testimony pertains to a collateral matter.

63. Daniel was an attorney who primarily practiced estate planning law. Peggy, another attorney, sued Daniel for breaching an oral agreement to sell his legal practice to her for $300,000. At trial, on behalf of Peggy, her secretary, Desmond, testified that he overheard Daniel personally offer to sell his practice to Peggy for $300,000. On cross-examination, Daniel's attorney asked Desmond, "Isn't it true that you work for Peggy, and that ever since your son lost a lawsuit you've hated attorneys?"

   If Peggy's attorney objects to this questioning, it is most likely that

A. The objection will be sustained because Daniel's attorney asked Desmond a leading question.

B. The objection will be sustained because the question's potential for prejudicing the jury outweighs its probative value.

C. The objection will be overruled because personal partiality/bias constitutes a proper basis for impeachment.

D. The objection will be overruled because Desmond's state of mind constitutes a proper basis for impeachment.

64. Doris sued Brad for breach of an oral contract. At the trial, Clara testified on behalf of Doris. She confirmed that a contract had, in fact, been made. On cross-examination by Brad's attorney, Clara was asked, "Weren't you caught cheating at a poker game last Saturday night?" Clara responded to this question with an unequivocal "No." Brad's attorney then called Dahlia, who was playing poker with Clara at that time. Dahlia was asked if Clara was caught cheating at poker that Saturday night. (You may assume that it's a misdemeanor to gamble in this jurisdiction.) Dahlia was prepared to testify that Clara had been caught dealing herself an ace from the bottom of the deck.

If Doris's attorney objects to this testimony, it is most likely that

A. The objection will be sustained because the misdemeanor in question clearly pertains to veracity.

B. The objection will be sustained because impeachment via extrinsic evidence is not permissible in this instance.

C. The objection will be overruled because it pertains to Clara's veracity.

D. The objection will be overruled because it pertains to whether Clara is law-abiding.

65. Larry sued Olivia for the serious injuries that he sustained when a car driven by Olivia collided with him while he was driving home from work. Winifred testified in Olivia's defense that Larry had "run a red light." For the purpose of impeaching Winifred, Larry's attorney called Jeanine to the stand. Jeanine testified that Winifred had "a very poor reputation for truthfulness in the community" and that, in her opinion, "Winifred was not trustworthy." Olivia's attorney then asked Jeanine, "Are you aware that Winifred recently brought a lost wallet containing $27 in cash to the police?"

If Larry's attorney objects to this question, it is most likely that

A. The objection will be overruled because Jeanine may be cross-examined about specific instances of Winifred's conduct pertaining to truthfulness or untruthfulness.

B. The objection will be overruled because Jeanine may be cross-examined about the extent of her knowledge about Winifred's reputation for honesty in the community.

C. The objection will be sustained because it pertains to a collateral matter.

D. The objection will be sustained because only the jury can determine whether to believe Jeanine.

66. Peter sued Don for breach of contract. The court admitted testimony by Peter that Don and his wife quarreled frequently, a fact of no consequence to the lawsuit. Don seeks to testify in response that he and his wife never quarreled. The court

A. Must permit Don to answer, if he had objected to Peter's testimony.

B. May permit Don to answer, whether or not he had objected to Peter's testimony.

C. May permit Don to answer, only if he had objected to Peter's testimony.

D. Cannot permit Don to answer, whether or not he had objected to Peter's testimony.

67. In a will case, Paula seeks to prove her relationship to the testator Terrence by a statement in a deed from Terrence, "I transfer to my niece Paula . . . " The deed was recorded pursuant to statute in the office of the county recorder and was retained there. Paula called Recorder as a witness, who authenticated a copy of the deed. The copy was made from microfilm records kept in the recorder's office pursuant to statute. The copy is

A. Admissible as a record of a document affecting an interest in property.

B. Admissible as recorded recollection.

C. Inadmissible as hearsay, not within any recognized exception.

D. Inadmissible under the Original Writing Rule.

Questions 68-73 are based on the following fact situation:

Driver ran into and injured Walker, a pedestrian. With Driver in his car were two of his friends, Paul and Ralph. Passerby saw the accident and called the police department, which sent Sheriff to investigate.

All of these people are available as potential witnesses in the case of *Walker v. Driver*. Walker alleges that Driver, while drunk, struck him as he walked in a duly marked crosswalk and that he (Walker), as a consequence, suffered physical harm to his leg and foot.

68. Counsel for Walker calls Paul to testify that just before the accident, Ralph exclaimed, "Watch out! We're going to hit that man in the cross-walk!" The trial judge should rule that this testimony is

   A. Admissible as a spontaneous utterance reflecting Ralph's impression at the time his statement was made.

   B. Admissible because it constitutes a declaration against interest as to the declarant, Ralph.

   C. Inadmissible because Ralph is available as a witness.

   D. Inadmissible because the statement preceded the accident.

69. Walker's counsel calls Sheriff to testify that, in Driver's presence, Paul said, "We hit him while he was in the crosswalk," and that Driver remained silent. The trial judge should rule this testimony

   A. Admissible because Driver, by his silence, has made Paul his agent and would thereby be bound by any admission Paul made.

   B. Admissible because Driver's silence constitutes an admission of a party-opponent.

   C. Inadmissible as "double hearsay" in that Driver's silence is being used to prove the truth of what Sheriff said Paul had stated.

   D. Inadmissible unless Driver is first called and asked to admit or deny the incident.

70. Walker's counsel seeks to introduce the testimony of Joe concerning Walker's statement three days after the accident that, "My ankle hurts so much, I'd bet almost anything that it's broken." The trial judge should rule that this testimony is

   A. Admissible as a statement of the declarant's pain and suffering.

   B. Admissible to prove that Walker's ankle was permanently injured.

   C. Inadmissible as a hearsay declaration.

   D. Inadmissible because proof of Walker's medical condition is a subject for expert testimony only.

71. Driver's counsel wants to introduce testimony from Sheriff concerning a discussion between Sheriff and Passerby at the police station two hours after the accident, wherein Passerby, in response to a question by Sheriff, excitedly exclaimed in a loud voice, "Walker ran out in the street and was not in the crosswalk!" Sheriff duly recorded Passerby's statement in an official police report. The trial judge should rule that Sheriff's oral testimony is

A. Admissible as an excited utterance.

B. Admissible as based on past recollection recorded.

C. Inadmissible because of the Original Writing Rule.

D. Inadmissible as hearsay.

72. Walker's counsel wants to have Sheriff testify to the following statement made to him by Ralph, out of the presence of Driver: "We were returning from a party at which we had each downed at least four beers." The trial judge should rule this testimony

A. Admissible as an admission of a party.

B. Admissible as a declaration against interest.

C. Inadmissible as hearsay, not within any exception.

D. Inadmissible as opinion.

73. On the evening of the day of the accident, Ralph wrote a letter to his sister in which he described the accident. After Ralph testified that he could not remember some details of the accident, Walker's counsel seeks to show him the letter to assist Ralph in his testimony on direct examination. The trial judge should rule that this is

A. Permissible under the doctrine of present recollection refreshed.

B. Permissible under the doctrine of past recollection recorded.

C. Objectionable, if Driver's counsel was not shown the letter prior to the time it was shown to Ralph.

D. Objectionable, unless the letter is read into evidence.

74. Owner, the sole owner of Oscar's Restaurants, hired Bellman to manage the restaurants. Bellman did so for the next five years, sending regular reports to Owner's headquarters and receiving irregular phone calls and written messages from Owner in reply. A week ago, Waiter arrived unannounced at Bellman's office, carrying a document that stated that Owner's restaurants and his agreement with Bellman had been transferred to him (Waiter). Waiter notified Bellman that, effective immediately, he was fired and that Waiter was taking over the management of the restaurants. Bellman claimed that Waiter could not fire him and that Owner's signature on the purported document was a forgery. He then brought an action to prevent Waiter from taking control of the restaurants. Bellman was called to testify that he and Owner had signed a contract when he was hired, wherein they had agreed that (1) Bellman would manage the restaurants for a ten-year period, and (2) he could be terminated only for unsatisfactory performance during that period. Which of the following objections by Waiter to Bellman's testimony is most likely to be sustained?

A. That the testimony violates the Statute of Frauds.

B. That the testimony violates the Original Writing Rule.

C. That the testimony violates the parol evidence rule.

D. That the testimony is irrelevant.

75. In a contract case, the plaintiff offered a purportedly signed original of the contract, bearing the defendant's signature. The trial judge can admit it

A. Subject to introduction of evidence that would support a finding of the genuineness of the signature.

B. Only if, in the trial judge's opinion, the contested signature bears a reasonable resemblance to that of the defendant.

C. Only if the trial judge finds that the genuineness of the defendant's signature is established as a matter of law.

D. Only if the plaintiff persuades the court that it is more likely than not that the signature is genuine.

76. Lyons is on trial for the murder of his wife. Lawyer, an attorney, is called by the prosecution to testify that the accused attempted to retain him as his defense counsel and, during their preliminary discussions, admitted having killed his wife. Lawyer eventually declined to represent Lyons. The trial judge should rule Lawyer's testimony

A. Admissible because Lawyer declined to represent Lyons.

B. Admissible because Lyons had advised Lawyer of a crime.

C. Inadmissible because the communication was privileged.

D. Inadmissible because Lawyer's testimony contains hearsay.

77. In a personal injury case, the plaintiff testified on his own behalf concerning his injury. On cross-examination, he was asked, "Isn't it true that you were convicted of perjury five years ago?" The plaintiff denied having ever been convicted of perjury. The defense then offered into

evidence a properly authenticated copy of the official court record of conviction. The trial judge should rule the record

A. Admissible because counsel may prove the conviction by extrinsic evidence.

B. Admissible because the perjury conviction helps to prove the defendant was free from negligence.

C. Inadmissible because the Original Writing Rule requires that the original court record of Lyons's conviction be produced.

D. Inadmissible because specific instances of misconduct of a witness may not be proved by the use of extrinsic evidence.

Questions 78-79 are based on the following fact situation:

ABC agreed to do the inspection and testing needed during construction by XYZ of a complex conveyer belt for an industrial plant. XYZ estimated completion in four months.

During negotiations, the parties had agreed that if overtime became necessary, it should be paid on a time-and-a-half basis. Their written contract, however, merely called for (1) ABC to expend 150 hours per month, and (2) XYZ to pay ABC $8,000 in four monthly installments of $2,000 each.

After three months, and after XYZ had paid ABC $6,000 in monthly installments, it became obvious that the conveyer would not be completed on time by XYZ. ABC requested, and XYZ orally agreed to pay ABC, $2,000 per month until the job was finished.

ABC submitted invoices on this basis for the fourth through the sixth months, when the job was finished. XYZ, having previously not paid the invoices contending it was short of cash, then paid ABC $2,000, but repudiated the oral agreement relying on the parol evidence rule. ABC sued XYZ for $4,000.

78. Will XYZ's parol evidence defense probably succeed?

A. Yes, because the oral agreement purports to vary the written contract on a subject included in it.

B. Yes, because the oral agreement purports to add to the written contract.

C. No, because the oral agreement in question was entered into after the written contract.

D. No, because the second agreement relates to a subject that was not dealt with in the original agreement.

79. If ABC offered to introduce evidence that, during negotiations prior to the written contract, XYZ had orally agreed that overtime should

be paid on a time-and-a-half basis, which of the following rules would provide the *most* support for ABC?

A. Parol evidence of collateral agreements is admissible where the writing was only a partial integration.

B. Parol evidence of negotiations is admissible in aid of interpretation.

C. Parol evidence is admissible to show an oral condition precedent to the existence of a contract.

D. Parol evidence is admissible to show fraud.

80. Alfred was charged with mail fraud. At trial, the defense called Joanna, who testified that she had known Alfred for 16 years and that he was an honorable, honest human being. On cross-examination, the prosecuting attorney asked Joanna if she had not been caught cheating while playing cards three weeks before. Joanna replied that she had not. The prosecuting attorney then offered to have Bill testify that he, Joanna, and four other persons were playing cards three weeks ago, and that Joanna was caught dealing an ace to herself from the bottom of the deck. Bill's testimony is

A. Admissible because it tends to discredit Joanna.

B. Admissible because Joanna had testified as to Alfred's character for honesty.

C. Inadmissible because Joanna has not been the subject of a criminal conviction as a consequence of the card-cheating incident.

D. Inadmissible if gambling is a federal crime.

81. John was charged with aggravated battery. At trial, the prosecution called Melvin to the stand to testify that he was present at a lineup and saw Jones point to John and state, "That's the guy who hit me." Jones passed away between his identification of John and the latter's trial. Melvin's testimony is

A. Inadmissible because Jones is not available to testify at the trial.

B. Inadmissible because Jones's identification of John constituted an opinion.

C. Admissible because Jones is unavailable.

D. Admissible because it is probative of John's motive for striking Jones.

82. Under the Mann Act, it is illegal to transport persons across state lines for the purpose of engaging in prostitution. Jack was prosecuted under

this statute for taking Sue from Boston to New York to work there as a prostitute. As part of its case-in-chief, the prosecution called Sue. However, she unexpectedly testified that (1) Jack hadn't driven her to New York, and (2) she had visited that city to shop for dresses. The prosecutor then offered into evidence a properly authenticated written statement made by Sue and delivered to the prosecution, wherein she had stated that Jack had driven her to New York City for the purpose of engaging in acts of prostitution in that city. The written statement is

A. Admissible for any purpose because it is hearsay.

B. Admissible as substantive evidence, but not for impeachment.

C. Admissible for impeachment, but not as substantive evidence.

D. Admissible for impeachment and as substantive evidence.

83. Josephina was arrested for driving under the influence of alcohol. At her trial, the prosecution seeks to introduce the written report of Officer Bones, one of the arresting officers. Officer Bones's report, made at the scene immediately after Josephina was handcuffed and placed in the back of the patrol car, stated that the defendant's speech was slurred at the time of the arrest. Officer Bones was not present at the trial because he had recently been in an accident. However, Officer Smith (Bones's partner for eight years) testified that the signature on the report was that of Bones. The report is

A. Inadmissible because it contains Bones's opinion as to an ultimate issue.

B. Inadmissible because it is hearsay.

C. Admissible because it has been properly authenticated.

D. Admissible because Officer Bones was unavailable.

84. In a personal injury suit by a pedestrian against a driver, Warren was called by the plaintiff to testify that the defendant had pleaded with him to testify falsely that the plaintiff had run in front of his car. The trial judge should rule that Warren's testimony is

A. Admissible because the defendant's offer to Warren was a statement against interest.

B. Admissible because Warren was called to testify by the pedestrian.

C. Inadmissible because it was hearsay, not within any exception.

D. Inadmissible because it was not relevant to the issue of whether the driver was, in fact, negligent.

85. Driver allegedly drove his car into the front of a store and injured Shopper, who was in the store. In a suit by Shopper against Driver, Driver called Samuel to testify. After Samuel stated that he and Driver had lived in the same community for 12 years, he testified that Driver enjoyed a reputation for being a safe and prudent driver. The trial judge should rule that Samuel's testimony is

A. Admissible because character evidence is admissible to prove the Driver acted in conformity with that character at the time in question.

B. Admissible if Samuel first testifies that he has personal knowledge of Driver's driving habits.

C. Inadmissible because evidence of Driver's reputation as a safe and prudent driver cannot be used to prove that he drove reasonably on the occasion in question.

D. Inadmissible because there are no civil actions in which character evidence is admissible.

86. On March 1, Computer Programs (CP) orally agreed with Holiday Department Store (HDS) to write a set of programs for HDS's computer and to coordinate the programs with HDS's billing methods. A subsequent memo, signed by both parties, provided in its entirety: "HDS will pay CP $20,000 in two equal installments within one month of completion if, by July 1, CP is successful in shortening by one-half the processing time for the financial transactions now handled on HDS's Zenon 747 computer." Tests by CP cut processing time by 51 percent, but were not coordinated with HDS's Zenon 747 computer. However, if HDS were to spend $5,000 to change its invoice preparation methods, as recommended by CP, the programs would cut processing time by a total of 58 percent, saving HDS $8,000 a year.

If HDS denies liability on the ground that CP had orally agreed to coordinate with HDS's methods of accounting, and CP seeks in litigation to bar testimony about that agreement because of the parol evidence rule, HDS's most effective argument is that

A. The parol evidence rule does not bar the introduction of evidence for the purpose of interpreting a written agreement.

B. The memorandum was not a completely integrated agreement.

C. HDS detrimentally relied on the oral promise of coordination in signing the memorandum.

D. The memorandum was not a partially integrated agreement.

87. Peter sued Dever, who was 19, for negligence after Peter was hit by a car driven by Dever while Peter was crossing a street. Peter asserted that Dever was exceeding the speed limit as he turned a corner. Dever answered that he was not speeding and, alternatively, that Peter was also negligent. Peter called James to the stand to testify that Dever always came around that corner at an excessive rate of speed. James's testimony is probably

   A. Admissible, to show that Peter was probably speeding on the occasion in question.

   B. Admissible, even though hearsay, because it would constitute an admission of the party-opponent.

   C. Inadmissible because it is hearsay and opinion.

   D. Inadmissible because it is character evidence.

88. Jerry sued Delbert for negligence, claiming that Delbert drove through a red light and hit Jerry's car in an intersection. Delbert counter-claimed, contending that Jerry entered the intersection while the light against him was yellow. After Jerry gave his version of the events of the accident, Malcolm, an eyewitness, was called to the stand and testified that Jerry's description of the accident was correct. Delbert's counsel then sought to introduce a properly authenticated report made by an investigator for Delbert's insurance company, who had died prior to the trial. In the report, the investigator claimed that Malcolm had advised him that the light was green for Delbert when he drove into the intersection. The report is

   A. Admissible for purposes of impeachment only.

   B. Admissible for purposes of impeachment and as substantive evidence.

   C. Inadmissible because it is hearsay.

   D. Inadmissible because Malcolm was never asked about the report prior to Delbert's attempt to introduce it into evidence.

89. Jack Jones was tried for the murder of Arthur Goodman. Walter testified on behalf of the defendant that he and Jones were playing cards during the evening on which the homicide occurred. On cross-examination of Walter, the prosecuting attorney asked if Jones had not threatened to kill him (Walter) about one week before the trial. Walter replied that Jones had not. The defense then sought to have Officer Oates testify that shortly after the crime he had interviewed Walter and that the latter had stated that he was playing cards with Jones on

the evening in question. Walter's statement had not been recorded, nor was it made under penalty of perjury. Officer Oates's testimony is

A. Admissible as substantive evidence.

B. Admissible under the business records exception to the hearsay rule.

C. Inadmissible because it was hearsay, not within any exception.

D. Inadmissible because proof of prior consistent statements by a witness is ordinarily not a permissible form of rehabilitation.

90. Jim Decker recently died. A will written by Decker was admitted to probate. However, a dispute has arisen between Decker's two sons, Oscar and Otto. A line was drawn through a provision of the will giving Decker's sports car to Otto. If this action was done by Decker with the intent of revoking the gift to Otto, the car would fall into the residuary clause (and thereby be inherited by Oscar). Otto claims that Oscar, who found the will, drew the line through the clause in question. Oscar seeks to introduce into evidence a statement by Ray, one of Decker's golfing partners, that Decker had told Ray about one year before he died that "I recently changed my will to leave the sports car to Oscar." Decker's statement is

A. Admissible because it pertains to the partial revocation of the declarant's will.

B. Admissible because it pertains to the declarant's then existing state of mind.

C. Inadmissible because it is hearsay, not within any exception.

D. Inadmissible because it violates a typical "Dead Man" statute.

91. Albert and Susan were involved in a traffic accident. Susan was taken to a hospital. The next day, a janitor at the hospital asked Susan, "What happened?" Susan, who sincerely believed that she was going to die, said quietly, "I'm very angry with myself; I was trying to put out my cigarette and lost control of the wheel for a second." Susan survived the accident and has now regained her health. When Albert sued Susan to recover for his personal injuries, Susan counterclaimed for her injuries and damages to her car. Albert sought to introduce testimony from the janitor recounting Susan's statement. The testimony is

A. Inadmissible because of the physician-patient privilege.

B. Inadmissible because it is hearsay.

C. Admissible under the dying declaration exception to the hearsay rule.

D. Admissible to prove the truth of what Susan's statement asserted.

92. Alex was involved in a motor vehicle accident with Milton. When a police officer arrived, he detected the smell of whiskey on Milton's breath. Milton was subsequently prosecuted for drunken driving. At the trial, Milton took the stand in his defense and asserted his innocence. When asked on cross-examination how many drinks he had ingested before the accident, he stated "three beers." Milton was subsequently acquitted of the drunk driving charge. In a civil lawsuit by Alex against Jones (the owner of the car that Milton was driving) for negligent entrustment, Alex sought to introduce into evidence a properly authenticated copy of the transcript of the criminal case that contained the foregoing question and answer. Milton had left the jurisdiction prior to the trial, and Alex has been unable to procure his attendance by process or otherwise. The evidence is

    A. Admissible under the former testimony exception to the hearsay rule.

    B. Admissible under the party-opponent exception to the hearsay rule.

    C. Inadmissible because it is hearsay, not within any exception.

    D. Inadmissible because Milton was acquitted in the criminal case.

93. Mitchell and Karl had been drinking and playing pool at a local restaurant-bar. Mitchell suddenly accused Karl of cheating by changing the position of one of the balls when Mitchell's back was turned. Karl stood his ground and asserted that Mitchell was an inferior player and a very poor sport. Mitchell abruptly reached toward his pocket. He wanted to withdraw a dollar to pay for the game, and then leave. However, before Mitchell could remove the money from his pocket, Karl swung his pool stick and struck Mitchell across the head (injuring him severely). Karl was charged with the crime of aggravated battery. Karl asserted the privilege of self-defense. In his defense, Karl sought to testify that his girlfriend, Sally, had told him that Mitchell usually carried a switchblade knife. In fact, this was incorrect and it is illegal to carry such an item in this jurisdiction. Sally died in an automobile accident about one week before the trial. Karl's testimony is

    A. Admissible, to show his belief that Mitchell was often armed with a knife.

    B. Admissible because a defendant in a criminal case is always entitled to introduce evidence of the victim's character by specific instances of misconduct.

    C. Inadmissible because it is hearsay, not within any exception.

    D. Inadmissible because character evidence pertaining to the victim is not admissible in a criminal case that does not involve homicide.

94. John owned Blackacre. One year ago, he handed a properly completed deed to the property to Milt, saying at the time, "When I die, this land is yours." (The deed made no mention of any requirement that Milt predecease John.) Six months later, however, John purported to transfer Blackacre via a deed to his niece, Nellie. John has recently been declared to be incompetent and both Milt and Nellie claim ownership to Blackacre. A conveyance of land does not occur in this jurisdiction unless the grantor has completed a valid deed with the intent that the transfer be immediately operative. Although Milt claims that John said nothing when the deed was tendered to him, Arthur was present at that time. Nellie seeks to have Arthur testify as to John's words to show that John did not intend that the conveyance be immediately operative when the deed was manually given to Milt. The evidence is

   A. Admissible because it is relevant and is not hearsay.

   B. Admissible because it is admissible under the "statement against interest" exception to the hearsay rule.

   C. Inadmissible under the parol evidence rule.

   D. Inadmissible because it is hearsay, not within any exception.

95. Albert and Banes were involved in a traffic accident. Garland witnessed the accident and told Officer Kane (who arrived shortly after the incident occurred) what he had seen. Kane wrote this information into an Accident Report, which he was required to write by law. Garland testified at the trial for Albert. On cross-examination, counsel for Banes asked Garland if he had looked at the Accident Report prior to the trial for the purpose of refreshing his memory. Garland admitted that he had. As a consequence,

   A. The entire report may be introduced on redirect for the purpose of rehabilitating Garland.

   B. Counsel for Banes may introduce into evidence the portion of the Accident Report dealing with Garland's testimony.

   C. Counsel for Banes may inspect the report and cross-examine Garland with respect to it, but cannot introduce any portion of it into evidence.

   D. Counsel for Banes is not permitted to introduce any portion of the Accident Report, if Garland's testimony was consistent with it.

96. Dr. Fine is suing the estate of Mr. Boone (who recently died), based on an alleged oral contract pursuant to which Dr. Fine performed an operation on the deceased. Mrs. Boone, the wife and executrix of Mr.

Boone's estate, seeks to testify that her husband had told her that Dr. Fine had offered to perform the operation gratuitously if Mr. Boone (a prominent person within the town) would permit use of his name in an advertising campaign that Dr. Fine planned to undertake, and that he (Mr. Boone) had accepted this offer. There is no "Dead Man" statute in this jurisdiction. If Dr. Fine objects to Mrs. Boone's testimony, it should be

A. Admissible because it is relevant.

B. Admissible under the "statement against interest" exception to the hearsay rule.

C. Inadmissible because it is hearsay.

D. Inadmissible under the confidential marital communications privilege.

97. Mr. and Mrs. Ballow are in litigation for the custody of their five-year-old child, Arturo. Seven years ago, Mr. Ballow was convicted of child abuse with respect to a young boy named Damien. Although an authenticated copy of this conviction could easily be obtained, Mrs. Ballow seeks to have Damien personally testify as to the beatings inflicted on him by Mr. Ballow. This evidence is

A. Inadmissible because character evidence is admissible only in criminal proceedings.

B. Inadmissible because character evidence (even though admissible) can be proved only by reputation in the community or opinion.

C. Admissible because evidence of prior acts bearing on whether Mr. Ballow should be given custody of Arturo is proper.

D. Inadmissible because under the Original Writing Rule the earlier conviction is the proper means of proving Mr. Ballow had struck Damien.

98. Paul was hurt when he was bitten by a large, unleashed, unusual-looking dog. Delmer, a person who lives about one mile from Paul, has an Australian Blue Hound. Paul sued Delmer for his injuries, and Delmer denied that his dog was involved in the attack. Wally is a neighbor of Paul's who had seen the incident from a distance of about 100 feet. He was called as a witness by Paul and testified that Paul had been attacked by an Australian Blue Hound. He was asked on cross-examination how he knew the exact type of dog that had attacked Paul. Wally replied that after the incident he had looked at a chart of various breeds of dogs in a library, and the one that looked most like the animal that attacked Paul

was labeled "Australian Blue Hound." On a motion to strike Wally's testimony, the best objection would probably be

A. Lack of personal knowledge by Wally.

B. Lack of adequate perception.

C. Improper opinion.

D. Bias in favor of Paul.

99. At a criminal trial, the prosecution seeks to introduce a videotape that depicts the defendant giving packages to people and telling them that the packages contain illegal drugs.

It is most likely that the videotape is

A. Admissible to show only the defendant's conduct but not as proof that the packages contained drugs.

B. Admissible to show the defendant's conduct and also as proof that the packages contained drugs.

C. Inadmissible hearsay unless it can be shown that it was made in the course of regular conduct of a business or a public agency, such as a surveillance tape from a security system.

D. Inadmissible under the Confrontation Clause if the tape was made by police or any other governmental actors.

100. Jeffers, a police officer, shot and killed Roland in the line of duty. Jeffers was so traumatized by the incident that he retired from the police force and underwent counseling with Karen, a licensed clinical social worker. In all, Jeffers attended approximately 50 counseling sessions.

The administrator of Roland's estate filed suit in federal district court alleging that Jeffers had violated Roland's constitutional rights by using excessive force during the encounter. During pretrial discovery, the administrator of the estate learned of the counseling sessions and sought access to Karen's notes concerning the sessions for use in cross-examining Jeffers. On objection by Jeffers, the court should rule that Karen's notes are

A. Inadmissible because the need for the disclosure is outweighed by the patient's privacy interests.

B. Inadmissible because the psychotherapist-patient privilege applies to confidential communications made to a licensed social worker.

C. Admissible because the communications were made solely to permit Karen to serve as an expert witness in the litigation.

D. Admissible as a present sense impression.

101. Darby is on trial for raping Wanda. The prosecution seeks to introduce testimony by Maria that 15 years ago, Darby raped her, an act for which he was never charged. Maria would testify that the rape took place when Darby, a stranger to her, attacked her in a parking lot. The rape of Wanda is alleged to have occurred following a date between the two. There are no meaningful similarities between the two crimes other than the fact that Darby was the alleged rapist. The prosecution's theory in seeking introduction of the Maria rape is that because Darby raped before, he's likely to have raped on the present occasion. Darby has not taken the stand as a witness. Maria's testimony is

A. Inadmissible because it seeks to put into evidence an unrelated offense.

B. Inadmissible because evidence of other crimes is not admissible to show that Darby acted in conformity with his character on this occasion.

C. Admissible and may be considered for its bearing on any matter to which it is relevant.

D. Admissible because character is in issue.

102. Duane is charged with molesting Victor, a ten-year-old boy. The prosecution seeks to present evidence that, 15 years ago, Duane molested Kara, a six-year-old girl, and was arrested for it but never charged. If counsel for Duane objects to the introduction of this evidence, it is most likely that the objection will be

A. Sustained because Duane was never convicted of a crime.

B. Sustained because this incident took place 15 years ago.

C. Overruled because Duane's character is an essential element of a claim or defense.

D. Overruled because in this case, evidence of prior child molestation is admissible.

103. Derek is on trial for burglary in a federal district court. While investigating the crime scene, detectives discovered a piece of cheese left at the scene with teeth marks in it. The prosecution claims that the teeth marks were made by Derek and seeks to offer testimony by Dr. Jacobs, a dentist who is an expert on dental identification. The prosecution would have Dr. Jacobs testify that there have been tests of the accuracy of such identifications, that the technique has been written up in peer-reviewed forensic journals, that it has a very low false positive rate, and that it is generally accepted by criminalists as a method of identification. Dr. Jacobs's testimony is

A. Admissible because there has been an adequate showing that bite-mark identification is scientifically valid.

B. Admissible because there has been an adequate showing that bite-mark identification is generally accepted in the field.

C. Inadmissible because the evidence is not relevant to an issue in the case.

D. Inadmissible because Dr. Jacobs is not qualified to be treated as an expert.

104. Helper pleads guilty to conspiring to sell stolen goods, pursuant to a plea agreement in which he agrees to testify for the government in exchange for the government's dropping all substantive counts against him. At the proceeding in which his plea is accepted, Helper admits in open court that he agreed with Boss to sell stolen computers. Helper dies one week later. At a subsequent trial of Boss for the same computer sales, the prosecution seeks to introduce evidence of what Helper said when he made his plea of guilty.

It is most likely that this evidence is

A. Inadmissible.

B. Admissible as a statement against penal interest.

C. Admissible as a prior statement made under oath at a proceeding.

D. Admissible it as a co-conspirator's statement.

105. During questioning by police, Daryl Defendant admitted committing a crime and described how he did it. He signed a written confession containing information about the crime. At his trial for that offense, a police officer who was present during the questioning seeks to testify about what Defendant said.

It is most likely that this testimony is

A. Admissible because it is relevant.

B. Admissible only if the prosecution also introduces the signed confession, a copy of it, or a reasonable explanation for its absence.

C. Inadmissible because the signed confession is the best evidence of its contents.

D. Inadmissible because the Confrontation Clause protects defendants from admission of out-of-court statements made in police interrogations.

106. In a civil suit governed by federal law, Plaintiff seeks to show that Defendant received a letter mailed by Plaintiff. Plaintiff introduces evidence sufficient to support a finding that Plaintiff addressed the letter to Defendant and mailed it properly. Defendant introduces no evidence about the letter.

The presumption that a properly mailed letter was received by the person to whom it was sent requires a finding that Defendant received the letter

A. Because the persuasion burden has been shifted to Defendant.

B. Because the production burden has been shifted to Defendant.

C. If the jury believes that a properly mailed letter will more likely than not be delivered to the person to whom it is addressed.

D. If the jury believes that Plaintiff addressed the letter to Defendant and mailed it properly.

107. John Johnson testifies for the prosecution at the criminal trial of Defendant. On cross-examination, Defendant's lawyer seeks to ask Johnson whether he is awaiting trial on a criminal misdemeanor charge.

The question is most likely

A. Permissible only if the misdemeanor charge involves dishonesty or false statement.

B. Permissible because it relates to bias.

C. Prohibited because it calls for irrelevant information.

D. Prohibited because it does not relate to a felony.

108. Willy Walker was run over by a truck driven by Dan Driver for his employer, TruckCo, a shipping company. Walker sought damages from TruckCo. At the trial, Driver testified that he drove carefully. To show that Driver had driven carelessly, Walker seeks to introduce evidence that one month after the accident, after having been fired by TruckCo, Driver told a friend that he had been asleep at the wheel when the accident occurred.

It is most likely that this evidence is

A. Not hearsay.

B. Admissible because it is an admission.

C. Admissible because it is covered by an exception to the hearsay exclusionary rule.

D. Inadmissible because of the hearsay exclusionary rule.

109. To prove that a bank employee was not frightened during a robbery attempt, the bank seeks to introduce testimony that during the robbery, a guard told the employee that the robber was not armed.

With regard to hearsay, this testimony is

A. Not hearsay.

B. Admissible because it is an admission.

C. Admissible because it is covered by an exception to the hearsay exclusionary rule.

D. Inadmissible because of the hearsay exclusionary rule.

110. Defendant is charged with a midnight robbery of a gas station. Shortly before the robbery occurred, a worker at the gas station told the station's manager that he had seen the defendant that morning, acting as if he was checking to see how the station's video surveillance cameras were operating. The manager seeks to testify about the worker's observations.

With regard to hearsay, this testimony is

A. Not hearsay.

B. Admissible because it is an admission.

C. Admissible because it is covered by an exception to the hearsay exclusionary rule.

D. Inadmissible because of the hearsay exclusionary rule.

111. In a contracts case, the plaintiff and a defendant owning an office-equipment leasing company agree that copying machines leased to the plaintiff by the defendant broke down more often than is usual. The parties dispute whether these breakdowns were caused by flaws in the machines or by careless use of the machines. The plaintiff seeks to introduce testimony by Frank Fixer, an experienced copy machine repair technician. Fixer will testify that the pattern of breakdowns is consistent with poor design of the machines and not consistent with careless use of the machines.

Fixer's testimony is most likely

A. Admissible if the trial court concludes that it is based on methods that have achieved general acceptance in the field of office-equipment maintenance and repair.

B. Admissible if the trial court concludes that it is based on reliable data, that the data can be verified, that Fixer's use of the data could be replicated or tested, and that Fixer's methods have achieved general acceptance in the field of office-equipment maintenance and repair.

C. Inadmissible because it is lay opinion.

D. Inadmissible because it represents an opinion on an ultimate issue.

112. At a private meeting, Nicholas Neville spoke with his lawyer, Opal Ormond, to get the lawyer's opinion about investment strategies. Neville wanted Ormond's opinion on whether investing in American stocks or in European stocks was a better strategy for long-term gains. Neville later invested a large amount of money in European stocks and suffered significant losses. Neville then sued his stockbroker, claiming that the broker wrongfully advised Neville to invest in European stocks and that Neville relied exclusively on the broker's advice. The defendant stockbroker seeks to question Ormond at the trial about her conversations with Neville about investment strategies, to show that Neville obtained investment advice from sources additional to the defendant.

It is most likely that

A. Neville is entitled to prevent Ormond from answering this question because of attorney-client privilege.

B. attorney-client privilege does not apply because the topic of Neville's conversation with Ormond did not involve legal advice.

C. Neville is entitled to prevent Ormond from answering this question because Neville's statements to Ormond are hearsay in this context.

D. the question is permissible because it calls only for proof of a prior inconsistent statement by Neville.

113. In a copyright case, Sam Songwriter seeks damages from Carol Composer, claiming that a popular song published by Composer was actually based on a song created earlier and performed by Songwriter at a "New Songs Festival" in 2009. As part of Composer's defense, Composer claims she never heard Songwriter's song and that her song was an entirely original composition. Songwriter seeks to prove that Composer's brother attended the festival and thus could have heard Songwriter's song and then sung or played it for Composer. To support this contention, Songwriter seeks to introduce evidence that early in 2008, Composer's brother said to a friend, "Next year, I'm going to go the New Songs Festival." It is most likely that this evidence is

A. Admissible because it shows the speaker's state of mind.

B. Admissible because it is a statement by a party opponent's agent.

C. Inadmissible because it is an out-of-court statement offered to prove the truth of what it asserts and is not covered by any hearsay exception.

D. Inadmissible because it is only conditionally relevant.

114. Bruce Bigman is on trial for the murder of Nathan Niceguy. Testifying in his own defense, Bigman admits having struck a fatal blow against Niceguy but claims that he did it in self-defense. He states, during his direct examination, that Niceguy came up to him in a bar and suddenly started to hit him and threaten to poke his eye out with a broken beer bottle. In response to this testimony, the prosecution may

A. Introduce testimony from Bob Buyer stating that Bigman once concealed a defect in a house he was selling

B. Introduce testimony from a bartender stating that Bigman once started a fight in a bar.

C. Introduce testimony from a neighbor of Niceguy stating that Niceguy had a reputation for being a peaceful and non-aggressive person.

D. Introduce testimony from a bartender stating that Niceguy once was gravely insulted in a bar and chose to ignore the insults.

115. Ralph Relative is on trial for committing sexual abuse against his young stepdaughter. A year before trial, an investigator hired by Relative interviewed Alice Aunt, an aunt of the alleged victim. Aunt has died, and Relative seeks to introduce testimony by the investigator, quoting Aunt as saying she had seen someone other than Relative committing a sexual assault against the stepdaughter in the location and at the time Relative is accused of having done so. The investigator's testimony is most likely

A. Admissible because the aunt's statement, though hearsay, is covered by the exception for statements against interest.

B. Admissible because it is a basis for an opinion by the investigator, in the investigator's capacity as an expert.

C. Inadmissible because the aunt's statement is hearsay outside the coverage of any exceptions.

D. Inadmissible because of the bias inherent in her relationships with Relative and her niece.

116. In a contract case, Customer sues Supplier and seeks damages for Supplier's failure to deliver goods on time. Customer seeks to testify that Supplier sent Customer an e-mail apologizing for the failure. The copy of the e-mail is most likely

    A. Admissible if Customer satisfies the requirements of the original writing rule.

    B. Admissible if Customer satisfies the requirements of authentication and the original writing rule.

    C. Inadmissible because it is hearsay.

    D. Inadmissible because an apology of this kind is excluded by FRE 408 barring evidence of statements made in an effort to settle a dispute.

117. Edward Elderly was a 95-year-old man dying of a terminal illness under hospice care. A day before he died, he said to a friend, "I've had a great life and I'm not nervous or afraid about the end, even though I know it's coming. The only thing I regret is that last year I hid some documents for my son-in-law, and now I think maybe he wanted me to hide them because they had something to do with fraud." In a lawsuit against Elderly's son-in-law, the plaintiff seeks to introduce testimony quoting Elderly's statement about hiding documents to prove that the son-in-law asked Elderly to hide documents. The testimony is most likely

    A. Admissible as a dying declaration because Elderly knew he was dying.

    B. Admissible as a statement against penal interest.

    C. Inadmissible because it is hearsay outside the coverage of any exceptions.

    D. Inadmissible because the dying declaration exception applies only in homicide cases.

118. Larry Landowner had a dispute with Nancy Neighbor about use of a driveway leading to both of their houses. In a suit between Landowner and Neighbor, a controverted issue was the frequency with which Neighbor drove on the driveway. Landowner testified that he kept a notebook of observations about the driveway and other parts of his property and that he regularly made entries in it. He sought to introduce the following statement from the notebook, "No recent activity, but last summer Neighbor used the driveway almost every day," as

proof that Neighbor had used the driveway almost every day during that summer. The statement is most likely

A. Admissible as a business record.

B. Admissible as a statement by a party-opponent.

C. Inadmissible because it is a prior consistent statement.

D. Inadmissible as hearsay outside the coverage of any exception.

119. Pamela Patient has brought a malpractice action against Sarah Surgeon, claiming that Surgeon's performance of an operation on Patient failed to follow the professional standard of care and that Patient was harmed by that failure. As part of her defense Surgeon seeks to introduce testimony from a colleague stating that he has observed Surgeon perform hundred of operations and that Surgeon always acts carefully in her work. This testimony is most likely

A. Admissible because it would prove the defendant's relevant character trait to support a finding of conduct in conformity with that trait.

B. Admissible because it describes a habit.

C. Inadmissible because it is hearsay.

D. Inadmissible because it would prove the defendant's character trait to support a finding of conduct in conformity with that character trait.

120. Inez Investor is suing Dan Developer. Investor claims that Developer misrepresented the likelihood of zoning approvals being granted for a proposed office building project. Developer testifies in his own defense. Investor knows that in the fairly recent past, Developer has committed fraud in another office building project and in a business transaction involving the purchase of some patent rights. To impeach Developer, Investor will most likely be permitted

A. To ask Developer if he committed fraud in patent rights transaction.

B. To ask Developer if he committed fraud in the other office building project.

C. To introduce testimony from a witness to prove that Developer committed fraud in the other office building project.

D. To introduce testimony from a witness to prove that Developer committed fraud in the patent rights transaction.

121. Bruce Browser was shopping at a large mall that has a central hall-way and many individual retail stores. He entered Fancy Clothes, a clothing store, and slipped and fell after he'd taken a few steps. He seeks damages from Fancy Clothes claiming that it had cleaned its floor with a product called XYZ that left the floor in a slippery con-dition that was unreasonably risky. A few days after Browser fell, the operator of the mall stopped using XYZ to clean the floors of the common areas of the mall and switched to a different product that it considered safer than XYZ. Fancy Clothes and the common areas of the mall have the same kind of floors. If Browser seeks to introduce evidence of the mall operator's switch away from XYZ to show that Fancy Clothes had acted unreasonably, it is most likely that the evi-dence is

    A. Admissible even though it is evidence of a subsequent remedial measure, because its proposed use is different from the uses for which subsequent remedial measures evidence is prohibited.

    B. Admissible even though it is evidence of a subsequent remedial measure, because the subsequent remedial measure was adopted by the mall operated and not by Fancy Clothes.

    C. Inadmissible because it is evidence of a subsequent remedial mea-sure and its proposed use is among the uses for which subsequent remedial measures evidence is prohibited.

    D. Inadmissible because Fancy Clothes does not have control over the conduct of the operator of the mall and is therefore not responsible for its actions.

122. The estate of Victor Victim has brought a products liability suit against FruitCo, a manufacturer of fruit-based diet supplements, claiming that Victim was killed by contaminants in a container of a FruitCo product. The estate seeks to introduce a hospital record with the following notation: "Victim's wife says Victim told her he had two glasses of FruitCo supplements a few hours ago." The number of out-of-court statements included in this evidence is

    A. One.

    B. Two.

    C. Three.

    D. Four.

123. To prove that Alan Able was a resident at a particular place, a party seeks to introduce a cell phone bill found at that place, addressed to Able and the address of that place. Able objects, arguing that the

hearsay rule prohibits introduction of the bill. The most likely ruling is that the bill is:

A. Admissible because the declarant's intended assertion was something different than to convey the fact that Able lives at that address.

B. Admissible because it is covered by the business records exception.

C. Admissible if it was generated by a data processing system since only humans can make hearsay statements.

D. Admissible because it is a statement by a party opponent.

124. Defendant killed Victim, with whom he had been living for about two years before the killing. In a prosecution for murder, Defendant claimed that Victim had attacked him, that the force he used in response was proportional, and that therefore he was not guilty of the charge. The prosecution seeks to persuade the jury that Defendant had acted violently against Victim on other occasions to suggest that Victim would not have risked being an aggressor in the circumstances that ended with Victim's death. Of the following items of evidence, the one most likely to be admissible if offered by the prosecution is

A. A diary entry by Victim from about three months before Defendant killed Victim saying "An hour ago after dinner Defendant punched me really hard—I'm very scared of Defendant."

B. Testimony by a police officer that Victim told him, about six months before Defendant killed Victim, that Defendant had attacked Victim violently three days earlier.

C. A note by Victim stating "To the police if I am found dead, investigate Defendant since he has hurt me in the past and has threatened to kill me."

D. Testimony by a bartender that Victim told him, about six months before Defendant killed Victim, that Defendant had attacked Victim violently three days earlier.

125. Dan Defendant is on trial for bank robbery. He testifies in his defense, claiming that he was not present at the scene of the crime and is a victim of mistaken identity. Several years ago, Defendant was convicted of a felonious violation of a state's consumer protection act. He contracted with numerous consumers to provide burglar alarm services and failed to give those consumers some required documents related to their rights as buyers at the time of the transactions.

The prosecution seeks to offer proof of this conviction to impeach Defendant's credibility. This evidence is

A. Admissible if the trial judge concludes that it relates to credibility and that its probative value exceeds the risk of unfair prejudice associated with it.

B. Admissible if the trial judge concludes that it relates to credibility and that its probative value and risk of unfair prejudice associated with it are about equal.

C. Admissible if the trial judge concludes that it relates to credibility and that its probative value is less than the risk of unfair prejudice associated with it.

D. Admissible without regard to the balance between probative value and risk of unfair prejudice.

126. Dan Driver drove his car into Walt Walker while Walker was crossing a street and had the right of way. In a tort suit by Walker against Driver, Walker seeks to show that Driver had notice that the brakes on his car were not operating properly before he drove it and hit Walker. Walker seeks to introduce evidence that the day before the incident, Driver typed "locations of brake repair shops near me" into a smartphone's search screen. If Driver objects on hearsay grounds, the most likely ruling is that the evidence is

A. Admissible because it is not an assertion.

B. Admissible because it is a statement by a party opponent.

C. Inadmissible because it is hearsay outside the coverage of any exception.

D. Inadmissible because it has not been authenticated.

127. Sam Shopper has sued BigStore, a large electronics store, to recover damages for injuries Shopper suffered when he slipped and fell in the store. Shopper claims that BigStore had allowed some small boxes to be stacked in an aisle, and that Shopper had tripped over those boxes. Bob Buyer, a customer who was in the store at the time saw Shopper fall, has testified at the trial, saying that he saw Shopper fall and that it looked to him as though Shopper tripped on some boxes. Gary Guard, a BigStore security employee, seeks to testify that several hours after Shoppe fell, Buyer told Guard, "I think I must have knocked Shopper over. I wasn't watching where I was going." If Guard's testimony is

offered to prove that Buyer knocked Shopper over, the strongest reason to *exclude* Guard's testimony is

A. Buyer's words were not against his pecuniary, proprietary or penal interests.

B. Buyer's words were not inconsistent with his testimony.

C. A declarant's words may not be quoted by another witness if the declarant testifies.

D. Buyer is available as a witness.

128. Dan Doctor, a physician, treated Pam Patient for a serious immune system disorder. The treatment required Patient to take five different kinds of pills at specific times each day. After a few months, Patient's disorder became worse. She has sued Doctor, claiming that the disorder became worse because the instructions Doctor gave her about when to take various pills were not clear. Because the instructions were confusing, Patient claims, she did not take the pills at the proper times and this led to the worsening of her disorder. To show that the instructions were clear, Doctor most likely would be permitted to introduce testimony

A. By himself, quoting the instructions he gave to Patient.

B. By an expert in immune system disorders, evaluating the clarity of Doctor's words.

C. By an expert in human communications, evaluating the clarity of Doctor's words.

D. By a lay witness who is another of Doctor's patients, stating his opinion about the clarity of similar instructions given to him by Doctor.

129. Daryl Defendant is on trial for bank robbery. The prosecution seeks to introduce a written report made by Alan Analyst, a police fingerprint analyst stating that a comparison between Defendant's fingerprints and fingerprints found at the scene of the crime indicates a positive match. In addition, the prosecution seeks to have a police department expert on fingerprint analysis, Edward Expert, explain the written report. Expert is experienced in fingerprint analysis and is also a supervisor at the office where Analyst works. Analyst is not available to testify. The strongest objection Defendant might make to this evidence is that

A. It violates the Original Writing Rule.

B. It violates the Confrontation Clause.

C. It incorporates hearsay for which there is no available exception.

D. It violates the personal knowledge requirement.

130. Max Manager was the chief of security for a large company. One morning some demonstrators occupied the lobby of the company's office building. Manager ordered his security staff to use force to remove the demonstrators. Later that day, Manager asked the company's lawyer whether his conduct might have exposed the company to liability, and the lawyer told Manager there was no risk to the company so long as the security staff had reasonably believed that they were facing severe threats of serious bodily injury. Manager then went to his office and typed a memo stating that during the morning's demonstration there had been lots of threats and reports of threats of violence by the demonstrators. A demonstrator has sued the company to recover damages for injuries allegedly inflicted by the company's security staff. To show that there were significant threats and reports of threats, the company seeks to introduce Manager's memo under the business records exception to the hearsay rule. The memo most likely would be

A. Admissible because its contents relate to the ordinary work of a chief of security.

B. Admissible because it was made soon after the events it describes.

C. Inadmissible because the circumstances indicate it lacks trustworthiness.

D. Inadmissible because lawyer-client privilege requires that a memo that reflects advice of counsel must be excluded from evidence.

131. David Defendant is on trial for murder. The prosecution's evidence would support a finding that Defendant and the victim shared a cell in a prison, and that Defendant poisoned the victim. Defendant testifies in his own defense, claiming that he did not commit the alleged crime. The prosecution will likely be permitted to introduce evidence showing

A. Defendant was convicted of perjury five years ago.

B. Defendant was convicted of arson five years ago.

C. Defendant has a reputation for being violent.

D. Defendant has falsely accused others in prison of violating prison rules.

132. A windstorm caused significant damage to a building, and the owner sought payment for the damage under an insurance policy. The insurance company refused to pay for the entire damage. It relied on a clause in the policy that excluded coverage for damage related to flaws in the building's structure that existed prior to the time that the insurance policy was issued. To prove that the building had suffered damage before the policy was issued, the insurance company sought to introduce a copy of a newspaper published 17 years prior to the trial that included a news story describing a lightning strike on the building that had caused significant structural damage. If the owner objects on hearsay grounds, the strongest response the insurance company could reasonably make is that the newspaper

A. Is an "ancient document."

B. Is properly the subject of judicial notice.

C. Is admissible under the residual hearsay exception.

D. Is a business record.

Multiple-Choice
Answers

1. **A** Ordinarily, the attorney-client privilege is assertable by a party's counsel on behalf of the client. The client may be a corporation. Because the records in question were already in existence when the Department of Commerce commenced its action against Exton, the work product privilege cannot be successfully asserted because these documents were not prepared in anticipation of litigation or for trial. Also because the communications are routine reports generated in the ordinary course of the corporation's business, they do not constitute confidential communications between an attorney and her client. Thus, the records are discoverable. Choice **B** is wrong because the attorney-client privilege can be asserted at the discovery stage. Also, the attorney (as well as his client) can ordinarily assert this privilege. Choice **C** is wrong because documents do not become insulated from discovery simply because they are delivered to one's attorney. Finally, choice **D** is wrong because documents do not become an attorney's work product or confidential communications simply because they are delivered to, or reviewed by, legal counsel.

2. **D** Only relevant evidence may be admitted. Evidence is relevant if it has any tendency to make the existence of a material fact more probable or less probable than it would be without the evidence. Joe's statement is relevant because it arguably links Bill to the crime. Choice **A** is wrong because the evidence does meet the definition of relevant evidence. Choice **B** is wrong because Joe's statement did not pertain to the treatment of his injury. Finally, choice **C** is wrong because a paramedic is ordinarily considered a "physician" for purposes of this privilege.

3. **B** An expert may be cross-examined with respect to learned treatises. Out-of-court statements made in writings that are contained in a learned treatise and called to the attention of an expert witness constitute an exception to the hearsay rule. Such evidence may be read into the record; FRE 803(18). Because an exception to the hearsay rule exists with respect to the out-of-court statements in question, they may be considered as substantive evidence (as well as for impeachment). Choice **A** is wrong because under this exception to the hearsay rule the statements are admissible as evidence. Choice **C** is wrong because, although the statements in question are hearsay, an exception to the hearsay rule exists in this instance. Finally, choice **D** is wrong because Cox's belief that the passages in question were not applicable to Post's condition would probably **not** be determinative. Because Dr. Freed testified that there is no difference between the two

types of arthritis, the court could conclude that the passages of the textbook were relevant. The court should probably let the jury decide which expert they considered more credible.

4. **B** Tangible evidence must ordinarily be authenticated or identified prior to its admissibility; FRE 901(a). This requirement may be satisfied by evidence sufficient to support a finding that the matter in question is what its proponent claims. If the court determines there is adequate evidence of the letter's authenticity, it is admissible. Choice **A** is wrong because corroboration of Harry's signature is not a required means of authentication (i.e., a writing can also be authenticated by a witness with knowledge or a distinctive characteristic). Choice **C** is wrong because the letter does tend to suggest that Harry was a co-conspirator. Finally, choice **D** is wrong because, although probably intended to be confidential in nature, the letter does not come within the purview of any recognized privilege.

5. **D** A hearsay statement is one made by an out-of-court declarant, which is offered into evidence to prove the truth of the matter asserted; FRE 801(c). Because the insurance adjuster is testifying as to an out-of-court statement by Martha to prove the truth of the matter asserted therein, it is hearsay (and therefore inadmissible). Choice **C** is wrong because, whether Martha is unavailable or not, her statement to the insurance adjuster is still hearsay. There is no rule permitting a hearsay statement simply because the out-of-court declarant is unavailable. (FRE 804 describes the particular situations where an unavailable out-of-court declarant's statement may be admitted.) Choice **A** is wrong because Martha is not a party to the action. Finally, choice **B** is wrong because Martha's statement was not an excited utterance (i.e., a statement relating to a startling event while under the stress of excitement caused by the event; FRE 803(2)). Martha's statement to the insurance adjuster was made three days after the incident had occurred.

6. **A** Pete's testimony as to how Jack had described Michael is relevant to show a motive for murder. With regard to hearsay, it is not offered for the truth of the matter asserted (i.e., that Michael really was a "sissy" or "scaredy cat") but rather to show that Michael had a motive to murder Jack. For that reason, it is not hearsay because a hearsay statement is one, other than one made by the declarant while testifying at the trial or hearing, that is offered into evidence to prove the truth of the matter asserted therein; FRE 801(c). Michael's objections are also out-of-court statements, but they are admissions and thus not barred

by the hearsay rule. Choice **B** is wrong because Pete's testimony is admissible whether or not Michael asserts his Fifth Amendment right against self-incrimination. Choice **C** is wrong because Pete's testimony is, as explained above, not hearsay. Finally, choice **D** is wrong because the statement is not offered to show that Michael acted in conformity with the character Jack had described on the occasion in question.

7. **A** Under the doctrine of present recollection refreshed, a witness may consult a document before giving testimony as part of pretrial preparation; FRE 612(2). Because that is what Mike did here, his testimony is admissible. Choice **B** is wrong because past recollection recorded pertains to a writing about a matter as to which the witness now has insufficient recollection to testify; FRE 803(5). The facts do not indicate that Mike, after taking the stand, had no recollection of the incident. Choice **C** is wrong because Mike is testifying from his personal knowledge (rather than reading from the report in question). Finally, choice **D** is wrong because the report, not having been admitted into evidence, need not have been authenticated.

8. **C** Where evidence of the content of a writing, recording, or photograph is sought, the original writing, recording, or photograph is ordinarily required; FRE 1002. This is especially true in transactions involving a contract, where the role played by the contract is so key that the contract really embodies the transaction. Because Deborah sought to testify about the precise provisions of the contract, the contract must be produced. Choice **A** is wrong because the contract is not a writing kept in the course of a regularly conducted business activity. Choice **B** is inapplicable because when a document embodies a transaction, such as the contract here that sets forth the requirements of performance, its contents cannot be proved by oral testimony. Finally, choice **D** is wrong because Deborah's testimony does not pertain to an alleged understanding that occurred prior to execution of the written agreement.

9. **C** Evidence of furnishing, or offering or promising to pay, medical expenses occasioned by an injury is not admissible to prove liability for that injury; FRE 409. Because a promise to pay another's medical bills is inadmissible, George's testimony about Paul's statement to Dora cannot be introduced. Choice **D** is wrong because Paul's intent in making the statement is irrelevant. It is inadmissible because his statement is expressly prohibited under the FRE. Choice **A** is wrong because, although George's testimony is a party-opponent admission,

the statement is inadmissible for reasons other than hearsay. Finally, choice **B** is wrong because, even though Paul's statement may be relevant, it is inadmissible.

10. **C** Relevant evidence is evidence having any tendency to make the existence of any fact of consequence more or less probable than it would be without that evidence; FRE 401. Because a plaintiff's fault is usually treated as a possible defense in products liability actions, evidence of Paul's failure to act reasonably is relevant. Choice **B** is wrong because Paul's testimony would not be hearsay. Choice **A** is wrong because, as discussed above, the evidence is relevant. Finally, choice **D** is wrong because nonassertive conduct, such as driving at a particular speed, cannot be hearsay.

11. **B** Although evidence that a person was or was not insured against liability is inadmissible on the issue of whether he acted negligently or wrongfully, it is admissible when offered for any other relevant purpose (i.e., proof of agency, ownership, control, bias, prejudice of a witness, etc.); FRE 411. If Dan had purchased liability insurance pertaining to the vehicle, such fact would suggest that he was a person "in control" of Amy's automobile. Choice **A** is wrong because Dan's purchase of insurance does not tend to show that it was more likely that Amy was at fault. Choice **C** is factually correct (i.e., the existence of insurance is irrelevant to fault), but this evidence does suggest that Dan was "in control" of the vehicle. Finally, choice **D** is wrong because, although possibly factually accurate (i.e., the availability of insurance tends to bias a fact finder against the insured party), the pertinence of this information with respect to the issue of whether Dan was "in control" outweighs the risk of juror misuse of the information.

12. **A** Evidence of offering, or promising, a valuable consideration to compromise (or attempting to compromise) a claim that is disputed is not admissible to prove liability; FRE 408. Because Jamison, on behalf of Frank's Market, made a compromise offer, the evidence is not admissible. Choice **B** is wrong because Jamison's statement is not hearsay (it is a party-opponent admission) and would arguably be relevant to show that the defendant knew that it was at fault; FRE 801(d)(2). Choice **C** is arguably correct (i.e., Jamison's statement tends to show that Frank's Market is liable), but is specifically made inadmissible by the FRE. Finally, choice **D** is wrong because there are no specific requirements of formality that govern whether

a conversation or other communication is or is not an offer to settle or a statement made in discussion of a settlement.

13. **A** When, after an event, measures are taken that, if taken previously, would have made the event less likely to occur, evidence of the subsequent measures are not admissible to prove culpable conduct in connection with such event; FRE 407. However, this rule does not exclude evidence of subsequent remedial measures offered for any other purpose (i.e., proving proof of ownership, control, feasibility of precautionary measures, or impeachment). Because merely painting a vehicle is not the type of measure that would have made the incident less likely to occur, the objection should be overruled. Choice **B** is wrong because evidence of remedial measures is not ordinarily admissible. Choice **C** is correct as a general statement of law, but the measure (i.e., the painting of the vehicle) undertaken in this instance is not remedial in nature. Finally, choice **D** is wrong because, as discussed above, the evidence is admissible in this particular situation.

14. **D** Evidence of subsequent remedial measures is not admissible to show negligence or culpable conduct in connection with such an event; FRE 407. Evidence of subsequent remedial measures is admissible, however, to prove ***ownership or control*** over the property that caused the accident. Evidence that Moneybags had the capability to order Cosgrove to install a retaining screen is relevant to determining whether Moneybags had control over the construction. Moneybags would be entitled, however, to a limiting instruction (i.e., that the judge advise the jurors that this evidence should not be used in their determination of whether Cosgrove or Moneybags was negligent, but should be considered only for the purpose of deciding whether Moneybags had retained control over the construction). Choice **C** is factually wrong. In fact, this evidence shows that Moneybags (rather than Cosgrove) had penultimate control of the construction. Choice **A** is wrong because evidence of remedial measures is admissible for the purpose of proving control over a particular activity. Finally, choice **B** is wrong because, although logically it may be true, the evidence is admissible for the purpose of showing Moneybags's control over the construction.

15. **B** Evidence of a party's character, or a trait of her character, is not admissible in civil cases for the purpose of proving action in conformity therewith on a particular occasion; FRE 404(a). Because Marla is attempting to introduce general character evidence about Ripoff,

the objection should be sustained. Choice **A** is wrong because there is a hearsay exception for evidence of reputation, applicable in cases where character evidence is otherwise admissible. Choice **C** is arguably factually correct. But, as discussed above, character evidence of Ripoff's unethical reputation is inadmissible. Finally, choice **D** is wrong for the reasons described above. Additionally, because this is not a criminal case, Ripoff cannot introduce positive character evidence about himself.

16. **A** Generally, evidence that would support a finding of a party's character, or a trait of his character (like the character trait of carelessness or inattentiveness), is not admissible in civil cases for the purpose of proving action in conformity therewith on a particular occasion; FRE 404(a). Here, however, because the evidence is presumably offered to show that Paul's parents knew (or should have known) about his negligent or reckless tendencies, it is admissible. In this situation, it is not offered to show that Paul acted in conformity with these tendencies. Counsel for Paul's parents could probably request a limiting instruction (i.e., that the jury be advised that it should only consider the evidence of Paul's prior conduct with respect to whether his parents knew, or should have known, that Paul's driving might result in an accident). Choice **B** is wrong because the evidence would not be admissible to show that Paul acted negligently or recklessly. Choice **C** is wrong because there is a hearsay exception for evidence of past convictions that applies in cases where those convictions are relevant. Finally, choice **D** is wrong because prior conduct might arguably tend to prove that the subject acted in conformity with those tendencies on the occasion in question. However, evidence is not admissible for that purpose.

17. **C** Evidence of prior crimes, wrongs, or acts is admissible for any purpose, other than to show the character of a person for the purpose of showing that he acted in conformity therewith on the occasion in question; FRE 404(b). Theresa's prior convictions are pertinent to undermine her contention that she was coerced into the crime in question because they show motive and perhaps show special knowledge related to crimes such as the one charged. (Of course, the jury could still believe her assertion, if they chose to do so.) Choice **D** is wrong because Theresa's identity is not in issue. She was arrested at the scene and has admitted committing the crime. Choice **A** is wrong because, as discussed above, prior convictions are admissible

in certain situations (such as the present one). Finally, choice **B** is wrong because Theresa's prior convictions are relevant to rebut her assertion that she was coerced into the crime in question.

18. **A** Although evidence of other crimes, wrongs, or acts is not admissible to prove character in order to show that a person acted in conformity therewith on the occasion in question, it may be admissible for any other relevant purpose (such as proof of motive, opportunity, intent, preparation, plan, knowledge, identity, or absence of mistake or accident); FRE 404(b). Because Magda had experienced a similar incident in which she had exited a store with an item that she had "tried on," the evidence should be admissible to rebut her assertion that an innocent mistake had been made. (Her attorney probably could obtain a limiting instruction—that the evidence be considered by the jury only on the issue of whether Magda had made a good-faith mistake.) The fact that no criminal charges were filed in the previous incident is of no significance. Choice **B** is wrong because it misstates the general proposition of law (i.e., prior conduct is not ordinarily admissible to prove conduct in conformity therewith). Choice **C** is wrong because the evidence is pertinent to Magda's assertion that she had made an innocent mistake. Finally, choice **D** is wrong because prior conduct, as explained above, is admissible in this situation.

19. **D** One who consults an attorney for the purpose of obtaining legal assistance is privileged to refuse to disclose, and to prevent the attorney (and his essential personnel) from disclosing, communications made for the purpose of facilitating the rendition of advice. The letter that Adams sent to Ladd was for the purpose of obtaining assistance with respect to the preparation of the deed. It would therefore be within the attorney-client privilege. The fact that Evans saw the letter would not result in forfeiture of the privilege because a legal secretary would presumably be considered "essential personnel" of her attorney-employer. Choice **A** is wrong because the document is clearly relevant on the issue of Adams's intent. Choice **B** is wrong because under the federal and most state rules, a copy is acceptable in lieu of the original. Choice **C** is wrong because any statement by Adams would be an admission if sought to be introduced by his opponent, Baker.

20. **D** Evidence is relevant if it has any tendency to make the existence of any fact of consequence to the determination of the matter more or less probable; FRE 401. The fact that there was a call from Bungler's

telephone to Harvey's store on the day on which a demand might have been made would permit an inference that Bungler was the extortionist. Choice **A** is wrong because directories that are generally used and relied on by the public constitute an exception to the hearsay rule; FRE 803(17). Choice **C** is wrong because the telephone directory was an original document; FRE 1003. Finally, Choice **B** is wrong because, although it is entirely possible that Bungler called Harvey's store for a business reason, it is also possible that he telephoned Harvey for the purpose of extorting money from him. Because the evidence has a tendency to prove that Bungler was the extortionist, it is relevant.

21. **C** Out-of-court statements that are offered into evidence to prove that the statement, in fact, was made or to show its effect on the listener, for example, to show that the listener had a certain emotion, had certain knowledge, or was put on notice (as opposed to proving the truth of any matter asserted therein or inferable thereby) are not hearsay. The note in question is admissible for the purpose of showing that the victim was being threatened with harm unless he complied with the demand to pay $50,000. It is ***not*** being offered to show that any statement in the note was, in fact, true. Therefore, it is not hearsay. Choice **D** is wrong because the note is not being offered into evidence for the purpose of proving that the defendant wrote it. The party-opponent exclusion to the hearsay rule is not applicable. Choice **B** is wrong because the note is not being offered into evidence to prove the truth of the matter asserted therein, but only that it was received and caused fear. Finally, choice **A** is wrong because the prosecution has offered the note into evidence only to show that the victim was in imminent fear of harm, not to show that it was written by the defendant.

22. **A** A witness who has testified with respect to the character of a person may be cross-examined with respect to relevant specific instances of conduct by that person; FRE 405(a). Because Blow testified as to Barker's character after the latter had testified, it was proper to cross-examine Blow with respect to prior acts of misconduct (although not resulting in prosecution) of Barker that are probative of the latter's truthfulness or untruthfulness. Because taking money from a cash register while working at an establishment (conduct probably constituting embezzlement or larceny) appears to be probative of truthfulness or untruthfulness, the question was proper. Choice **B** is wrong because Blow has been asked about prior acts of misconduct

not of himself but of ***another*** (i.e., the defendant, Barker). Choice **C** is wrong because embezzlement or larceny are crimes having similar ingredients as burglary and would probably be viewed as bearing on truthfulness or untruthfulness. Therefore, the fact that Barker's prior conduct is somewhat different from that with which he is now charged is not pertinent. Finally, choice **D** is wrong because there is no requirement that ***Barker*** be asked about his prior misconduct to make Blow's testimony proper or relevant.

23. **C** Out-of-court statements about an event or condition made while the declarant was observing that event or condition, or immediately thereafter, are admissible as an exception to the hearsay rule. Because Brown made his comment to Jock while he smelled the gas, his statement would be admissible; FRE 803(1). Choice **B** is wrong because there is no indication from the facts that Brown believed that his death was imminent. Choice **D** is wrong because there is nothing to indicate that the gas was viewed by Brown as a "startling" event or condition. In fact, because Brown apparently continued to perform his work, there is no indication that he felt unusual stress. Finally, choice **A** is wrong because the statement could not reasonably have been characterized as contrary to Brown's penal or pecuniary interest at the time he made it.

24. **C** Evidence of a person's habit is relevant to prove that the person's conduct on a particular occasion was in conformity with such habit or routine practice; FRE 406. Arlene's testimony is basically "habit" evidence because it describes conduct that is fairly "automatic" and is repeated without significant conscious thought. Therefore it should be admissible. Choice **D** is wrong because it sets forth a wrong proposition of law (i.e., prior conduct is not generally admissible to prove conduct in conformity therewith on a particular occasion). Choice **A** is wrong because Arlene seeks to testify about a habit, rather than specific prior conduct. Finally, choice **B** is wrong because Arlene's claim against the manufacturer does not preclude her from contesting Clyde's action against her.

25. **D** Evidence of a person's character, or trait of character, is ordinarily inadmissible for the purpose of proving conduct in conformity therewith on a particular occasion; FRE 404(a). Matthew's character is not in issue because proof that he is a thieving or cheating type of person is not a required element of the plaintiff's legal theory. Also, the evidence is not being offered to offset Matthew's impeachment. Choice **C** is wrong because reputation of a person's character

constitutes an exception to the hearsay rule; FRE 803(21). Choice **B** is wrong because, although Matthew's character is in issue, the evidence is not admissible. Finally, choice **A** is wrong because it sets forth an erroneous rule of law (i.e., character evidence is not generally admissible in civil cases).

26. **A** Evidence of past acts is not admissible to prove the character of a person to show that she acted in conformity therewith. However, it may be admissible for any other relevant purpose; FRE 404(b). Because Carlyle's character is directly in issue, the evidence is admissible to show that he lacked the mental competence necessary to modify a will. Testimony about Carlyle's actions, which are nonverbal conduct not intended as assertions, does not constitute hearsay; FRE 801(a). Also, testimony reporting that he had said things indicating he believed he was shooting people would also be outside of the hearsay definition because it would be introduced to show that the statements (though made) were false. Choice **B** is wrong because character evidence is not ordinarily admissible. Choice **D** is generally a correct statement of law, but specific acts of Carlyle are nevertheless admissible in this situation. Finally, choice **C** is wrong because when a person's character is in issue in a case, proof of specific acts that support conclusions about that character is admissible (FRE 405(b)).

27. **B** Evidence of a person's character is ordinarily not admissible for the purpose of showing that he acted in conformity therewith on a particular occasion. However, an accused may offer evidence of a pertinent trait of his character; FRE 404(a)(1). Because honesty and fair dealing are not pertinent to the crime for which Bill has been charged (i.e., murder), the evidence is not admissible. In this situation, only evidence of a peaceable character would be pertinent. Choice **A** is wrong because Bill may introduce evidence of certain pertinent character traits. Choice **C** is wrong because, even in a homicide case, the character trait in question must pertain to the crime for which the defendant has been charged. Finally, choice **D** is wrong because evidence of his own character, when offered by an accused, must relate to the criminal activity involved.

28. **A** Although evidence of a person's character is ordinarily not admissible for the purpose of showing that he or she acted in conformity therewith on a particular occasion, an accused may offer evidence of a pertinent trait; FRE 404(a)(1). Because Sharon is charged with a crime that pertains to honesty, her reputation pertaining to

truthfulness is pertinent. Choice **B** is wrong because Sharon does not have a general right to introduce evidence of all possible positive character traits. Choice **D** is a misstatement of the law (in a criminal case, an accused may introduce evidence of a pertinent trait of his character). Finally, choice **C** is also a wrong statement of law. Proof of reputation is admissible; FRE 405(a).

29. **D** This is an instance of reputation evidence being relevant solely because a party to the case was aware of that reputation. The reputation evidence is not being used to show that Shawna was unduly aggressive during the incident in question, but it is being used, properly, to support a claim by Kellie that she reasonably anticipated serious injury and that therefore the degree of force she used was justified in self-defense. For this reason, the ordinary prohibition against use of character evidence to show action in conformity with that character does not apply. Choice **A** is wrong because the prohibition against character evidence in civil cases only applies when the character evidence is introduced for the purpose of proving that a person acted in conformity therewith on a particular occasion; FRE 404(a). Choice **B** is wrong because Shawna's reputation is relevant to assessing Kellie's self-defense claim. Choice **C** is wrong because neither Shawna nor Kellie has been charged with a crime.

30. **C** Evidence of a pertinent character trait offered by a criminally accused is admissible; FRE 404(a)(1). In all cases in which character evidence is admissible, proof may be made by testimony as to reputation; FRE 405(a). Because the evidence offered by Jimmy is directly pertinent to the crime for which he is charged, it is admissible. Choice **D** is a wrong statement of law (reputation evidence is admissible). Choice **B** is wrong because opinion evidence as to Jimmy's character is admissible in this situation; FRE 405(a). Finally, choice **A** is a wrong statement of law. As discussed above, character evidence is admissible in this instance.

31. **A** Evidence of the victim's character for peacefulness may be offered by the prosecution in a homicide case to rebut an assertion that the deceased victim was the initial aggressor; FRE 404(a)(2). Because Tanya contends that Rita attacked her first and is charged with homicide, the prosecution may introduce evidence of Rita's peaceable character. Choice **B** is wrong because it constitutes an overly broad statement of law (if the ***prosecution*** seeks to introduce evidence about a victim's character, it may do so only in a homicide case to rebut evidence that the victim was the first aggressor or to

rebut character evidence in other criminal cases introduced by the defendant). Choice **C** is wrong because there is no precondition that the prosecution have introduced evidence of Tanya's character during its case-in-chief. Finally, choice **D** is wrong because, in this situation, the prosecution may initiate evidence pertaining to the victim's peaceable character.

32. **A** Except in the case of a homicide, evidence of a pertinent character trait of the victim of a crime can be offered by the prosecution only to rebut similar evidence to the contrary offered by an accused; FRE 404(a)(2). Because the prosecution, as part of its case-in-chief, is offering character evidence pertaining to the victim, and the particular crime is not a homicide, the evidence is not admissible. Choice **B** is wrong because "any type" of character evidence cannot be offered by Mark. Although the accused may introduce evidence of the victim's character, such evidence must pertain to a pertinent trait. Choice **C** is wrong because, as explained above, the prosecution cannot (except in the case of a homicide) initially offer evidence of the victim's character. Finally, choice **D** is wrong because, in this situation, no type of character evidence pertaining to the victim is admissible by the prosecution in its case-in-chief.

33. **A** In a criminal case in which a person is accused of rape, reputation or opinion evidence of the past sexual behavior of the victim is not admissible; FRE 412(a). Choice **A** conforms to this rule. Choice **B** is wrong because the statement is too broad. Past instances of the victim's sexual behavior are admissible only on the issue of whether the accused was or was not the source of semen or the victim's injury; FRE 412(b)(2)(A). In this case, it is conceded that a sexual act occurred between Alan and Betty. Choice **C** is wrong because such evidence, though arguably relevant, is not admissible unless the theory for its relevance is so strong that excluding the evidence would violate the defendant's constitutional right to present a defense. Finally, choice **D** is wrong because the fact that Betty had voluntarily gone into Alan's room does not establish that she consented to the sexual act.

34. **D** Standard rules of relevance apply here because this case does not involve alleged sexual misconduct. Even if it were a criminal case in which a person is accused of rape where evidence of a victim's past sexual behavior is not admissible, evidence that pertains to past relations with persons other than the accused that is offered by the accused on the issue of whether he was the source of semen or the victim's injury is admissible; FRE 412(b)(2)(A). Similarly, in this

civil case, Cindy's sexual behavior with men other than Steve would be admissible, provided these relationships occurred approximately at the time during which she could have become pregnant. Choice **C** is wrong because, as discussed above, past sexual behavior is admissible if it bears on the source of semen. Choice **A** is wrong because it states the applicable legal principle too broadly. Cindy's prior sexual behavior with men other than Steve must encompass the time period during which she could have been impregnated. Finally, choice **B** is wrong because evidence of prior sexual behavior with other men would not be pertinent to whether Cindy consented to the sexual act that produced her child.

35. B Hearsay is a statement, other than one made by the declarant while testifying at the trial or hearing, that is offered to prove the truth of the matter asserted therein; FRE 801(c). Because Terry is testifying as to what Bud told him, Terry's testimony is hearsay. Thus, it is not admissible. Choice **A** is wrong because the testimony is relevant. If the glasses were in perfect condition when shipped, it would tend to prove that Brenda's assertion of minute cracks is erroneous. Choice **C** is wrong because the party-opponent admission is a statement by the other side in the litigation. Here, the attorney for Bill is seeking the testimony of one of his client's employees as to a statement by another of his employees. Thus, the party-opponent exclusion from the hearsay rule is inapplicable. Finally, choice **D** is wrong because Bud's statement to Terry is offered to prove the truth of the matter asserted.

36. C A statement that, by itself, gives rise to legal consequences (sometimes called an "operative fact" or a "verbal act") is not hearsay because it is offered for the fact that it was said, rather than for the truth of what its words assert. The statement in question was offered simply to show that Jack said those words. The legal system, not Jack, is the source of meaning or consequences for those words. Choice **D** is wrong because a dying declaration is one made by a declarant who believes death is imminent. Additionally, a dying declaration must concern the cause or circumstances of death; FRE 804(b)(2). Choice **A** is wrong because, as discussed above, Lou's statement would not constitute hearsay. Finally, choice **B** is wrong because Jack's statement would be relevant, whether or not the executor had contended that Jack was incompetent.

37. A A statement that, by itself, gives rise to legal consequences (sometimes called an "operative fact" or a "verbal act") is not hearsay because it is offered for the fact that it was said, rather than for the truth of the matter asserted therein. Carol's testimony is offered simply to prove that the words were said, not to prove that Mr. Revered is a crook, so her testimony is not hearsay. Choice **B** is wrong because Carol's testimony is not hearsay. Additionally, the "present state of mind" exception to the hearsay rule does not include statements of belief to prove the fact believed; FRE 803(3). Choice **C** is wrong because Miss Gribbins's statement was in the nature of a fact, rather than mere opinion. Finally, choice **D** is wrong because proof of Miss Gribbins's competency is not a precondition to introduction of the testimony about what she said.

38. A Hearsay is a statement, other than one made by the declarant while testifying at the trial or hearing, offered to prove the truth of the matter asserted therein; FRE 801(c). Jane's testimony is not offered to prove the truth of the matter asserted (i.e., that Susan hit Amy). It is relevant in showing Claire's motivation in going to Susan's home. Choice **B** is wrong because Claire's motivation for being at Susan's home is relevant (i.e., it shows that she did not necessarily go to Susan's house for the purpose of attacking her). Choice **C** is wrong because evidence is precluded due to the possibility of prejudicing the jury only if the risk of unfair prejudice substantially outweighs the probative value of the evidence. Finally, choice **D** is wrong because Jane's testimony is, for the reasons described above, not hearsay.

39. B A statement that is relevant because of its effect on the hearer, regardless of whether the statement is true, is not hearsay because it is offered for the fact that it was said, rather than for the truth of the matter asserted therein. Conrad's testimony is not hearsay because it is not offered to prove the truth of the matter asserted (i.e., that MegaBank actually had a large amount of money in its vault on Friday). Rather, the testimony sought to show that Peter had a motivation to rob MegaBank on that day. Choice **A** is wrong because the evidence is admissible whether or not Donald is "unavailable." Choice **C** is wrong because Conrad's testimony is not hearsay. Finally, choice **D** is wrong because, as explained above, Conrad's testimony is relevant to whether Peter robbed MegaBank.

40. D In federal court and in most states, control of the spousal testimonial privilege is placed in the hands of the testifying spouse. The marital communications privilege does not bar Winona's testimony because it protects only communications (i.e., oral or written statements, or nonverbal assertions). It ordinarily does not cover testimony about physical appearances. Choice **A** is wrong because assertion of the testimonial privilege is controlled by the testifying spouse. Choice **B** is wrong because Winona is not testifying as to a communication made by Harry. Finally, choice **C** is also wrong because Winona is not testifying as to a communication.

41. **D** Where an out-of-court declarant testifies at the trial and is subject to cross-examination concerning the statement, and the statement is consistent with his testimony and offered to rebut an assertion of improper influence, the statement is not hearsay if the out-of-court statement was made before the declarant had a motive to lie; FRE 801(d)(1). Thus, Morgan's testimony about what Bob told him is not hearsay. Bob made his statement before he and Jack became business partners. Morgan's testimony both rehabilitates Bob and can be used as substantive evidence (because it helps establish that Tina was the party at fault). Choice **C** is wrong because Morgan's testimony can be used as substantive evidence, in addition to mere rehabilitation. Choice **A** is wrong because the testimony, as discussed above, is not excluded by the hearsay rule. Finally, choice **B** is wrong because the testimony is a proper means of rehabilitation.

42. **B** Evidence is relevant if it has a tendency to make the existence of any fact of consequence more or less probable; FRE 401. Vic's testimony tends to prove that Dan was acting negligently on the occasion in question. Choice **A** is wrong because under the FRE one may always impeach his witness (including situations where the party was surprised by his witness's testimony); FRE 607. Choice **D** is wrong because a party is ***not*** bound by the testimony of his witness. Finally, choice **C** is wrong because a party may impeach his own witness.

43. **D** Although contradiction of prior testimony is ordinarily a proper means of impeachment, it cannot be achieved by extrinsic evidence where it pertains to a collateral matter (i.e., one which is not related to the substantive issues of the litigation). In this instance, Talker is being contradicted over the statement that he has never been drunk in his life. Because whether Talker was intoxicated two years ago does not pertain to the issues of the case, a court would probably rule that Friend's testimony (which would constitute extrinsic evidence) is inadmissible. Choice **C** is wrong because it wrongly states the law. A witness can be impeached ***intrinsically*** by specific acts of

misconduct that bear on his truthfulness or veracity; FRE 608(b). Additionally, a witness may ordinarily be impeached extrinsically with respect to prior criminal convictions; FRE 609(a). A witness may be impeached intrinsically (i.e., out of his own mouth) with respect to specific, prior acts bearing on his truthfulness or veracity. Choice **A** is wrong because Friend's impeaching testimony does **not** pertain to Talker's recollection of a recent event. Finally, choice **B** is wrong because the impeachment involved in this instance does not establish whether Talker was being truthful about his condition at the time of the accident.

44. C A witness may be impeached by evidence of his reputation or character for truthfulness or veracity, even if the evidence is an opinion; FRE 608(a). Zemo is apparently about to testify that Observer's reputation for veracity in his community is poor. Because this is a proper ground for impeachment, the question was proper. Choice **D** is wrong because it is not necessary that an impeaching witness personally know the party about whom he is testifying (it is only necessary that the witness know of that person's reputation in the community). Choice **A** is wrong because Observer's veracity cannot be a collateral issue. Finally, choice **B** is wrong because a witness's reputation for lack of truthfulness or veracity is among the kinds of proof permitted to show that a witness's testimony may not be truthful.

45. B Evidence is relevant if it has a tendency to make the existence of any fact of consequence more or less probable; FRE 401. Conduct not intended as an assertion is not hearsay under the FRE; 801(a)(2). Assuming that the persons who were on the bus entered the hospital as a consequence of the accident, the doctor's testimony would be relevant in showing that Pat's neck injury was also caused by the collision. Additionally, there is no hearsay problem because the statements made by the other passengers about their neck pains would be admissible under the "then existing physical condition" or "medical diagnosis or treatment" exceptions to the hearsay rule; FRE 803(3) and (4), respectively. Choice **A** is wrong because the doctor's testimony does not pertain to a medical matter. He is testifying only as to the fact that three persons requested medical assistance for back pains at City Hospital. Choice **D** is wrong because the Original Writing Rule is not applicable in this instance (i.e., Pat is not attempting to introduce testimony about the contents of a document). Finally, choice **C** is wrong because, as explained above, the statements of the three persons who were admitted to the hospital come within exceptions to the hearsay rule; FRE 803(3) and (4).

46. **A** A prior inconsistent statement of a witness, who is subject to cross-examination, is not hearsay, if that statement was (1) made under oath; and (2) made at a prior trial, hearing, or other proceeding, or in a deposition; FRE 801(d)(1). Because Beth's prior inconsistent testimony was made in a deposition (which is made under oath), it is not hearsay. It is admissible as substantive evidence against Samantha (i.e., the jury may consider this evidence in determining if Tim has satisfied his burden of proof). Choice **B** is wrong because Beth's deposition testimony can be used as substantive evidence. Choice **C** is wrong because admissibility of the deposition testimony is not dependent on whether Samantha's attorney was present and had the opportunity to question Beth. Finally, choice **D** is wrong because, as discussed above, Beth's deposition testimony is not hearsay.

47. **A** If called to the attention of an expert witness on cross-examination, statements contained in a published treatise, on the subject of history, medicine, or other science or art, established as a reliable authority by the testimony or admission of the witness are not excluded by the hearsay rule. If admitted, the statements may be read into evidence (but may not be received as exhibits); FRE 803(18). Because Dr. Frank was acknowledged as an expert by Dr. Evans, the portion of the former's book pertaining to sterility occasioned by toxic emissions may be read into evidence. Choice **B** is wrong because the portion of Dr. Frank's book read into evidence can be considered for substantive (as well as impeachment) purposes. Choice **C** is wrong because an exclusion from the hearsay rule exists in this situation. Finally, choice **D** is wrong because the portion of Dr. Frank's book described above may be read into evidence, whether or not he is available to testify.

48. **A** Evidence of a final judgment entered after a trial or on a plea of guilty, adjudging a person guilty of a crime punishable by death or imprisonment in excess of one year, to prove any fact essential to sustain a judgment, is not excluded by the hearsay rule; FRE 803(22). Because the crime in question was punishable by a term of up to five years, Justin's prior guilty plea is admissible to prove negligence with respect to his collision with William. Choice **B** is wrong because there is no express requirement that a guilty plea be made under

oath to constitute an exclusion from the hearsay rule. Choice **C** is wrong because proper authentication of the guilty plea is not a basis for upholding the objection to its admissibility. Finally, choice **D** is wrong because, as explained above, the guilty plea in this situation constitutes an exclusion from the hearsay rule.

49. **B** Evidence of a final judgment, entered after a trial, adjudging a person guilty of a crime punishable by death or imprisonment in excess of one year, which is offered to prove an essential fact in a subsequent proceeding, is covered by an exception to the hearsay rule. However, this exception does **not** apply when such evidence is "offered by the government, in a criminal prosecution for purposes other than impeachment, judgments against persons other than the accused"; FRE 803(22). Because the prosecution is offering Mel's conviction of conspiracy for other than impeachment purposes, the evidence is excluded by the hearsay rule. Choice **A** is wrong because the judgment against Mel for conspiracy to rob the Abco Bank with Duane would arguably make it "more probable" that Duane had committed the crime for which he has been charged; FRE 401. Choice **C** is wrong because there is no general rule that prior criminal convictions constitute an exception to the hearsay rule (the conviction must ordinarily involve a crime punishable by death or more than one year in prison). Finally, choice **D** is wrong because the prior criminal conviction is being offered by the prosecution during its case-in-chief (not as impeachment).

50. **C** A statement that was, at the time of its making, so contrary to the declarant's pecuniary interest that a reasonable man in his position would not have made the statement, unless he believed it to be true, is (assuming the declarant is unavailable as a witness) not excluded by the hearsay rule; FRE 804(b)(3). Because Alvin has died and admitted owing Jim $1,000, his statement to Carl is admissible. (Additionally, it might also constitute an admission because the executor probably "stands in the shoes" of Alvin.) Choice **B** is wrong because the dying declaration exception requires that the statement pertain to the cause or circumstances of the declarant's death. Choice **D** is wrong because the statement in question was being introduced as evidence of the truth of the declarant's belief, not just to show that the declarant believed it. Finally, choice **A** is wrong because, as discussed above, Alvin's statement is within the coverage of an exclusion from the hearsay rule.

51. A Out-of-court statements made by an unavailable declarant that would tend to subject him to civil or criminal liability are excluded from the hearsay rule; FRE 804(b)(3). Because Tim's statement exposed himself to criminal liability and he is no longer available (he has relocated to India), his statement to Jeff is not excluded by the hearsay rule. Choice **B** is wrong because Tim is not being sued by Mary. Thus, he is not a party to this action. Choice **C** is wrong because the statement is not inadmissible simply due to a lack of "direct proof." There is no such prerequisite. Finally, choice **D** is wrong because, as discussed above, Tim's comment to Jeff is a "statement against interest" and is therefore not excluded by the hearsay rule.

52. D Ben's testimony contains one level of hearsay: the out-of-court words attributed to Kerry. Those words express two mental states (love and hatred) and are therefore within the coverage of the hearsay exception for statements of a then-existing mental condition. The testimony is relevant because it supports a theory that Kerry had a motive to murder Margaret. Choice **A** is wrong because this privilege must be asserted by either Kerry or Ben. The latter apparently has chosen not to assert the privilege, and the former is not at the trial. Choice **B** is wrong because the testimony contains only one level of hearsay (the out-of-court words of Kerry). Choice **C** is wrong because Kerry is not a party, and therefore her words fail to satisfy the definition of admission: a party's statement introduced against that party.

53. B "Testimony given at another hearing . . . or a different proceeding, by an unavailable declarant, is not excluded by the hearsay rule, if the party against whom the testimony is now offered, or, in a civil action . . . , a predecessor in interest, had an opportunity and similar motive to develop the testimony by direct, cross, or redirect examination"; FRE 804(b)(1). Jane would be considered a predecessor in interest of Megan because she had a like motive to develop the same testimony about the same material facts. Therefore the "former testimony" exclusion from the hearsay rule applies and the evidence is admissible. Choice **A** is wrong because the evidence falls under the "former testimony" exclusion from the hearsay rule. Choice **C** is wrong because the fact that Dr. Peters's transcript was authenticated does not overcome a hearsay objection. Finally, choice **D** is wrong because the fact that Dr. Peters was an expert is irrelevant to the hearsay problem.

54. A If a witness is not testifying as an expert, his testimony in the form of opinion or inference is limited to those opinions or inferences that are (1) rationally based on his perception; and (2) helpful to a clear understanding of his testimony or the determination of a fact in issue; FRE 701. Martin's testimony that Trish was "clearly speeding" is certainly helpful to a determination of who was at fault. Choice **B** is wrong because Trish's nonverbal conduct was not intended as an assertion and is therefore not hearsay; FRE 801(a)-(c). Choice **C** is wrong because layperson opinion is admissible in many circumstances, as explained above. Finally, choice **D** is wrong because opinion testimony can be admitted whether or not there is an independent means of verifying it.

55. A Facts or data in a particular case on which an expert bases an opinion may be those perceived by, or made known to, him at or before the hearing. If such facts are of the type reasonably relied on by experts in that particular field in forming opinions, the facts or data need not be admissible in evidence; FRE 703. Because Dr. Martin presumably qualifies as an expert with respect to the extent of Angie's injuries, his opinion can be based on the lab technician's evaluation of the X-rays, if this is the type of information reasonably relied on by experts in the field. Choice **B** is wrong because there is no requirement that Dr. Martin must have personally examined Angie to render an opinion with respect to the permanency of her injuries. Choice **C** is wrong because, as described above, an expert may render an opinion on facts or data not otherwise admissible in evidence. Finally, choice **D** is wrong because, as discussed above, the applicable FRE rule permits Dr. Martin's opinion to be based on the lab technician's analysis of Angie's X-rays.

56. C The credibility of a witness may be attacked by any party, including the one calling him; FRE 607. Extrinsic evidence of a prior inconsistent statement by a witness is not admissible, unless (1) he is afforded an opportunity to explain or deny the same; and (2) the opposing party is afforded an opportunity to interrogate him thereon, or, the interests of justice otherwise require; FRE 613(b). Assuming Jim was given the opportunity to explain his statement to Jason and was available for redirect examination (i.e., had not left the courtroom), Jason's testimony is admissible. Choice **D** is wrong because, as explained above, William must be available for redirect examination pursuant to FRE 613(b). Choice **A** is wrong because impeachment testimony is not offered to prove the truth of the matter asserted therein. It is being introduced into evidence only to impugn a witness's credibility. Finally, choice **B** is wrong because under the FRE a party may impeach his own witness.

57. **B** The credibility of a witness may be attacked by opinion or reputation evidence, but the evidence must refer to his character for truthfulness or untruthfulness; FRE 608(a). Because evidence that Tom had a reputation for having an "aggressive, impetuous nature" does not pertain to credibility, the testimony is not admissible. Choice **A** is wrong because a specific hearsay exception applies to statements about reputation. Choice **C** is wrong because there is no requirement that a character witness initially state that he believes that he is personally familiar with the former witness's character. Finally, choice **D** is wrong because having an "aggressive, impetuous nature" probably does not impair a witness's credibility.

58. **B** Questions leading to impeachment must have a tendency to discredit the witness's credibility. The fact that a witness is an alcoholic arguably would not tend to indicate that he would have a tendency to lie on the witness stand. Choice **A** is wrong because bias in favor of the party for whom the witness is testifying is a proper basis for impeachment. Choice **C** is wrong because prior misconduct (not resulting in a criminal conviction) is a proper ground of intrinsic impeachment where it pertains to truthfulness or veracity. Deliberately failing to report income would show a tendency to be untruthful and therefore would be a proper ground for intrinsic impeachment. Finally, choice **D** is wrong because one may be impeached by prior criminal convictions that involve dishonesty or false statements; FRE 609.

59. **D** A person may claim the privilege against self-incrimination whenever there is a reasonable possibility that her testimony will incriminate her. Bystander is entitled to remain silent if there is a reasonable possibility that her answer could incriminate her. Choices **C** and **B** are wrong because it is not necessary that there be (1) a preponderance of evidence, or (2) clear and convincing evidence that the testimony will be self-incriminating to assert the Fifth Amendment. Finally, choice **A** is wrong because it is not necessary that the judge be convinced; he must believe only that there is a reasonable possibility that the testimony by the witness will incriminate her.

60. **A** An expert may base his opinion on information gained about the case by listening to other witnesses who testify before he does. This is usually done by use of a hypothetical question: the questioner asks

the expert to assume that the prior testimony is true and then to give an inference or opinion. Because Dr. Jones, an expert in this area, was asked to give his opinion based on listening to the prior testimony of Phillips and to assume that the testimony was true, his opinion is admissible. Choice **B** is wrong because the jury determines issues of credibility. Choice **D** is wrong because an expert's testimony may be based on facts or data perceived by her even as a result of lay testimony at the trial. Finally, choice **C** is wrong because a hypothetical question may be based on prior testimony at the trial.

61. **B** The facts or data on which an expert bases an opinion may be those perceived or made known to her at or before the hearing. If of a type reasonably relied on by experts in that particular field in forming an opinion, the facts or data on which an expert bases her opinion need not have been admitted into evidence; FRE 703. Because the reports in question are (presumably) reasonably relied on in medical practice, Dr. Black could render an opinion that the plaintiff's injuries were permanent. Choice **A** is wrong because, although the laboratory reports probably come within the "business records" exception to the hearsay rule, these items are not themselves being offered as evidence. Choice **C** is wrong because there is no requirement that an expert be qualified to conduct the tests on which she is basing her opinion. Finally, choice **D** is wrong because there is no requirement that an expert's opinions be based on tests that were done under her supervision. The data considered must only be of the type that is reasonably relied on by experts in that field in forming their opinions.

62. **D** Impeachment by contradiction as to a collateral matter may ordinarily not be accomplished by extrinsic evidence. It can be achieved only by intrinsic evidence—statements made from the witness's own mouth while on the stand. Because the question of why (not if) Walter was standing on Second and Maple is a collateral matter, contradicting Walter on this point cannot be accomplished by extrinsic evidence (i.e., calling another witness to dispute his testimony). Choice **C** is wrong because Shirley's testimony has nothing to do with substantive proof of fault. The only question presented by this factual pattern is whether her testimony constitutes a proper mode of impeachment. Choice **A** is wrong because, even though Shirley's testimony impeaches Walter's veracity, it is inadmissible because it pertains to a collateral matter. Finally, choice **B** is wrong because, despite arguably undermining Walter's memory, for the reasons described above, the testimony is not admissible.

63. **C** A witness's personal partiality or bias constitutes a proper basis for impeachment. The fact that Desmond worked for Peggy suggests he would be partial to her. Additionally, the possibility that he hated attorneys is also a proper question because Daniel is a member of that group. Presumably, Daniel's attorney had a good-faith basis for the second question. (It might be noted that Peggy's attorney could have objected to this inquiry on the ground that it was a compound question because Daniel's attorney, in effect, asked two questions.) Choice **D** is wrong because a witness's state of mind is not per se a proper basis for impeachment. Choice **A** is wrong because leading questions are ordinarily permissible on cross-examination. Finally, choice **B** is wrong because the potential for prejudicing the jury is not outweighed by Daniel's attorney's right to cross-examine Desmond.

64. **B** Impeachment with respect to prior bad acts not resulting in a conviction ordinarily cannot be accomplished by extrinsic evidence. Because Dahlia's testimony constitutes extrinsic evidence, the objection should be sustained. Choice **A** is wrong because the impeachment in this situation goes to improper conduct that has not resulted in a conviction and is sought to be accomplished by extrinsic evidence—Dahlia's testimony. Choice **C** is wrong because Clara's veracity is a proper basis for impeachment. Finally, choice **D** is wrong because, although the prior negative act in question pertains to veracity, it cannot be proven by extrinsic evidence in this situation.

65. **A** Where a witness testifies with respect to the character for truthfulness of someone else who has testified, that character witness may be cross-examined with respect to specific instances of conduct by the person whose character he or she has testified about, so long as the conduct pertains to truthfulness or untruthfulness; FRE 608(b). Because Jeanine testified as to Winifred's lack of trustworthiness, Olivia's attorney had the right to ask her if she was aware that Winifred had recently returned a lost wallet (with cash inside of it) to the police. Choice **B** is wrong because it does not constitute a basis for determining whether Jeanine could be asked about Winifred's recent act of exceptional honesty. Choice **C** is wrong because this type of rehabilitation is expressly authorized by the FRE. Finally, choice **D** is wrong because, although the jury can still decide whether to believe Jeanine, the rehabilitation described in this situation is expressly authorized by the FRE.

66. **B** A court is entitled to exercise reasonable control over the mode and order of interrogating witnesses and the presentation of evidence; FRE 611. Ordinarily, however, a court will not permit evidence that is irrelevant to the issues. Once the evidence is in, however, the court may permit the other side to show that the evidence is not true to discredit the party offering the evidence. Choice **D** is wrong because the determination whether to permit Don to impeach Peter by extrinsic evidence (i.e., Don's testimony) is discretionary with the court. Choice **A** is wrong because it was not necessary for Don to object to Peter's testimony to preserve the right to impeach, and the court had discretion not to permit Don to testify further on a collateral issue. Choice **C** is wrong because Don did not have to object.

67. **A** For purposes of establishing its content, execution, and delivery, recitals contained in a deed that has been recorded in a public office pursuant to a statute authorizing such recordation are admissible as an exception to the hearsay rule; FRE 803(14), (15). Although the statement of Paula's relationship is hearsay, because it comes contained in the deed, it is hearsay within this exception. Choice **B** is wrong because the "past recollection recorded" exception to the hearsay rule is applicable only where a witness testifies that she has no present recollection about a writing made or adopted by her when the document was fresh in her mind. Choice **C** is wrong because the testimony comes within an exception to the hearsay rule that is present in this instance. Finally, choice **D** is wrong because authenticated duplicates of a deed are ordinarily admissible in place of the original; FRE 1003.

68. **A** Out-of-court statements pertaining to a startling event, made by a declarant while under the stress of the excitement caused by the event, are admissible as an exception to the hearsay rule; FRE 803(2). The imminent collision between Driver's car and Walker would constitute a "startling" situation, and Paul's exclamation would be an "excited utterance." Choice **C** is wrong because the "excited utterance" exception to the hearsay rule does not require that the declarant be unavailable as a witness. Choice **D** is wrong because the startling event was the imminent collision with Walker. The fact that the statement preceded the accident strengthens the sense of excitement that must have prompted Paul. Choice **B** is wrong because Ralph's statement was not a declaration against his interest, which must involve a risk to the speaker's pecuniary, proprietary, or penal interests; FRE 804(b)(3). The statement can be admitted only if the

declarant is unavailable. The facts fail to indicate any reason why Driver's negligent operation of his car would result in liability to Ralph.

69. **B** The Federal Rules treat admissions as nonhearsay. Out-of-court statements made by another in the presence of a party-opponent, who fails to object to or deny the statements, are deemed to be adopted as admissions by the party-opponent and do not constitute hearsay; FRE 801(d)(2)(B). Driver's failure to object to or deny Paul's statement that Walker was hit while in the crosswalk would probably constitute an adoptive admission. Paul's statement, in effect, would be attributed to Driver. Under the FRE, admissions of a party-opponent are not hearsay. Choice **A** is wrong because Driver's silence would not, in itself, make Paul his agent. Choice **C** is wrong because adoptive admissions are treated in the same way as admissions of a party; they are not hearsay. Finally, choice **D** is wrong because there is no necessity that a party-opponent be given an opportunity to admit or deny a statement before he may be deemed to have adopted or admitted it.

70. **A** Out-of-court statements made by a declarant pertaining to his contemporaneous state of mind, physical condition, or pain are admissible as an exception to the hearsay rule; FRE 803(3). Walker's statements described a simultaneous physical sensation or condition. Joe's testimony about Walker's statement would be admissible as an exception to the hearsay rule. Choice **B** is wrong because Walker's statement to Joe is admissible only to show how the elbow felt at the time the statement was made, which does not show whether or not the injury was permanent. Choice **D** is wrong because Walker's description of the severe pain that he is experiencing does *not* require confirmation by expert testimony. Finally, choice **C** is wrong because, although Joe's testimony is hearsay, it comes within an exception to the hearsay rule.

71. **D** An oral or written statement, made to the witness out-of-court that is offered into evidence at trial to prove the truth of the statement, is hearsay. Hearsay evidence is inadmissible unless some exception to the hearsay rule exists; FRE 801(c). Because Sheriff is testifying as to what Passerby stated to him, his statement is not admissible unless some exception to the hearsay rule exists. Choice **C** is wrong because Sheriff is not trying to prove the contents of a document. Choice **A** is wrong because Passerby was not "under the stress of excitement" caused by the accident (Passerby made his statement two hours

after the accident). Finally, choice **B** is wrong because the statement involved was made by Passerby, who did not record his recollection. Sheriff was not recording his own recollection but Passerby's.

72. **C** Hearsay evidence is inadmissible unless some exception to the hearsay rule exists; FRE 801(c). Because Sheriff is testifying as to what Ralph told him out-of-court, the latter's statement is hearsay. It therefore would be inadmissible unless some exception to the hearsay rule exists. Choice **D** is wrong because Ralph's remark that each of the persons in Driver's car had "downed" at least four cans of beer is a statement of fact, rather than opinion. Choice **A** is wrong because Ralph is not a party to the lawsuit. Finally, choice **B** is wrong because there is no relationship between Ralph and Driver that would make Ralph liable for Driver's operation of the vehicle; Ralph's statement would not appear to be against his pecuniary, proprietary, or penal interests. Further, Ralph is available at trial, which would preclude application of the "statement against interest" exception.

73. **A** A witness's recollection of something about which he or she had prior personal knowledge may be refreshed by virtually any means (including writings). Where a witness's memory is refreshed by a writing, the opposing party is entitled to introduce into evidence those portions of the writing that relate to the witness's testimony; FRE 612. Because Walker's attorney is merely attempting to refresh Ralph's recollection, the judge should rule that Ralph may be shown the letter that he wrote to his sister. Choice **B** is wrong because the doctrine of past recollection recorded is *not* applicable until the witness testifies that he has no present recollection with respect to the statements made in the writing. Walker's attorney is not attempting to prove the contents of the letter but to refresh Ralph's recollection about some details of the accident. Choice **C** is wrong because there is no requirement that opposing counsel must be shown the "refreshing" writing prior to the time it is used. Finally, choice **D** is wrong because there is no requirement that an item that refreshes a witness's memory (if, in fact, Ralph's letter to his sister had this effect) must be read into evidence. If the doctrine of past recollection recorded were made applicable, Walker's attorney would *then* be entitled to have the letter read into evidence.

74. **B** Under the Original Writing Rule, testimony about the contents of a writing is allowed only if the proponent of the testimony introduces the original document or a copy, or has an acceptable excuse for failure to produce the original or copy; FRE 1002. Because Bellman is

testifying as to the contents of a writing (his contract with Owner), he would be required to introduce the original agreement, a copy, or an excuse before his testimony would be allowed. Choice **C** is wrong because the parol evidence rule applies when an effort is made to introduce evidence pertaining to prior or contemporaneous understandings that vary or modify the terms of an integrated writing. In this instance, Bellman is seeking only to establish the existence of a contract with Owner (not to modify or vary it). Choice **A** is wrong because there is a written contract as required by the Statute of Frauds, which is not violated. Finally, choice **D** is wrong because the testimony would be relevant (tend to prove or disprove a fact or consequence) because Waiter (as Owner's assignee) would be bound by the agreement to retain Bellman for ten years.

75. **A** Preliminary questions concerning the admissibility of evidence are ordinarily determined by the court. However, where the relevancy of evidence depends on the proof of a fact, the court will admit it subject to the introduction of evidence sufficient to support a finding of that fact; FRE 104(a) and (b). The contract is relevant only if the signature is authentic. Absent such signature, the document would not be relevant. Thus, the court could admit the contract subject to the introduction of adequate evidence by the plaintiff that the signature was authentic. Choice **D** is wrong because the fact finder (rather than the judge) would determine whether the signature is genuine (assuming, of course, sufficient evidence to permit this conclusion is introduced). Choice **C** is wrong because the judge is not obliged to conclude that the signature is genuine as a matter of law. Rather, the fact finder would decide by a preponderance of the evidence, whether the signature was genuine. Finally, choice **B** is wrong because the authenticity of a signature is not determined by the trial judge.

76. **C** One who consults an attorney for the purpose of obtaining professional assistance is privileged to refuse to disclose, and to prevent the attorney (and his essential personnel) from disclosing, communications made for the purpose of facilitating such services (whether or not the attorney is actually retained). Because Lyons approached Lawyer for the purpose of obtaining his services, the fact that Lawyer declined to represent Lyons is irrelevant and does not destroy the latter's attorney-client privilege. Choice **A** is wrong because, as long as Lawyer was a party to statements by Lyons, the attorney-client privilege is applicable. Choice **B** is wrong because Lyons is privileged

to prevent Lawyer from disclosing his admission that he committed the crime for which he is charged. A defendant must be permitted to disclose his involvement in a crime to enable the attorney to represent him adequately and to prepare his plea. (Disclosures with respect to *prospective* illegal conduct are, however, *not* within the attorney-client privilege.) Finally, choice **D** is wrong because Lawyer's testimony with respect to Lyons's statement, if admissible, would have been covered by the party-opponent exclusion to the hearsay rule; FRE 801(d)(2)(A).

77. **A** A witness may be impeached intrinsically or *extrinsically* by proving an outstanding conviction for a crime that involves dishonesty or false statements; FRE 609(a)(2). Prior convictions for perjury are a proper means of impeachment and may be proven by extrinsic evidence (i.e., a properly authenticated copy of the court record of the conviction). Choice **D** is wrong because impeachment through specific instances of misconduct relating to perjury *that have resulted in a conviction* may be shown by extrinsic evidence. Choice **B** is wrong because it states the wrong reason for admitting the testimony. A conviction for perjury does not tend to prove anything; it only provides a basis for disbelieving the witness's credibility. Finally, choice **C** is wrong because public records are ordinarily admissible in lieu of the original writing (FRE 1003); and they are covered by an exception to the hearsay rule; FRE 803(8).

78. **C** Under the parol evidence rule, where the parties intended a writing to be the final and complete expression of their contract, the document is a total integration, and evidence of any prior or contemporaneous oral or written understandings that vary, contradict, or add to the terms of the document is not admissible. Because the agreement in question was made *after* the written contract, the parol evidence rule would not be applicable. Choice **D** is wrong because the fact that a particular subject was not dealt with in the written agreement would *not* preclude subsequent modification of the original contract. Finally, choices **A** and **B** are wrong because the parol evidence rule does not apply to agreements made *subsequent* to the integration; subsequent agreements may vary the original and may add to it.

79. **A** Under the parol evidence rule, if the parties intended a writing to be the final and complete expression of their understandings with respect to those items recited (but not their entire agreement), the document is a partial integration, and evidence of any prior or

contemporaneous oral or written understandings that do not contradict the terms of such writing is admissible. If the court can be
persuaded that the writing was merely a partial (as opposed to a
total) integration, evidence of collateral agreements that does not
contradict the writing is ordinarily admissible. Because the "overtime" provision would not necessarily conflict with the term calling
for a fixed number of hours and for regular monthly installments,
evidence of the collateral agreement would probably be admissible.
Choice **B** is wrong because prior negotiations are not ordinarily
admissible unless there has not been a total integration. Choice **C**
is wrong because, although parol evidence is ordinarily admissible
to show an oral condition precedent to the existence of a contract,
ABC is not seeking to prove a condition precedent to the existence
of the written agreement. Finally, choice **D** is wrong because there is
no suggestion of fraud in the facts or by the parties.

80. **C** Specific instances of misconduct (other than those resulting in the
conviction of a crime) by a witness other than the defendant for the
purpose of impeaching the witness may **not** be proved by extrinsic
evidence; FRE 608(b). Because Joanna's cheating at the card game
has not apparently resulted in a criminal conviction, she may **not** be
impeached by extrinsic evidence (i.e., by means other than out of her
own mouth). Testimony by Bill is inadmissible. Choice **D** is wrong
because it is irrelevant whether gambling is a federal crime. Bill's testimony is inadmissible because Joanna's conduct has not resulted in
a conviction. Choice **A** is wrong because, although the card-cheating
incident might impugn Joanna's credibility, the evidence is nevertheless inadmissible. Finally, choice **B** is wrong because the fact that
Joanna had given her opinion of Alfred's character did **not** make
her misconduct admissible because the conduct did not result in
conviction.

81. **A** A statement is not hearsay (1) if the declarant testifies at the trial
or hearing; (2) he is subject to cross-examination concerning the
statement; and (3) the statement is one of identification of a person
made after perceiving him; FRE 801(d)(1)(C). Because Jones passed
away prior to John's trial, he obviously was not available to testify.
Melvin's testimony is hearsay and therefore inadmissible. Choice **B**
is wrong because Jones's identification of John was a statement of
fact, rather than opinion (i.e., John was the person who had attacked
him). Choice **C** is wrong because the fact that a witness is unavailable does not make his out-of-court statement admissible. Finally,

choice **D** is wrong because, although Jones's statement is probative of John's motive, it is nevertheless hearsay.

82. **C** A statement is not hearsay if (1) declarant testifies at the trial or hearing; (2) the statement is the subject of cross-examination; and (3) the statement is inconsistent with the testimony and was given under oath at a trial, hearing, or other proceeding, or in a deposition; FRE 801(d)(1)(A). However, because the facts indicate that Sue's statement was simply delivered to the prosecution (i.e., it was **not** made under oath at a prior proceeding or deposition), it is hearsay and may not be admitted as substantive evidence. It is outside the coverage of the hearsay exception for statements against penal interest because that exception applies only when the declarant is unavailable at trial. Choices **B** and **D** are wrong because Sue's statement is hearsay and not admissible as substantive evidence. However, her statement, inconsistent with her testimony at trial, may be used to impeach her. Choice **A** is wrong because Sue's statement is hearsay, hence it is admissible only for impeachment. The statement is not being introduced to prove the truth of its contents. It is being used to discredit Sue's credibility by showing that, at a different time, she made conflicting statements. It should be noted that, under the FRE, no foundation need be laid prior to impeaching a witness via a prior inconsistent statement. It is necessary only that the witness be afforded an opportunity to explain or deny the prior inconsistent statement.

83. **B** An oral or written statement, other than one made by a declarant while testifying at the trial or hearing, which is offered into evidence at trial to prove the truth of the contents, is hearsay. Hearsay evidence is inadmissible unless some exception to the hearsay rule exists; FRE 801(c)-(d). The public records exception does not apply because this evidence is offered against the defendant in a criminal case; FRE 803(8). Officer Bones's report is therefore hearsay (it is an out-of-court written statement by Officer Bones describing Josephina's speech at the time of the arrest). The fact that Officer Smith can authenticate the report because of his familiarity with Bones's signature does not cure the hearsay objection. Choice **C** is wrong because proper authentication of Bones's report does not cure the hearsay problem. Choice **D** is wrong because the fact that Officer Bones is unavailable does not constitute a reason for overcoming the hearsay objection. Finally, choice **A** is wrong because it states the wrong reason for excluding the report: Bones's statement

that Josephina's speech was slurred is probably a statement of fact, rather than opinion, because it describes an objective symptom of Josephina's condition.

84. **B** A statement is not hearsay if offered against a party and it is his own statement; FRE 801(d)(2)(A). Although Warren is testifying as to what the defendant said out-of-court, the statement is not hearsay because it was made by the party against whom the evidence is offered. Choice **A** is wrong because the defendant's statement is against his penal interest, but the defendant is available to testify. Choice **D** is wrong because an inference may be drawn that a party who attempts to induce false testimony was culpable with respect to the incident in question. Finally, choice **C** is wrong because the defendant's statement is *not* hearsay.

85. **C** Evidence of a person's character is *not* admissible in a civil lawsuit for the purpose of proving that his actions on a particular occasion were consistent with his reputation; FRE 404(a). Because this is a civil action, Driver cannot introduce evidence of his reputation for being a safe and prudent driver. Choice **D** is wrong because character evidence is admissible in civil litigation where a person's character is directly in issue (e.g., in a negligent entrustment case or defamation action). Choice **A** is wrong because evidence of one's reputation to prove conduct in conformity therewith on a particular occasion is inadmissible in a civil lawsuit. Finally, choice **B** is wrong because the character evidence is inadmissible whether or not a foundation had been laid by the testifying witness.

86. **B** Under the parol evidence rule, where the parties intended a writing to be the final and complete expression of their contract, the document is a total integration, and evidence of any prior or contemporaneous oral or written understanding that varies, contradicts, or adds to the terms of the writing is not admissible. The "most effective argument" of HDS is that the writing was not intended by the parties to be the complete expression of their agreement. If this argument prevailed, the memorandum would not preclude evidence of additional, consistent terms. Choice **A** is wrong because, although stating a valid rule of law, the understanding that CP desires to introduce does *not* appear to be necessary in interpreting any of the provisions of the writing. Choice **C** is wrong because detrimental reliance does *not* preclude application of the parol evidence rule. Finally, choice **D** is wrong because it would be inconsistent with HDS's position (HDS would argue that the memorandum was a partial integration,

a finding that would permit evidence of additional terms agreed on orally).

87. **A** Evidence of a person's prior habitual conduct is relevant to prove that his conduct on a particular occasion was in conformity with his habits; FRE 406. Because Dever "always" came around that *particular* corner at an excessive rate of speed, his conduct probably rises to the level of a "habit." Thus, the evidence is admissible to prove that Dever acted in conformity with his habit (a habit is a person's regular response to a particular type of situation) on the occasion in question. A witness who is not an expert may render an opinion (i.e., that Dever's driving exceeded the speed limit) where it is (1) rationally based on his perception; and (2) helpful to the determination of a fact in issue; FRE 701. Choice **B** is wrong because (1) Dever's conduct is not hearsay because it was *not* intended as an assertion; FRE 801(a)(2). Choice **D** is wrong because James's statement is *not* character evidence (rather it describes particular acts of the defendant on earlier occasions). Finally, choice **C** is wrong because, as described above, the evidence is neither hearsay nor inadmissible opinion. Although prior conduct to prove the same conduct on a later occasion is ordinarily *not* admissible, evidence of conduct conforming to a habit is admissible; FRE 404(b) and 406.

88. **A** A statement is not hearsay and may be admitted as substantive evidence if (1) the declarant testifies at the trial or hearing; (2) the declarant is subject to cross-examination; and (3) the statement is inconsistent with his testimony and was given under oath at a trial, hearing, other proceeding, or in a deposition; FRE 801(d)(1)(A). Prior inconsistent statements of the witness are always a proper means of impeachment whether or not hearsay. Choice **B** is wrong because the report is double hearsay (the investigator is stating what Malcolm said). There is no indication that Malcolm's statement to the investigator for the insurance company was made under oath at a trial, at a proceeding, or in a deposition. Thus, it is hearsay and not admissible as substantive evidence. The investigator's statement might come within the "business records" exception to the hearsay rule, if it is deemed to be trustworthy. However, because *all* levels of hearsay within a statement must qualify as exceptions, the report is inadmissible. Choice **C** is wrong because, although the written report of the investigator is hearsay, it is nevertheless admissible for the purpose of impeachment. In that context, the evidence is being offered to discredit the witness, rather than for the purpose

of proving whether the prior statement was true or not. Choice **D** is wrong because it is not necessary that a witness first be asked to explain a prior inconsistent statement. Extrinsic evidence of a prior inconsistent statement is admissible if the witness is afforded an opportunity (before or after his testimony) to explain or deny the statement; FRE 613(b). Because Malcolm was on the stand, he would have an opportunity to explain or deny the statement purportedly given to the insurance company's investigator.

89. **A** Statements are not hearsay if (1) the declarant testifies at the trial or hearing; (2) the declarant is subject to cross-examination concerning the statement; (3) the statement is consistent with his testimony; and (4) the statement is offered to rebut an express or implied charge of recent fabrication by, or improper influence on, the declarant; FRE 801(d)(1)(B). Although Officer Oates is testifying as to what Walter said out-of-court, his testimony is not hearsay under this provision of the FRE. Choice **B** is wrong because the "business records" exception to the hearsay rule is applicable only to data compilations (i.e., something written or, possibly, tape-recorded). Choice **C** is wrong because the statement is not considered hearsay under the FRE. Finally, choice **D** is wrong because, although proof of a prior consistent statement by a witness is ordinarily *not* admissible, an exception to that rule exists under the FRE where the statement is offered to rebut an assertion of recent fabrication or improper influence (i.e., the threat to murder Walter one week ago); FRE 801(d)(1)(B).

90. **A** Statements made by a decedent pertaining to his belief with respect to the execution, revocation, identification, or terms of his will, for the purpose of proving the fact believed, are admissible as an exception to the hearsay rule; FRE 803(3). Although Ray's statement with respect to what Decker told him is hearsay, it proves Decker's belief that he had revoked a portion of his will. Because the evidence is being introduced to prove that Decker deleted the clause in question with the intention of preventing Otto from inheriting the sports car, it is covered by the FRE 803(3) exception. Choice **B** is wrong because the statement in question does not pertain to the declarant's "then existing" state of mind, but to his intent in deleting the clause. Choice **D** is wrong because "Dead Man" statutes apply to litigation about a transaction between the deceased and a survivor and limit testimony by the survivor. Finally, choice **C** is wrong because, although Ray's statement of what Decker said out-of-court is hearsay, it is within an exception recognized by the FRE.

91. D A party's words or acts may be offered as evidence against him or her. This rule, for an admission by a party-opponent, applies only where the out-of-court statement is made by a party to the present proceeding, and where the statement is offered against, not for, the party who made it. There is no requirement that the party who made the statement be available to testify. Because Susan's statement meets these requirements, her statement is admissible as an admission by a party-opponent; FRE 801(d)(2)(A). Choice **A** is wrong because the physician-patient privilege usually pertains only to statements made to a physician. Thus, Susan's statement to a janitor is outside the purview of this privilege. Choice **B** is wrong because Susan's statement, the admission of a party-opponent, would not constitute hearsay; FRE 801(d)(2)(A). Finally, choice **C** is wrong because the dying declaration exception to the hearsay rule is available only where the out-of-court declarant is unavailable; FRE 804(b)(2). (Note, however, that the federal rule does not require that the declarant have died.) Because Susan has now regained her health and counterclaimed, she is presumably capable of being called as a witness.

92. C Milton's statement was made outside of the present courtroom and is therefore hearsay. Choice **A** is wrong because prior statements made under oath by an unavailable declarant constitute an exception to the hearsay rule only if the party against whom the statements are offered had an opportunity and similar motive to question the declarant at the time the statements were made; FRE 804(b)(1). Jones did not have the opportunity to cross-examine Milton in the criminal case. Choice **B** is wrong because Milton is not the party-opponent of Alex (Jones is the litigant in the present lawsuit). Finally, choice **D** is wrong because the fact that Milton was acquitted in the prior criminal case is not material in deciding whether his statement is admissible in the present litigation.

93. A An out-of-court statement that is offered into evidence not to prove the truth of the contents of the statement, but simply to show that the statement was made, is not hearsay. Sally's statement is being offered into evidence not to prove that Mitchell ordinarily carried a switchblade knife, but that Karl reasonably believed that Mitchell might have been reaching for a weapon. Choice **B** is wrong because a defendant in a criminal case is usually restricted to reputation and opinion evidence about a victim's character; FRE 405(a) and 405(b). Choice **C** is wrong because Sally's statement was not hearsay, as explained above. Finally, choice **D** is wrong because evidence of a victim's character is admissible in nonhomicide cases if it is pertinent.

94. **A** When an ambiguous physical act is accompanied by words that resolve the ambiguity, the accompanying words are called the "verbal part of the act" and are not hearsay because they are not offered into evidence to prove the truth of the matter asserted. Because the words in question tend to show that John did not intend the gift to Milt to be immediately operative, the words clarify the ambiguous physical act of John's handing the deed over to Milt. These words are the verbal part of the act, and are not hearsay. Choice **B** is wrong because the "statement against interest" exception to the hearsay rule is not applicable (John's statement is not hearsay at all, and there is no showing that the statement was against his interest). Choice **C** is wrong because evidence pertaining to a condition precedent to the effectiveness of a document that appears to be complete on its face constitutes a recognized exception to the parol evidence rule. In such a case, the evidence is not being offered to modify or supplement the writing, but to show only that the document was not to become effective until the occurrence of a particular condition. Finally, choice **D** is wrong because John's statement is not hearsay.

95. **B** If a witness uses a writing to refresh his memory before testifying, the court, in its discretion and if it determines that it is necessary in the interests of justice, may permit an adverse party to (1) have the writing produced at the hearing; (2) inspect it; (3) cross-examine the witness thereon; and (4) introduce into evidence those portions of the writing that relate to the testimony of the witness; FRE 612. Because Garland used the Accident Report to refresh his memory prior to the trial, counsel for Banes may, with the court's permission, introduce into evidence the portion of the report dealing with Garland's testimony. Choice **C** is wrong because the cross-examining party may introduce into evidence that portion of the writing that was used to refresh the witness's memory. Choice **D** is wrong because Banes may be permitted to introduce into evidence the portion of the writing that related to Garland's testimony, whether or not it was consistent with Garland's testimony. Finally, choice **A** is wrong because only that part of the report introduced by Banes's attorney may be used on redirect. The entire report may not be introduced.

96. **C** Mrs. Boone's testimony is double hearsay because she is testifying to a statement made by her husband asserting that Dr. Fine had made a statement. Dr. Fine's words are an out-of-court statement made

by a party-opponent and therefore are not hearsay, but Mr. Boone's words are relevant only if they are true and are therefore hearsay. No exception applies to Mr. Boone's words, so the testimony must be excluded as hearsay. Choice **A** is wrong because, although the information in the testimony is relevant, it is hearsay (as explained above) and therefore must be excluded. Choice **B** is wrong because the statement by Mr. Boone was not against his interest at the time he made it. Finally, choice **D** is wrong because, even if Mr. Boone related Dr. Fine's statement to his wife in confidence, the privilege against testifying belonged to the husband or the wife, not to Dr. Fine.

97. **C** In cases in which character, or a trait of character, of a person is an essential element of a charge, claim, or defense, proof may be made of specific instances of prior conduct showing that trait; FRE 405(b). Because an individual's character is very much in issue in determining whether he should have custody of a child, proof of specific instances of prior misconduct is admissible. Choice **D** is wrong because the Original Writing Rule is applicable only where the witness is attempting to prove the contents of a document. Damien is testifying about what personally occurred to him (not about the contents of a document). Choice **A** is wrong because character evidence may be admissible in noncriminal proceedings where a party's character is relevant in any way different from supporting a conclusion that the party acted in conformity with that character on a specific occasion. Finally, choice **B** is wrong because specific instances of conduct are admissible where an individual's character is an essential element of the case.

98. **C** Where specialized knowledge will assist the fact finder to understand the evidence or to determine a factual issue, a person qualified as an expert by her knowledge, skill, experience, training, or education may testify with respect thereto; FRE 702. The determination whether a particular dog was an Australian Blue Hound probably requires an expert opinion. Because Wally apparently was not an expert about rare dog breeds, his opinion as to the type of dog that attacked Paul (formed only from looking at a photo in the library) was impermissible opinion. Additionally, because Wally is testifying about the contents of a writing, the Original Writing Rule would also be applicable (i.e., counsel for Paul would be obliged to introduce into evidence the pages of the book that Wally had reviewed). Wally's testimony is subject also to the objection that it violates the

hearsay rule because he is testifying about the contents of a writing (i.e., the pictures and "Australian Blue Hound" designation contained in the book). Choice **D** is wrong because, although bias is a proper form of impeachment, it would not constitute a basis for striking Wally's testimony, which has no apparent element of bias. Choice **A** is wrong because Wally, having witnessed the attack on Paul, does have personal knowledge of the incident and of his conduct at the library. Finally, choice **B** is wrong because 100 feet is not such a great distance as to preclude Wally from being capable of identifying the type of dog that attacked Paul. The possible defect in Wally's perception caused by the distance is a proper point to raise on cross-examination, but it is not a basis for excluding Wally's entire testimony.

99. **B** The videotape is admissible evidence of the conduct it depicts (the defendant's actions). It is also admissible to show that the defendant made statements about drugs. Those statements are admissible for their truth because they are admissions (statements made by a person introduced against that person at trial). Choice **A** is wrong because the defendant's statements are admissible evidence on the issue of what the packages contained. Choice **C** is wrong because the tape is a mechanical recording of conduct and is therefore not hearsay; the assertions by defendant contained in the tape are not hearsay because they are admissions. Choice **D** is wrong because the Confrontation Clause applies only when statements are "testimonial" and no definition of testimonial would cover statements made by one participant in a drug sale to another participant in such a sale; furthermore, the declarant is the defendant, so the declarant is present at trial and available to testify about the statement and the events it describes.

100. **B** The federal psychotherapist-patient privilege applies to confidential communications made to psychiatrists, psychologists, and licensed social workers in the course of psychotherapy; FRE 501; *Jaffee v. Redmond*. Because Jeffers received counseling from a licensed clinical social worker, the notes from these sessions are protected by the psychotherapist-patient privilege. Choice **A** is wrong because the federal psychotherapist-patient privilege is an absolute, not a qualified, one, and therefore is not guided by a balancing test. Choice **C** is wrong because Jeffers consulted with Karen for the purpose of receiving counseling, not to permit her to serve as an expert in the case. Choice **D** is wrong because the

comments contained in the notes were not made immediately after Jeffers shot Roland, but were made during the course of 50 counseling sessions.

101. **C** In a criminal case in which the defendant is accused of a sexual assault, evidence of the defendant's commission of another sexual assault is admissible and may be considered for its bearing on any matter to which it is relevant; FRE 413(a). So the fact that Darby raped Maria is admissible to show that "if he did it before, he probably did it again." The weight but not the admissibility of this evidence would be affected by the facts that the circumstances surrounding the two crimes are quite different, the prior crime took place a long time ago, and Darby was never charged with or convicted of the prior crime. Choice **A** is wrong because, although the rape of Maria is separate from and unrelated to the rape of Wanda, evidence of the defendant's commission of another rape is admissible. Choice **B** is wrong because, in a criminal case involving sexual assault, evidence that the defendant committed a prior sexual assault is admissible and may be considered on any matter to which it is relevant. Choice **D** is wrong because character is not in issue (the prosecution is not required to establish anything about Darby's character in order to secure a conviction).

102. **D** In a criminal case in which the defendant is accused of child molestation, evidence of a previous commission of child molestation by the defendant is admissible and may be considered for its bearing on any matter to which it is relevant; FRE 414(a). So evidence of the previous child molestation may be admitted to show that "if he did it before, he probably did it again." Choice **A** is wrong because evidence of a previous child molestation is admissible even if there was no conviction. Choice **B** is wrong because FRE 414 imposes no time limit on the other-crimes evidence. Choice **C** is wrong because Duane's character need not be proved in order to support a conviction of the charged crime.

103. **A** When an expert's testimony concerns a scientific test or principle, it must be shown that the scientific test or principle is "scientifically valid" and that it is relevant to an issue in the case; FRE 702. Some of the factors used in determining whether evidence is scientifically valid are (1) whether the test can be reliably tested; (2) whether it's been subject to peer review and publication; (3) its error rate; and (4) whether it's generally accepted in the field. Because Dr. Jacobs's testimony meets these criteria and the testimony is relevant to a

determination as to whose teeth marks are on the cheese, the testimony should be admissible. Choice **B** is wrong because, in determining whether scientific evidence is admissible, the standard of whether the evidence is "generally accepted" has been replaced by the standard of whether the evidence is "scientifically valid." General acceptance is still a factor, although no longer the sole factor to be considered. Choice **C** is wrong because the evidence is relevant to an issue in the case, the identity of the perpetrator. Choice **D** is wrong because Dr. Jacobs, with his knowledge and skill in bite-mark identification, is qualified to be treated as an expert.

104. **A** Helper's statements at the proceeding in which his plea was accepted were hearsay, and for purposes of the Confrontation Clause they were ***testimonial*** hearsay, because they were made to the government and referred to details of past criminal conduct. Because Boss did not have a chance to cross-examine Helper when Helper made the statements, and because Helper has died since making those statements, the Confrontation Clause prohibits their use against Boss. Choices **B**, **C**, and **D** are wrong because overcoming the hearsay bar is not equivalent to overcoming the restrictions required by the Confrontation Clause.

105. **A** The words Daryl said to the police are relevant to his guilt of the charged offense, and they are not hearsay because they are his own words introduced against him (and therefore are an admission). The police officer can testify from personal knowledge that Daryl said the words. Choice **B** is wrong because the police officer is not testifying about what the written confession said, but rather is testifying about what Daryl said when Daryl was describing the crime. Even if a written document containing the same ideas does exist (Daryl's signed confession), testimony about the facts in that confession does not violate the Original Writing Rule if the witness has a basis other than the document for his testimony. Choice **C** is wrong because the testimony was ***not*** an effort to prove the contents of the confession; it was an effort to prove what words Daryl had said at the same time as he wrote his confession. Choice **D** is wrong because the declarant is the defendant himself, not some other witness, and is available as a witness at trial.

106. **D** Under the "bursting bubble" theory of presumptions adopted in FRE 301, a presumed fact (in this case, receipt of the letter) is treated as having been established if the proponent persuades the trier of fact that a basic fact (in this case, proper addressing and

mailing of the letter) is true and the opponent of the presumption fails to satisfy the burden of production with regard to the presumed fact. Because Defendant introduced no evidence about the letter, if the jury believes that the basic fact is established, Plaintiff is entitled to a finding that Defendant received the letter. Choice **A** is wrong because presumptions under the FRE do not shift the persuasion burden. Choice **B** is wrong because the presumption operates only if the trier of fact is persuaded that the basic fact has been established. Choice **C** is wrong because the presumption is a legal doctrine that a jury must follow, regardless of whether the jury would or would not otherwise believe that there is a logical connection between the mailing of a letter and an addressee's receipt of the letter.

107. **B** Establishing that Johnson is awaiting trial on a misdemeanor charge would show that there is a current relationship between Johnson and the prosecution; furthermore, the relationship could influence Johnson to shade his testimony in favor of the prosecution in the hope that the prosecution would then be lenient with him in connection with his misdemeanor charge. For that reason, the misdemeanor charge is proper evidence of possible bias. Choice **A** is wrong because the misdemeanor charge is relevant to show bias, not to show intentional lying because Johnson has the character trait of untruthfulness. Choice **C** is wrong because proof of a witness's bias is always relevant. Choice **D** is wrong because regardless of whether the pending charge involves a misdemeanor or a felony, the fact that there is a pending charge places Johnson and the prosecution in a relationship that could lead Johnson to be biased in favor of the prosecution.

108. **D** The evidence is offered to prove the truth of what the statement asserted, that Driver had fallen asleep while driving. For this substantive use (distinct from a possible impeachment use), the evidence is hearsay. No exception would allow its admission. Choice **A** is wrong because the out-of-court statement had to be true in order for it to have its claimed relevance. Choice **B** is wrong because Driver is not a party, and his statement cannot be an employee's admission properly introduced against an employer, because he did not make the statement during the existence of the employee-employer relationship; FRE 801(d)(2)(D). Choice **C** is wrong because the most likely exception, covering statements against interest, cannot be used here because it requires that the declarant

be unavailable. Driver is available because he has testified at the trial.

109. **A** Regardless of whether the out-of-court statement was true, it is relevant to show its likely effect on the employee who heard it. If the employee heard the statement, it would likely have made her relatively unafraid. For that reason, it is not hearsay. Choices **B** and **C** are wrong because the statement is not hearsay, so consideration of an exclusion or exemption from the hearsay rule would have no bearing on its admissibility. Choice **D** is wrong because the statement is not hearsay.

110. **D** The worker's statement to the manager would be relevant only if it were true. For that reason, it is hearsay. No hearsay exclusion or exception applies, so the evidence is inadmissible. Choice **A** is wrong because the statement's relevance depends on its truth. Choice **B** is wrong because the declarant's words are not being introduced against the declarant. Choice **C** is wrong because no exception applies. The present sense impression exception is the closest fit, but it applies only when the statement is made immediately after the declarant has perceived what the declarant's statement describes; FRE 803(1).

111. **B** Fixer's testimony is best characterized as expert testimony of the "experience-based" variety. In *Kumho Tire*, the United States Supreme Court held that the *Daubert* guidelines for admission of expert testimony apply not only to scientific testimony but also apply to experience-based expert testimony. The factors set out in Choice **B** are some of the *Daubert* factors the trial court would be required to consider. Choice **A** is wrong because it treats the *Frye* test for admission of expert testimony as conclusive. Under *Daubert*, that test is among the appropriate factors for a judge to consider, but it is no longer conclusive. Choice **C** is wrong because Fixer would likely be characterized as an expert witness. Choice **D** is wrong because FRE 704(a) permits opinion testimony on ultimate issues of this type.

112. **B** Attorney-client privilege would not apply to these conversations between Neville and his lawyer because the conversations were for the purpose of obtaining investment advice, not legal advice. Choice **A** is wrong because privilege applies only if the communications were for the purpose of obtaining legal advice. Choice **C** is wrong because the fact that the conversations took place, not the

truth of anything said in them, is relevant to Neville's claim that he relied exclusively on the defendant broker's advice in deciding to invest in the European stocks. For this purpose, the out-of-court statements are not hearsay. Choice **D** is wrong because the asserted relevance of the inquiry is to prove that Neville obtained advice, not just to show that Neville testified falsely.

113. A This testimony quotes an out-of-court statement that would be relevant only if its contents were true. Its relevance depends on its being treated as substantive proof that the speaker did have a plan to go to the festival. Further, statements of plan or intention are treated by FRE 803(3) as within the "state of mind" exception. Thus, the brother's statement would be admissible to show the brother's state of mind, and to support a conclusion that he acted in accordance with that state of mind (that intention or plan). Choice B is wrong because the defendant's brother was not the defendant's agent. Choice C is wrong because the statement is covered by the state of mind exception in FRE 803(3). Choice D is wrong because conditionally relevant evidence is ordinarily admissible if it satisfies any other applicable requirements as well.

114. C In a homicide case, whenever the defense claims in any way that the victim was the first aggressor, the prosecution is entitled to introduce evidence of the victim's character trait of peacefulness, under FRE 404(a)(2)(C). Choice A describes an effort to impeach the credibility of Bigman, but it violates FRE 608(b) because it seems to introduce extrinsic evidence of a past act related to truth-telling. The Rule allows only inquiry into such acts. Choice B is wrong because it seeks to attack Bigman's character with proof of a specific past act, while the permissible method for attacking his character is to use opinion or reputation evidence. The conduct is too common to be permitted under a rationale that it shows motive or absence of mistake. Choice D is wrong for the same reason that Choice B is wrong: it attempts to prove Niceguy's character with a kind of proof that is forbidden for that purpose.

115. C The aunt's statement is relevant only if the information it contains is true since identifying someone other than Relative as the perpetrator is the point of its introduction. No exception to the hearsay exclusion rule could reasonably apply. Choice A is wrong because the Aunt's statement was not against her proprietary, pecuniary, or penal interest when she made it. Witnessing a crime does not affect any of those interests. Choice B is wrong because the investigator is not described in the question as an expert. If the investigator could be considered an expert, FRE 703 would allow the investigator to base an opinion on inadmissible material typically relied on by experts. Admission of such material under that Rule, however, is discretionary and unlikely under these circumstances. Choice D is wrong because bias is not usually a basis for excluding testimony; the testimony is ordinarily admitted and the opponent is then entitled to prove aspects of bias that could affect a jury's evaluation of the testimony.

116. **B** This e-mail would be relevant since it admits a fact that is significant in Customer's case, and it would not be hearsay because it is a statement by a party opponent. Therefore, if it is authenticated, and if a court deems the printed copy of the e-mail to be an "original," it would be admissible. Choice A is wrong because it ignores the Original Writing Rule requirement. Choice C is wrong because the e-mail is a statement by a party opponent and therefore is not hearsay. Choice D is wrong because an apology is not a settlement offer. FRE 408 about settlements applies only when there is a dispute about the validity or amount of a claim.

117. **C** The testimony includes hearsay since Elderly's words are relevant for their stated purpose only if they were an accurate report of what the son-in-law said. No hearsay exception would cover them. Choice A is wrong because the dying declaration exception applies only to statements about the cause of an impending death, and Elderly's statement was on a different subject. Choice B is wrong because a person who is about to die would not reasonably be concerned about criminal consequences of his statements, and therefore the rationale for the statement against interest exception would not apply. Choice D is wrong because the dying declaration exception applies in homicide cases *and* in all civil cases.

118. **D** Landowner's written statement is hearsay since it was made out of court and it is being introduced to prove the truth of what it asserts. No exception would cover it. Choice A is wrong because Landowner may not be deemed to have been conducting a regular activity and because a business record must contain information recorded at or near the time of the events it describes (not, for example, events that happened "last summer"). Choice B is wrong because Landowner is seeking to introduce his own statement, not a statement by his opponent. Choice C is wrong because the mere fact that a statement is consistent with trial testimony does not

make it inadmissible if it qualifies for admission under some other rationale.

119. **D** This testimony would be relevant only if a juror used it to conclude that because Surgeon is usually careful, she was careful on a particular occasion. This inference is prohibited in civil cases and in most instances in criminal cases. Choice A describes the prohibited propensity inference. Choice B represents that strongest possible argument for admissibility, but it is an argument that would fail. Evidence that shows habit is admissible to prove conduct in conformity with the habit, but it must describe conduct that is almost automatic in nature, and that is highly specific. Just "acts carefully" is too general to fit the definition of habit. Choice C is wrong because the problem does not involve a quotation of an out-of-court statement. It involves out-of-court conduct.

120. **A** Subject to the FRE 403 balancing test for probative value and unfair prejudice, a party may ask a witness about his or her past conduct that relates to the character trait of truthfulness. Fraud in a patent rights transaction relates to one's character for truthfulness. Revealing to the jury that the Developer has once done something fraudulent relating to patents is not likely to lead the jury to make an unfair assumption about Developer's conduct in the current office building project, so the FRE 403 balancing test would be passed. Choice B is wrong because—unlike the situation in Choice A—the risk of unfair prejudice is high. A juror who finds out that Developer committed a fraud in a past office building project is likely to assume that Developer has a propensity to commit frauds in that context and to use that assumption improperly against Developer in the current case. Another factor that cuts against allowing this question is Investor's ability to impeach Developer with the information about the patent transaction. Denying Investor the chance to question Developer about the older office building project still leaves Investor with a strong method for impeaching Developer: inquiry about the patent rights transaction. Choices C and D are wrong because extrinsic proof of past acts (other than convictions) is prohibited for the impeachment purpose of establishing a witness's bad character for truthfulness.

121. **B** Browser seeks to introduce this evidence to show that Fancy Clothes had acted unreasonably in its floor maintenance. Evidence that the mall operator switched from XYZ suggests that XYZ is

a poor choice for that maintenance. It is not prohibited by FRE 407 about subsequent remedial measures because the defendant Fancy Clothes did not engage in the remedial measure. The rule bars evidence only of a *defendant's* post-accident conduct. Choice A is wrong because the proposed use is specifically a use that FRE 407 prohibits, when FRE 407 applies. Choice C is wrong because FRE 407 prohibits evidence only of a *defendant's* post-accident conduct. Choice D is wrong because even if Fancy Clothes does not control the mall operator's conduct, that conduct could still be relevant to analyzing the quality of the cleaning work that Fancy Clothes carried out for maintaining its floor.

122. **C** In analyzing out-of-court statements for the purpose of applying the hearsay rules, it is important to identify each declarant and link each declarant with a statement. In this example there are three declarants. Something like "I had two glasses" was a statement by Victim, something like "My husband said he had two glasses" was a statement by Victim's wife, and something like "Victim's wife says . . ." was a statement (in writing) by an unnamed hospital worker. Thus there were three out-of-court statements. Choices A, B, and D are wrong because each one identifies an incorrect number of statements.

123. **A** The most likely ruling is that conveying the idea "Able lives here" was *not* the purpose of the written out-of-court statement. When an unintended implication of a statement has relevance at a trial, most courts will admit the statement on the ground that it does not implicate the prohibition against introducing out-of-court statements to prove the truth of what they assert. Choice B is wrong because there could be some doubt about whether all the information associated with this statement was generated by actors in the enterprise – some of it was probably provided to the enterprise by a third party. Choice C is wrong because a human communication was necessarily involved in created the record that has afterwards been maintained electronically. Choice D is wrong because Able, against whom the statement is sought to be introduced, is not the party who made the statement. Therefore it is not an opposing party's statement in the sense required by that hearsay exemption.

124. **A** The diary statements are relevant to show both that Defendant punched Victim and that Victim was afraid of Defendant. The reference to punching would be a present sense impression, and the reference to being scared would be covered by the exceptions for

statements of mental state. Choices B and C are wrong because their introduction would violate the Confrontation Clause. They are testimonial hearsay (spoken in Choice B and written in Choice C), and there is no showing that Defendant killed Victim to prevent Victim from being a witness. Choice D is wrong because the out-of-court statement to the bartender is hearsay that is not covered by any exception.

125. **A** Under FRE 609(a)(1)(B), in a criminal case evidence of this kind may be admitted against a criminal defendant only if its probative value with regard to the defendant's truthfulness outweighs its prejudicial effect to the defendant. Choices B and C describe balances between probative value and risk of unfair prejudice that are different from the required balance. Choice D is also wrong; when falsehoods are required to be proved or admitted in order to sustain a conviction of a particular crime, evidence of that conviction may be introduced without any balancing test at all, but this question is ambiguous as to whether or not the conviction fits that description since the crime apparently involved only failure to provide certain required information.

126. **B** The words typed by Defendant are a party's words introduced against the party. This fits them within the FRE definition of non-hearsay under FRE 801(d)(2)(A). Choice A is wrong because the statement is roughly equivalent to "I need to know the locations of brake shops." If a court rejected that analysis, Choice A is still a less likely ruling than the one described in Choice B because the statement by party opponent rationale avoids any doubt about how to interpret Driver's words. Choice C is wrong because the statement is not hearsay. Choice D is wrong because an authentication problem has no relevance to consideration of an objection based on hearsay.

127. **D** Buyer's words are hearsay. They come close to qualifying for admissibility under the statement against interest exception, but that exception requires the unavailability of the declarant. Buyer is available, so that exception does not apply. Buyer's availability requires exclusion of Guard's testimony. Choice A is wrong because Buyer's words were against his pecuniary interest since they exposed him to potential tort liability. Choice B is wrong because Buyer's words at trial contradict his statement to Guard. Choice C is wrong because even if a declarant does testify, the declarant's words may be quoted by other witnesses if they are

offered for a nonsubstantive purpose or if they are offered for a substantive purpose and they are covered by a hearsay exemption or exclusion.

128. **A** Doctor can quote his own words since they are being introduced to prove that they were said, not to prove that any meaning they convey is an accurate description of some past reality. They are relevant since the jury can evaluate them based on its own experiences. Choices B and C are wrong because expert testimony is admissible only if it can help the jury understand something that is ordinarily beyond the knowledge or comprehension of typical jurors. The clarity of language is something that jurors would likely be able to understand on their own. Choice D is wrong because a lay witness usually must testify about facts, not opinions. Furthermore, the lay witness's opinion about clarity would not be helpful to the jury because the jury itself is capable of assessing the clarity of Doctor's words without assistance from witnesses.

129. **B** A report made by a "police fingerprint analyst" would clearly be testimonial hearsay since it was an out-of-court statement intended for use against someone in the process of law enforcement and criminal prosecution. It violates the Confrontation Clause to introduce such hearsay unless the declarant is unavailable and the defendant has earlier had a chance to cross-examine the declarant about the statement. Choice A is wrong because the Original Writing Rule allows testimony about a writing so long as the writing is introduced. Choice C is wrong because many courts would rule that the business records or public records exception could apply to this document. Choice D is wrong because experts are not covered by the personal knowledge requirement.

130. **C** The business records exception is withdrawn when the circumstances of the making of the record indicate a lack of trustworthiness. In this case, the memo was made only after a lawyer essentially told Manager what facts would be helpful to the company. Memos made in anticipation of litigation will rarely be covered by the business records exception. Choices A and B are wrong because satisfying some of the requirements of the exception does not mean that the record will be admitted when other requirements (such as the one about trustworthiness) have not been met. Choice D is wrong because the memo is not a communication to a lawyer and because the client, in this case the defendant company, is seeking to introduce it and has the right to waive a privilege if a privilege exists.

131. **A** When a witness testifies, the opponent may introduce evidence that the witness has been convicted of a truth-telling crime for the purpose of impeachment. Choice B is wrong because it represents an effort to establish the propensity inference, that because Defendant did an arson once, Defendant has some character traits such as violence and unlawfulness that make it more likely that he committed the charged murder. Choice C is wrong because character evidence of this type is allowed only if the defendant has earlier introduced evidence of good character. Choice D is wrong because past acts showing untruthfulness may be used for impeachment by inquiring about them on cross-examination, but extrinsic evidence about them is forbidden.

132. **C** The residual exception allows admission of hearsay that has guarantees of trustworthiness similar to those of enumerated exceptions if some additional requirements are also satisfied. The "ancient documents" rule would cover this newspaper story if it were 20 years old, instead of just 17 years old. This is quite close and could be a basis for admission. Choice C is the right answer here, additionally, because each of the other choices is clearly wrong. Choice A is wrong because the rule applies only to documents that are at least 20 years old. Choice B is wrong because judicial notice may be used only for facts that are well-known or subject to verification from sources such as standard reference works. Choice D is wrong because the statement is not one that is used in the ordinary conduct of an enterprise for that enterprise's inherent functions; rather, it is the work-product of an enterprise whose business is the creation of statements.

Table of References to the Federal Rules of Evidence

Index